World Summit
for
Social Development

WORLD SUMMIT
FOR
SOCIAL DEVELOPMENT

Editor

Dr. Digumarti Bhaskara Rao

M.Sc. M.A., M.A., M.ED., Ph.D.

Secretary Academy of Communication, Culture,
Education, Science and Service,
D-43, Srinivasa Nagar Colony, Guntur-522006
Andhra Pradesh, (India)

1998

Discovery Publishing House

New Delhi-110002

First Published-1998

ISBN 81-7141-420-6

Published by:
Discovery Publishing House
4831/24, Ansari Road, Prahlad Street,
Daryaganj, New Delhi-110002 (*INDIA*)
Phone: 3279245
Fax: 91-11-3253475

Printed at:
Trun Offset Printers,
518/14, Anup Market, Maujpur, Delhi - 53.
☎ 2260794

Foreword

The Copenhagen Declaration and Programme of Action together comprise a new social contract at the global level. The presence of so many world leaders at the World Summit for Social Development has given immense political weight to these agreements. Never before have so many leaders come together for such a purpose—to fight poverty, to create productive jobs and to strengthens the social fabric.

The spirit of the Summit's agreements is one which, above all, reflects a sense of solidarity within nations and between nations. We cannot permit those who are privileged to ignore those who are poor, vulnerable or disadvantaged. The letter of this contract, as outlined in the ten commitments of the Declaration, engages nations to undertake a concerted Programme of Action.

The acute social ills of today—crime, drugs, disease, disaffection, urban decay and declining standards of education—all have crucial consequences for human security in its largest sense. These social problems, which once could be confined within borders, now spread across the world. Once considered to be the exclusive responsibility of national Governments, these problems are now of global scale and require global attention.

The potential for cooperation has never been greater. The east-west divide has disappeared and the north-south confrontation is gradually giving way to a more global approach. The new economic and social challenge is not confrontation but divergence—the widening divide between those who can make it on their own and those who cannot will need the cooperation of the international community. But not even the strongest economies today—developed, developing or transitional—can escape the problems of social development, of poverty, unemployment and social disintegration.

True and lasting success in putting the Copenhagen agreements into action will require a coalition of all societal actors, working together towards the same objectives. Governments will need to act in partnership with experts, parliamentarians, grass-roots and religious organisations, trade unions, businesses and non-governmental organizations, harnessing their talent and enthusiasm. Together we must continue our collective efforts to help shape a better common future for all nations, communities and people.

Boutros Boutros-Ghali
Former Secretary-General, United Nations

Educate to Empower

As borders shift, technologies change, currencies fluctuate and people migrate, access to information—and the skills to manage new knowledgeis critical to the survival and success of people in rich and poor nations alike.

The Social Summit's core themes—poverty, unemployment and social integration—touch upon the real and pressing concerns of people worldwide. Indeed, this is the first gathering of Heads of State ever called to focus explicitly on the problems of ordinary people. It is also the first such meeting in which empoverment and integration—not dependence—are seen as forces which will unite countries, instead of dividing them, in the discussion of social development.

Social development is about enabling people to satisfy basic human needs while at the same time taking responsibility for their own lives and for the well-being of their communities; it is based on values of personal dignity and mutual respect. It attempts to release the positive forces of creativity and full human potential.

The Social Summit has begun a process of dialogue and public outreach on empowerment. This concept is the linchpin of social development in the twenty-first century and beyond. Education in all of its forms—from primary schooling to university training, from vocational education to training and re-training of workers of all ages and abilities—is critical to empowerment. Governments, people's organizations and the private sector must find new ways to work together to promote social development as the world becomes more interdependent. This is why the Social Summit's Declaration and Programme of Action highlight the central role of education to empowerment.

The Declaration commits world leaders to take action in key areas, focusing on Commitments which can be fulfilled only in partnership with civil society. These include commitments to eradicate the most extreme forms of poverty; to enable all people to attain secure and sustainable livelihoods through freely-chosen productive employment to promote social integration; and to full equality between women and men.

Empowering people through education is central to fulfilling these promises. That is why education figures centrally within the *Declaration's* commitments and in policy options outlined in the *Programme of Action*. The poverty commitment explicitly includes universal primary education among the human needs every government commits itself to fulfil, while the employment commitment refers directly to the importance of ensur[ing] that workers and employers have the training needed to adapt to changing economic conditions.

The social integration commitment, in turn, cites the role of education systems and communication media in encouraging the protection and integration of disadvantaged groups, enhancing respect for cultural diversity and human rights, and promoting respect for the identity, culture and interests of various groups. Throughout the Summit's agenda, the empowerment of women through lifelong education is highlighted as central to social development.

Let the summit be a moment in which those who educate for empowerment take time to gather, to pause, to reflect and to renew their energies—students and teachers of today and tomorrow.

Ambassador Juan Somavia
Chair, Preparatory Committee,
World Summit for Social Development

Preface

The World Summit for Social Development was organised by the United Nations in Copenhagen, Denmark from 6 to 12 March 1995 to find a global strategy to combat poverty, unemployment and social disintegration in way that people will be at the centre of social development.

The Summit was attended by heads of State or Government or their representatives and made statements and pledged on behalf of their countries. Alongwith these observers or representatives of regional commissions, United Nations bodies and programmes, specialised agencies, intergovernmental agencies, and a large number of non-governmental agencies have also enriched the Summit. In all, over 14,000 participants attended the Summit.

The Summit was organised in a world situation where: More than one billion people live in poverty—with little or no access to jobs, basic necessities and education. Most of these are in rural areas of Asia and Africa, although millions can also be found in the cities of the industrialised countries as well as the developing world. The benefits of the unprecedented material progress that witnessed by the world in the last half of the present century have not been distributed equally, and the gulf between the haves and have-nots has widened dramatically in recent years—between rich and poor nations and between rich and poor citizens. Also, worldwide, one out of every five people, more than one billion, live below the poverty line, and an estimated 13 to 18 million die annually of poverty-related causes. The ranks of those living in extreme poverty will quadruple within one lifetime if current economic and demographic trends continue. And an estimated thirty per cent of the global labour force, over eight hundred million people, is not productively employed. They are either hunting vainly for jobs or are under-employed, working at tasks that do not allow them to make ends meet, and majority of them live in developing countries.

The participants of the Summit adopted on March 12, 1995 the

Copenhagen Declaration on Social Development and the Programme of Action of the World Summit for Social Development. And also decided to request the General Assembly of the United Nations to hold a special session in the year 2000 for an overall review and appraisal of the implementation of the outcome of the Summit and to consider further actions and initiatives. The commitments and actions adopted for social development were included in the Declaration and Programme of Action for their implementation to bring the expected social development.

Let us hope that the World Summit for Social Development shall move the people for people's development. Long live the spirit of the summit and bring glory to human race.

Dr. Digumarti Bhaskara Rao
R.V.R. College of Education
Nagarjuna University, Guntur- 522006

Acknowledgements

I
extend my cordial thanks
and
deep sense of appreciation
to
Mr. Boutros Boutros-Ghali
Mr. Poul Nyreep Rasmussen
Mr. Juan Somavia
Gloria Kan
United Nations Organisation
the General Assembly of the United Nations
the Secretariat of the United Nations
the Secretariat of the Summit
the Heads of State or Government
UNESCO's EFA 2000 Bulletin
UN Bodies and Programmes and Specialised Agencies
UN Information Centre in India
who
made this publication possible
to
realise the commitments and actions of the Summit.

D.B. RAO
ACCESS

Contents

Foreword *v*
Educate to Empower *vii*
Preface *ix*
Acknowledgments *xi*

1. Copenhagen Declaration on Social Developoment 1

2. Programme of Action of the World Summit for Social Development 35

APPENDICES

1. Resolutions Adopted by the Summit 126

2. Attendance and Organisation of Work 130

3. General Exchange of Views 140

4. Report of the Main Committee 145

5. Adoption of the Copenhagen Declaration on social Development and the Programme of Action of the World Summit for Social Development 149

6. Report of the Credentials Commitee 160

7.	Meeting of Heads of state or Government	161
8.	Adoption of the Report of the Summit	170
9.	Closure of the Summit	171
10.	Opening Statements Statement by Poul Nyrup Rasmussen, President of the Summit Statement by Boutros Boutros-Ghali, Secretary General of the United Nations	172
11.	Closing Statement	180
12.	Heads of State or Government	182
13.	Background Papers Attacking Poverty Towards a Society for All	192
14.	Fact Sheets Helping the Poor to Help Themselves Health: Cornerstone of Social Development Agriculture and Social Development Rural Poverty : The Struggle to Survive Shelter, Employment and the Urban Poor Refugees: Victims of Social Disintegration International Migration: Focus on Women A New Age for Old Age	215

1
Copenhagen Declaration on Social Development

1. For the first time in history, at the invitation of the United Nations, we gather as heads of State and Government to recognize the significance of social development and human well-being for all and to give to these goals the highest priority both now and into the twenty first century.
2. We acknowledge that the people of the world have shown in different ways an urgent need to address profound social problems, especially poverty, unemployment and social exclusion, that affect every country. It is out task to address both their underlying and structural causes and their distressing consequence in order to reduce uncertainty and insecurity and in the life of people.
3. We acknowledge that our societies must respond more effectively to the material and spiritual needs of individuals, their families and the communities in which they throughout our diverse countries and regions. We must do so not only as matter of urgency but also as a matter of sustained and unshakeable commitment through the years ahead.
4. We are convinced that democracy and transparent and accountable governance and administration in all sectors of

society are indispensable foundations for the realization of social and people-centered sustainable development.

5. We share the conviction that social development and social justice are indispensable for the achievement and maintenance for peace and security within and among our nations. In turn, social development and social justice cannot be attained in the absence of peace and security or in the absence of respect for all human rights and fundamental freedoms. This essential interdependence was recognized 50 years ago in the Charter of the United Nations and since grown ever stronger.

6. We are deeply convinced that economic development, social development and environmental protection are interdependent and mutually reinforcing components of sustainable development, which is the framework for our efforts to achieve a higher quality of life for all people. Equitable social development that recognizes empowering the poor to utilize environmental resources sustainably is a necessary foundation for sustainable development. We also recognize that broad-based and sustained economic growth in the context of sustainable development is necessary to sustain social development and social justice.

7. We recognize, therefore, that social development is central to the needs and aspirations of people throughout the world and to the responsibilities of Governments and all sectors of civil society. We affirm that, in both economic and social terms, the most productive policies and investments are those that empower people to maximize their capacities, resources and opportunities. We acknowledge that social and economic development cannot be secured in a sustainable way without the full participation of women and that equality and equity between women and men is a priority for the international community and as such must be at the centre of economic and social development.

8. We acknowledge that people are at the centre of our concerns for sustainable development and that they are entitled to a healthy and productive life in harmony with the environment.

9. We gather here to commit ourselves, our Governments and

our nations to enhancing social development throughout the world so that all men and women, especially those living in poverty, may exercise the rights, utilize the resources and share the responsibilities that enable them to lead satisfying lives and to contribute to the well-being of their families, their communities and humankind. To support and promote these efforts must be the overriding goals of the international community, especially with respect to people suffering from poverty, unemployment and social exclusion.

10. We make this solemn commitment on the eve of the fiftieth anniversary of the United Nations, with a determination to capture the unique possibilities offered by the end of the cold war to promote social development and social justice. We reaffirm and are guided by the principles of the Charter of the United Nations and by agreements reached at relevant international conferences, including the World Summit for Children, held at New York in 1990; the United Nations Conference on Environment and Development, held at Rio de Janeiro in 1992; the World Conference on Human Rights, held at Vienna in 1993; the Global Conference on the Sustainable Development of Small Island Developing States, held at Bridgetown, Barbados in 1994; and the International Conference on Population and Development, held at Gairo in 1994. By this Summit we launch a new commitment to social development in each of our countries and a new era of international cooperation between Governments and peoples based on a spirit of partnership that puts the needs, rights and aspirations of people at the centre of our decisions and joint actions.

11. We gather here in Copenhagen in a Summit of hope, commitment and action. We gather with full awareness of the difficulty of the tasks that lie ahead but with a conviction that major progress can be achieved, must be achieved and will be achieved.

12. We commit ourselves to this Declaration and Programme of Action for enhancing social development and ensuring human well-being for all throughout the world now and into the twenty-first century. We invite all people in all countries and in all walks of life, as well as the international commu-

nity, to join us in our common cause.

A. Current Social Situation and Reasons for Convening the Summit

13. We are witnessing in countries throughout the world the expansion of prosperity for some, unfortunately accompanied by an expansion of unspeakable poverty for others. This glaring contradiction is unacceptable and needs to corrected through urgent actions.

14. Globalization, which is a consequence of increased human mobility, enhanced communications, greatly increased trade and capital flows, and technological developments, opens new opportunities for sustained economic growth and development of the world economy, particularly in developing countries. Globalization also permits countries to share experiences and to learn from one another's achievements and difficulties, and promotes a cross-fertilization of ideals, cultural values and aspirations. At the same time, the rapid processes of change and adjustment have been accompanied by intensified poverty, unemployment and social disintegration. Threats to human well-being, such as environmental risks, have also been globalized. Furthermore, the global transformations of the world economy are profoundly changing the parameters of social development in all countries. The challenge is how to manage these processes and threats as to enhance their benefits and mitigate their negative effects upon people.

15. There has been progress in some areas of social and economic development:

    a. The global wealth of nations has multiplied sevenfold in the past 50 years and international trade has grown even more dramatically;

    b. Life expectancy, literacy and primary education, and access to basic health care, including family planning, have increased in the majority of countries and average infant mortality has been reduced, included in developing countries;

    c. Democracies pluralism, democracies institutions and fundamental civil liberties have expanded. Decolonization efforts have achieved much progress, while the elimination of apartheid is a historic achievement.

16. Yet we recognize that far too many people, particularly women and children, are vulnerable to stress and deprivation. Poverty, unemployment and social disintegration too often result in isolation, marginalization and violence. The insecurity and many people, in particular and vulnerable people, face about the future-their own and their children's-is intensifying:

a. Within many societies, both in developed and developing countries, the gap between rich and poor has increased. Furthermore, despite the fact that some developing countries are growing rapidly the gap between developed and many developing countries, particularly the least developed countries, has widened;

b. More than one billion people in the world live in abject poverty, most of whom go hungry every day. A large proportion, the majority of whom are women, have very limited access to income, resources, education, health care or nutrition, particularly in Africa and the least developed countries;

c. There are also serious social problems of a different nature and magnitude in countries with economies in transition and countries experiencing fundamental political, economic and social transformations;

d. The major cause of the continued deterioration of the global environment is the unsustainable pattern of consumption and production, particularly in industrialized countries, which is a matter of grave concern, aggravating poverty and imbalances;

e. Continued growth in the world's population, its structure and distribution, and its relationship with poverty and social and gender inequality challenge the adaptive capacities of Governments, individuals, social institutions and the natural environment;

f. Over 120 million people worldwide are officially unemployed and many more are underemployed. Too many young people, including those with formal education, have little hope of finding productive work;

g. More women than men live in absolute poverty and the imbalance continues to grow, with serious consequences for women and their children. Women carry a disproportionate share of the problems of coping with poverty, social disintegration, unemployment, environmental degradation and the effects of war;

h. One of the world's largest minorities, more than 1 to 10, are people with disabilities, who are too often forced into poverty, unemployment and social isolation. In addition, in all countries older persons may be particularly vulnerable to social exclusion, poverty and marginalization;

i. Millions of people worldwide are refugees or internally displaced persons. The tragic social consequences have a critical effect on the social stability and development of their home countries, their host countries and their respective regions.

17. While these problems are global in character and affect all countries, we clearly acknowledge that the situation of most developing countries, and particularly of Africa and the least developed countries, is critical and requires special attention and action. We also acknowledge that these countries, which are undergoing fundamental political, economic and social transformation, including countries in the process of consolidating peace and democracy, require the support of the international community.

18. Countries with economies in transition, which are also undergoing fundamental political, economic and social transformation, require the support of the international community as well.

19. Other countries that are undergoing fundamental political, economic and social transformation require the support of the international community as well.

20. The goals and objectives of social development require continuous efforts to reduce and eliminate major sources of social distress and instability for the family and for society. We pledge to place particular focus on and give priority attention to the fight against the worldwide conditions that pose severe threats to the health, safety, peace, security and well-being

of our people. Among these conditions are chronic hunger; malnutrition; illicit drug problems; organized crime; corruption; foreign occupation; armed conflicts; illicit arms trafficking; terrorism, intolerance and incitement to racial, ethnic, religious and other hatreds; xenophobia; and endemic, communicable and chronic diseases. To this end, coordination and cooperation at the national level and especially at the regional and international levels should be further strengthened.

21. In this context, the negative impact on development of excessive military expenditures, the arms trade, and investment for arms production and acquisition must be addressed.

22. Communicable diseases constitute a serious health problem in all countries and are a major cause of death globally; in many cases, their incidence is increasing. These disease are a hindrance to social development and are often the cause of poverty and social exclusion. The prevention, treatment and control of these diseases, covering a spectrum from tuberculosis and malaria to the human immunodeficiency virus/acquired immunodeficiency syndrome (HIV/AIDS), must be given the highest priority.

23. We can continue to hold the trust of the people of the world only if we make their needs our priority. We know the poverty, lack of productive employment and social disintegration are an offence to human dignity. We also know that they are negatively reinforcing and represent a waste of human resources and a manifestation of ineffectiveness in the functioning of markets and economic and social institutions and processes.

24. Our challenge is to establish a people-centered framework for social development to guide us now and in the future, to build a culture of cooperation and partnership, and to respond to the immediate needs of those who are most affected by the human distress. We are determined to meet this challenge and promote social development throughout the world.

B. Principles and Goals

25. We heads of State and Government are committed to a political, economic, ethical and spiritual vision for social development that is based on human dignity, human rights, equality, respect, peace, democracy, mutual responsibility and cooperation, and full respect for various religious and ethical values and cultural backgrounds of people. Accordingly, we will give the highest priority in national, regional and international policies and actions to the promotion of social progress, justice and the betterment of the human condition, based on full participation by all.

26. To this end, we will create a framework for action to:

a. Place people at the centre of development and direct our economics to meet human needs more effectively;

b. Fulfil our responsibility for present and future generations by ensuring equity among generations and protecting the integrity and sustainable use of our environment;

c. Recognize that, while social development is a national responsibility, it cannot be successfully achieved without the collection commitment and efforts of the international community;

d. Integrate economic, cultural and social policies so that they become mutually supportive, and acknowledge the interdependence of public and private spheres of activity;

e. Recognize that the achievement of sustained social development requires sound, broadly economic policies;

f. Promote democracy, human dignity, social justice and solidarity at the national, regional and international levels; ensure tolerance, non-violence, pluralism and non-discrimination, with full respect for diversity within and among societies;

g. Promote the equitable distribution of income and greater access to resources through equity and equality of opportunity for all;

h. Recognize the family as the basic unit of society, and

acknowledge that it plays a key role in social development and as such should be strengthened, with attention to the rights, capabilities and responsibilities of its members. In different cultural, political and social systems various forms of family exist. It is entitled to receive comprehensive protection and support;

i. Ensure that disadvantaged and vulnerable persons and groups are included in social development, and the society acknowledges and responds to the consequences of disability by securing the legal rights of the individual and by making the physical and social environment accessible;

j. Promote universal respect for, and observance and protection of, all human rights and fundamental freedoms for all, including the right to development; promote the effective exercise of rights and the discharge of responsibility at all levels of society; promote equality and equity between women and men; protect the rights of children and youth; and promote the strengthening of social integration and civil society;

k. Reaffirm the right of self-determination of all peoples, in particular of peoples under colonial or other forms of alien domination or foreign occupation, and the importance of the effective realization of this right, as enunciated, *inter alia*, in the Vienna Declaration and Programme of Action adopted at the World Conference on Human Rights;

l. Support progress and security for people and communities whereby every member of society is enabled to satisfy his or her basic human needs and to realize his or her personal dignity, safety and creativity;

m. Recognize and support indigenous people in their pursuit of economic and social development, with full respect for their identity, traditions, forms of social organization and cultural values;

n. Underline the importance of transparent and accountable governance and administration in all public and private national and international institutions;

o. Recognize that empowering people, particularly women, to strengthen their own capacities is main objective of development and its principal resource. Empowerment requires the full participation of people in the formulation, implementation and evaluation of decisions determining the functioning and well-being of our societies;

p. Assert the universality of social development and outline a new and strengthened approach to social development, with a renewed impetus for international cooperation and partnership;

q. Improve the possibility of older persons achieving a better life;

r. Recognize that the new information technologies and new approaches to access to and use of technologies by people living in poverty can help in fulfilling social development goals, and therefore recognize the needs to facilitate access to such technologies;

s. Strengthen policies and programmes that improves, ensure and broaden the participation of women in all sphered of political, economic, social and cultural life, as equal partners, and improve their access to all resources needed for the full exercise of their fundamental rights;

t. Create the political, legal, material and social conditions that allow for the voluntary repatriation of refugees in safety and dignity to their countries of origin, and the voluntary and safe return of internally displaced persons to their places of origin and their smooth reintegration into their societies;

u. Emphasize the importance of the return of prisoners of war, persons missing in action and hostages to their families, in accordance with international conventions, in order to reach full social development.

27. We acknowledge that it is the responsibility of State to attain these goals. We also acknowledge that these goals cannot be achieved by State alone. The international community, the

United Nations, the multilateral financial institutions, all regional organizations and local authorities, and all actors of civil society and need to positively contribute their own share of efforts and resources in order to reduce inequalities among people and narrow the gap between developed and developing countries in a global effort to reduce social tensions, and to create greater social and economic stability and security. Radical political, social and economic and changes in the countries with economies in transition have been accompanied by a deterioration in their economic and social situation. We invite all people to express their personal commitment to enhancing the human condition through concrete actions in their own fields of activities and through assuming specific civic responsibilities.

C. Commitments

28. Our global drive for social development and the recommendations for action contained in the Programme of Action are made in spirit of consensus and international cooperation, in full conformity with the purposes and principles of the Charter of the United Nations, recognizing that the formulation and implementation of strategies, policies, programmes and actions for social development are the responsibility of each country and should take into the account the economic, social and environmental diversity of conditions in each country, with full respect for the various religious and ethical values, cultural backgrounds and philosophical convictions of its people, and in conformity with all human rights and fundamental freedoms. In this context, international cooperation is essential for the full implementation of social development programmes and actions.

29. On the basis of our common pursuit of social development, which aims at social justice, solidarity, harmony and equality within and among countries, with full respect for national sovereignty and territorial integrity, as well as policy objectives, development priorities and religious and cultural diversity, and full respect for all human rights and fundamental freedoms, we launch a global drive for social progress and development embodied in the following commitments.

Commitment 1

We commit ourselves to creating an economic, political, social cultural and legal environment that will enable people to achieve social development.

To this end, at the national level, we will:

a. Provide a stable legal framework, in accordance with our constitutions, laws and procedures, and consistent with international law and obligations, which includes and promotes equality and equity between women and men, full respect for all human rights and fundamental freedoms and the rule of law, access to justice, the elimination of all forms of discrimination, transparent and accountable governance and administration and the encouragement of partnership with free and representative organizations of civil society;

b. Create an enabling economic environment aimed at promoting more equitable access for all to income, resources and social service;

c. Reinforce, as appropriate, the means and capacities for people to participate in the formation and implementation of social and economic policies and programmes through decentralization, open management of public institutions and strengthening the abilities and opportunities of civil society and local communities to develop their own organizations, resources and activities;

d. Reinforce peace by promoting tolerance, non-violence and respect for diversity, and by settling disputes by peaceful means;

e. Promote dynamic, open, free markets, while recognizing the need to intervene in markets, to the extent necessary, to prevent or counteract market failure, promote stability and long-term investment, ensure fair competition and ethical conduct, and harmonize economic and social development, including the development and implementation of appropriate programmes that would entitle and enable people living in poverty and the disadvantaged, especially women, to participate fully and productively in the economy and society;

f. Reaffirm, promote and strive to ensure the realization of the rights set out in relevant international instruments and declarations, such as the Universal Declaration of Human Rights, the Covenant on Economic, Social and Cultural Rights and the Declaration on the Right to Development, including those relating to education, food, shelter, employment, health and information, particularly in order to assist people living in poverty;

g. Create the comprehensive conditions to allow for the voluntary repatriation of refugees in safety and dignity to their countries of origin, and the voluntary and safe return of internally displaced persons to their places of origin and their smooth reintegration into their society.

At the international level, we will:

h. Promote international peace and security and make and support all efforts to settle international disputes by peaceful means in accordance with the Charter of the United Nations;

i. Strengthen international cooperation for achieving social development;

j. Promote and implement policies to create a supportive external economic environment, through, *inter alia*, cooperation in the formulation and implementation of macroeconomic policies, trade liberalization, mobilization and/or provision of new and additional financial resources that are both adequate and predictable and mobilized in a way that maximizes the availability of such resources for sustainable development, using all available funding sources and mechanism, enhanced financial stability, and more equitable access of developing countries to global markets, productive investments and technologies and appropriate knowledge, with due consideration to the needs of countries with economies in transition;

k. Strive to ensure that international agreement relating to trade, investment technology, debt and official development assistance are implemented in a manner that promotes social development;

l. Support, particularly through technical and financial cooperation, the efforts of developing countries to achieve rapid, broadly based sustainable development. Particular consideration should be given to the special needs to small island and land-locked developing countries and the least developed countries;

m. Support, through appropriate international cooperation, the efforts of countries with economies in transition to achieve rapid broadly based sustainable development;

m. Reaffirm and promote all human rights, which are universal, indivisible, interdependent and interrelated, including the right to development as a universal and inalienable right and an integral part of fundamental human rights, and strive to ensure that they are respected, protected and observed.

Commitment 2

We commit ourselves to the goal of eradicating poverty in the world, through decisive national actions and international cooperation, as an ethical, social, political an economic imperative of humankind.

To this end, at the national level, in partnership with all actors of civil society and in the context of a multidimensional and integrated approach, we will:

a. Formulate or strengthen, as a matter of urgency, and preferably by the year 1996, the International Year for the Eradication of Poverty, national policies and strategies geared to substantially reducing overall poverty in the shortest possible time, reducing inequalities and eradicating absolute poverty by a target date to be specified by each country in its national context;

b. Focus our efforts and policies to address the root causes of poverty and to provide for the basic needs of all. These efforts should include the elimination of hunger and malnutrition; the provision of food security, education, employment and livelihood, primary health-care services including reproductive health care, safe drinking water and sanitation, and adequate shelter; and participation in social and cultural life. Social priority will be given to the needs and rights of women and children, who often bear the greatest burden of poverty, and to the needs of vulnerable and disadvantaged groups and persons;

c. Ensure that people living have access to productive resources, including credit, land, education and training, technology, knowledge and information, as well as to public services, and participate in decision-making on a policy and regulatory environment that would enable them to benefit from expanding employment and economic opportunities;

d. Develop and implement policies to ensure that all people have adequate economic and social protection during unemployment, ill health, maternity, child-rearing, widowhood, disability and old age;

e. Ensure that national budgets and policies are oriented, as necessary, to meeting basic needs, reducing inequalities and targeting poverty, as a strategic objectives;

f. Seek to reduce inequalities, increase opportunities and access to resources and income, and remove any political, legal, economic and social factors and constraints that foster and sustain inequality.

At the international level, we will;

g. Strive to ensure that the international community and international organizations, particularly the multilateral financial institutions, assist developing countries and all countries in need in their efforts to achieve our overall goal of eradicating poverty and ensuring basic social protection;

h. Encourage all international donors and multilateral development banks to support policies and programmes for the attainment, in a sustained manner, of the specific efforts of the developing countries and all countries in need relating to people-centered sustainable development and to meeting basic needs for all; to assess their existing programmes in consultation with the concerned developing countries to ensure the achievement of the agreed programme objectives; and to seek to ensure that their own policies and programmes will advance the attainment of agreed development goals that focus on meeting basic needs for all and eradicating absolute poverty. Efforts should be made to ensure that participation by the people concerned is an integral part of such programmes;

i. Focus attention on and support the special needs of countries and regions in which there are substantial concentrations of people living in poverty, in particular in South Asia, and which therefore face serious difficulties in achieving social and economic development.

Commitment 3

We commit ourselves to promoting the goal of full employment as a basic priority of our economic and social policies, and to enabling all men and women to attain secure and sustainable livelihoods through freely chosen productive employment and work.

To this, end at the national level, we will:

a. Put the creation of employment, the reaction of unemployment and the promotion of appropriately and adequately remunerated employment at the centre of strategies and policies of Governments, with full respect for workers' rights and with the participation of employers, workers and their respective organizations, giving special attention to the problems of structural, long-term unemployment and underemployment of youth, women, people with disabilities, and all other disadvantaged groups and individuals;

b. Develop policies to expand work opportunities and productivity in both rural and urban sectors by achieving economic growth, investing in human resource development, promoting technologies that generate productive employment, and encouraging self-employment, entrepreneurship, and small and medium-sized enterprises;

c. Improve access to land, credit, information, infrastructure and other productive resources for small and microenterprises, including those in the informal sector, with particular emphasis on the disadvantaged sectors of society;

d. Develop policies to ensure that workers and employers have the education, information and training needed to adapt to changing economic conditions, technologies and labour markets;

e. Explore innovative options for employment creation and seek new approaches to generating income and purchasing power;

f. Foster policies that enable people to combine their paid work with their family responsibilities;

g. Pay particular attention to women's access to employment, the protection of their position in the labour market and the promotion of equal treatment of women and men, in particular with respect to pay;

h. Take due account of the importance of the informal sector in our employment development strategic with a view to increasing its contribution to the eradication of poverty and to social integration in developing countries, and to strengthening its linkages with the formal economy;

i. Pursue the goal of ensuring quality jobs, and safeguard the basic rights and interests of workers and to this end, freely promote respect for relevant International Labour Organization conventions, including those on the prohibition of forced and child labour, the freedom of association, the right to organize and bargain collectively, and the principle of non-discrimination.

At the international level, we will:

j. Ensure the migrant workers benefit from the protections provided by relevant national and international instruments, take concrete and effective measures against the exploitation of migrant workers, and encourage all countries to consider the ratification and full implementation of the relevant international instruments on migrant workers;

k. Foster international cooperation in macroeconomic policies, liberalization of trade and investment so as to promote sustained economic growth and the creation of employment, and exchange experiences on successful policies and programmes aimed at increasing employment and reducing unemployment.

Commitment 4

We commit ourselves to promoting social integration by fostering societies that are stable, safe and just and that are based on the promotion and protection of all human rights, as well as on non-discrimination, tolerance, respect for diversity, equality of opportunity, solidarity, security, and participation of all people, including disadvantaged and vulnerable groups and persons.

To this end, at the national level, we will:

a. Promote respect for democracy, the rule of law, pluralism and diversity, tolerance and responsibility, non-violence and solidarity by encouraging educational systems, communication media and local communicates and organizations to raise people's understanding and awareness of all aspects of social integration;

b. Formulate or strengthen policies and strategies geared to the elimination of discrimination in all its forms and achievement of social integration based on equality and respect for human dignity;

c. Promote access for all to education, information technology and know-how as essential means for enhancing communication and participation in civil, political, economic, social and cultural life, and ensure respect for civil, political, economic, social and cultural rights;

d. Ensure the protection and full integration into the economy and society of disadvantaged and vulnerable groups and persons;

e. Formulate or strengthen measures to ensure respect for an protection of the human rights of migrants, migrant workers and their families, to eliminate the increasing acts of racism and xenophobia in sectors of many societies, and to promote greater harmony and tolerance in all society;

f. Recognize and respect the right of indigenous people to

maintain and develop their identity, culture and interests, support their aspirations for social justice and provide an environment that enables them to participate in the social, economic and political life of their country;

g. Foster the social protection and full integration into the economy and society of valerians, including veterans and victims of the Second World War and other wars;

h. Acknowledge and encourage and contribution of people of all age groups as equally and vitally important for the building of a harmonious society, and foster dialogue between generations in all parts of society;

i. Recognize and respect cultural, ethnic and religious diversity, promote and protect the rights of persons belonging to national, ethnic, religious or linguistic minorities, and take measures to facilitate their full participation in all aspects of the political, economic, social religious and cultural life of their societies and in the economic progress and social development of their countries;

j. Strengthen the ability of local communities and groups with common concerns to develop their own organizations and resources and to propose policies relating to social development, including through the activities of non-governmental organizations;

k. Strengthen institutions that enhance social integration, recognizing the central role of the family and providing it with an environment that assures its protection and support. In different cultural, political and social systems, various forms of the family exists;

l. Address the problems of crime, violence, and illicit drugs as factors of social disintegration.

At the international level, we will:

m. Encourage the ratification of, the avoidance as far as possible of the resort to reservations to, and the implementation of international instruments and adherence to internationally recognized declarations relevant to the elimination of discrimination and the promotion and protection of all human rights;

n. Further enhance international mechanisms for the provision of humanitarian and financial assistance to refugees and host countries and promote appropriate shared responsibility:

o. Promote international cooperation and partnership on the basis of equality, mutual respect and mutual benefit.

Commitment 5

We commit ourselves to promoting full respect for human dignity and to achieving equality and equity between women and men, and to recognizing and enhancing the participation and leadership roles of women in political, civil, economic, social and cultural life and in development.

To this end, at the national level, we will:

a. Promote changes in attitudes, structures, policies, laws and practices in order to eliminate all obstacles to human dignity, equality and equity in the family and society, and promote full and equal participation of urban and rural women and women with disabilities in social, economic and political life, including in the formulation, implementation and follow-up of public policies and programmes;

b. Establish structure, policies, objectives and measurable goals to ensure gender balance and equity in decision-making processes at all levels, broaden women's political, economic, social and cultural opportunities and independence, and support the empowerment of women, including through their various organizations, especially those of indigenous women, those at the grass-roots level, and those of poverty-stricken communities, including through affirmative action, where necessary, and also through measures to integrate a gender perspective in the design and implementation of economic and social policies;

c. Promote full and equal access of women to literacy, education and training, and remove all obstacles to their access to credit and other productive resources and to their ability to buy, hold and sell property and land equally with men;

d. Take appropriate measures to ensure, on the basis of equality of men and women, universal access to the widest range of health-care services including those relating to reproductive health care, consistent with the Programme of Action of the International Conference on Population and Development;

e. Remove the remaining restrictions on women's rights to own land, inherit property or borrow money, and ensure women's equal right to work;

f. Establish policies, objectives and goals that enhance the equality of status, welfare and opportunity of the girl child, especially in regard to health, nutrition, literacy and education, recognizing that gender discrimination starts at the earliest stages of life;

g. Promote equal partnership between women and men in family and community life and society, emphasize the shared responsibility of men and women in care of children and support for elder family members, and emphasize men's shared responsibility and promote their active involvement in responsible parenthood and responsible sexual and reproductive behaviour ;

h. Take effective measures, including through the enactment and enforcement of laws, and implement policies to combat and eliminate all forms of discrimination, exploitation, abuse and violence against women and girl children, in accordance with relevant international instrument and declarations;

i. Promote and protect the full and equal enjoyment by women of all human rights and fundamental freedoms;

j. Formulate or strengthen policies and practices to ensure that women are enabled to participate fully in paid work and in employment through such measures as positive action, education, training, appropriate protection under labour legislation, and facilitating the provision of quality child care and other support services:

At the international level, we will:

k. Promote and protect women's human rights and encourage the ratification of, if possible by the year 2000, the avoidance, as far as possible, of the resort to reservations to, and the implementation of the provisions of the Convention on the Elimination of All Forms of Discrimination against Women and other relevant instruments, as well as the implementation of the Nairobi Forward-looking Strategies for the Advancement of Women, the Geneva Declaration for Rural Women, and the Programme of Action of the International Conference on Population and Development;

l. Give specific attention to the preparation for the Fourth World Conference on Women, to be held at Beijing in September 1995, and to the implementation and follow-up of that conclusions of that Conference;

m. Promote international cooperation to assist developing countries, at their request, in their efforts to achieve equality and equity and the empowerment of women;

n. Devise suitable means to recognize and make visible the full extent of the work of women and all their contributions to the national economy, including contributions in the unremunerated and domestic sectors.

Commitment 6

We commit ourselves to promoting and attaining the goals of universal and equitable access to quality education, the highest attainable standard of physical and mental health, and the access of all to primary health care, making particular efforts to rectify inequalities relating to social conditions and without distinction as to race, national origin, gender, age or disability; respecting and promoting our common and particular cultures; striving to strengthen the role of culture in development; preserving the essential bases of people-centered sustainable development; and contributing to the full development of human resources and to social development. The purpose of these activities is to eradicate poverty, promote full and productive employment and foster social integration.

To this end, at the national level, we will:

a. Formulate and strengthen time-bound national strategies for the eradication of illiteracy and universalization of basic education, which includes early childhood education, primary education and education for the illiterate, in all communities, in particular for the introduction, if possible, of national language in the educational system and by support of the various means of non-formal education, striving to attain the highest possible standard of learning;

b. Emphasize lifelong learning by seeking to improve the quality of.education of ensure that people of all ages are provided with useful knowledge, reasoning ability, skills, and the ethical and social values required to develop their full capacities in health and dignity and to participate fully in the social, economic and political process of development. In this regard, women and girls should be considered a priority group;

c. Ensure that children, particularly girls, enjoy their rights and promote the exercise of those rights by making education, adequate nutrition and health care accessible to them, consistent with the Convention on the Rights of the Child, and recognizing the rights, duties and responsibilities of parents and persons legally responsible for children;

d. Take appropriate and affirmative steps to enable all children and adolescents to attend and complete school and to close the gender gap in primary, secondary, vocational and higher education;

e. Ensure full and equal to education for girls and women, recognizing that investing in women's education is the key element in achieving social equality, higher productivity and social returns in terms of health, lower infant mortality and the reduced need for high fertility;

f. Ensure equal educational opportunities at all levels for children, youth and adults with disabilities, in integrated settings, taking full account of individual differences and situations;

g. Recognize and support the right of indigenous people to

education in a manner that is responsive to their specific needs, aspirations and cultures, and ensure their full access to health care;

h. Develop specific educational policies, with gender perspective, and design appropriate mechanisms at all levels of society in order to accelerate the conversion of general and specific information available worldwide into knowledge, and the conversion of that knowledge into creativity, increased productive capacity and active participation in society;

i. Strengthen the links between labour market and education policies, realizing that education and vocational training are vital elements in job creation and in combating unemployment and social exclusion in our societies, and emphasize the role of higher education and scientific research in all plans of social development;

j. Develop broad-based education programmes that promote and strengthen respect for all human rights and fundamental freedoms, including the right to development, promote the values of tolerance, responsibility and respect for the diversity and rights of others, and provide training in peaceful conflict resolution, in recognition of the United Nations Decade for Human Rights Education (1995-2005);

k. Focus on learning acquisition and outcome, broaden the means and scope of basic education, enhance the environment for learning and strengthen partnerships among Governments, non-governmental organizations, the private sector, local communities, religious groups and families to achieve the goal of education for all;

l. Establish or strengthen both social-based and community-based health education programmes for children, adolescents and adults, with special attention to girls and women, on a whole range of health issues, as one of the prerequisites for social development, recognizing the rights, duties and responsibilities of parents and other persons legally responsible for children consistent with the Convention on the Rights of the Child;

m. Expedite efforts to achieve the goals of national Health-for-All strategies, based on equality and social justice in line with the Alma-Ata Declaration on Primary Health Care, by developing or updating country action plans or programmes to ensure universal, non-discriminatory access to basic health services, including sanitation and drinking water, to protect health, and to promote nutrition education and preventive health programmes;

n. Strive to ensure that persons with disabilities have access to rehabilitation and other independent living services and assistive technology to enable them to maximize their well-being, independence and full participation in society;

o. Ensure an integrated and intersectoral approach so as to provide for the protection and promotion of health for all in economic and social development, taking cognizance of the health dimensions of policies in all sectors;

p. Seek to attain the maternal and child health objectives, especially the objectives of reducing child and maternal morality, of the World Summit for Children, the United Nations Conference on Environment and Development and the International Conference on Population and Development;

q. Strengthen national efforts to address more effectively the growing HIV/AIDS pandemic by providing necessary education and prevention services, working to ensure that appropriate care and support services are available and accessible to those affected by HIV/AIDS, and taking all necessary steps to eliminate every form of discrimination against and isolation of those living with HIV/AIDS;

r. Promote, in all educational and health policies and programmes, environmental awareness, including awareness of unsustainable patterns of consumption and production.

At the International level, we will:

s. Strive to ensure that international organizations, in particular the international financial institutions, support these objectives, integrating them into their policy programmes and operations as appropriate. This should be complemented by renewed bilateral and regional cooperation;

t. Recognize the importance of the cultural dimension of development to ensure respect for cultural diversity and that of our common human cultural heritage. Creativity should be recognized and promoted;

u. Request the specialized agencies, notably the United Nations Education, Scientific and Cultural Organization and the World Health Organization, as well as other international organizations dedicated to the promotion of education, culture and health, to give greater emphasis to the overriding goals of eradicating poverty, promoting full and productive employment and fostering social integration;

v. Strengthen intergovernmental organizations that utilize various forms of education to promote culture; disseminate information through education and communication media; help spread the use of technologies; and promote technical and professional training and scientific research;

w. Provide support for stronger, better coordinated global actions against major diseases that take a heavy toll of human lives, such as malaria, tuberculosis, cholera, typhoid fever and HIV/AIDS; in this context, continue to support the joint and co-sponsored United Nations programmes on HIV/AIDS;

x. Share knowledge, experience and expertise and enhance creativity, for example by promoting the transfer of technology, in the design and delivery of effective education, training and health programmes and policies, including substance-abuse awareness, prevention and rehabilitation programmes, which will result, *inter alia*, in endogenous capacity-building;

y. Intensify and coordinate international support for education and health programmes based on respect for human dignity and focused on the protection of all women and children, especially against exploitation, trafficking and harmful practices, such as child prostitution, female genital mutilating and child marriages.

Commitment 7

We commit ourselves to accelerating the economic, social and human resource development of Africa and the least developed countries;

To this end, we will:

a. Implement, at the national level, structural adjustment policies, which should include social development goals, as well as effective development strategies that establish a more favorable climate for trade and investment, give priority to human resource development and further promote the development of democratic institutions;

b. Support the domestic efforts of Africa and the least developed countries to implement economic reforms, programmes to increase food security, and commodity diversification efforts through international cooperation, including South-South cooperation and technical and financial assistance, as well as trade and partnership;

c. Find effective, development-oriented and durable solutions to external debt problems, through the immediate implementation of the terms of debt forgiveness agreed upon in the Paris Club in December, 1994, which encompass debt reduction, including cancellation or other debt-relief measures; invite the international financial institutions to examine innovative approaches to assist low-income countries with a high proportion of multilateral debt, with a view to alleviating their debt burdens; and develop techniques of debt conversion applied to social development programmes and projects in conformity with Summit priorities. These actions should take into account the mid-term review of the United Nations New Agenda for the Development of Africa in the 1990s and the Programme of Action for the Least Developed Countries for the 1990s, and should be implemented as soon as possible;

d. Ensure the implementation of the strategies and measures for the development of Africa decided by the international community, and support the reform efforts, development strategies and programmes decided by the Africa countries and the least developed countries;

e. Increase official development assistance, both overall and for social programmes, and improve its impact, consistent with countries' economic circumstances and capacities to assist, and consistent with commitments in international agreements;

f. Consider ratifying the United Nations Convention to Combat Desertification in Those Countries Experiencing Serious Drought and/or Desertification, Particularly in Africa, and support African countries in the implementation of urgent action to the combat desertification and mitigate the effects of drought;

g. Take all necessary measures to ensure that communicable diseases, particularly HIV/AIDS, malaria and tuberculosis, do not restrict or reverse the progress made in economic and social development.

Commitment 8

We commit ourselves to ensuring that when structural adjustment programmes are agreed to they include social development goals, in particular educating poverty, promoting full and productive employment, and enhancing social integration.

To this end, at the national level, we will:

a. Promote basic social programmes and expenditures, in particular those affecting the poor and vulnerable segments of society, and protect them from budget reductions, while increasing the quality and effectiveness of social expenditures;

b. Review the impact of structural adjustment programmes on social development, including, where appropriate, by means of gender-sensitive social impact assessments and other relevant methods, in order to develop policies to reduce their negative effects and improve their positive impact, the cooperation of international financial institutions in the review could be requested by interested countries;

c. Promote, in the countries with economies in transition, an integrated approach to the transformation process, addressing the social consequences of reforms and human resource development needs;

d. Reinforce the social development components of all adjustment policies and programmes, including those results from the globalization of markets and rapid technological chance, by designing policies to promote more equitable and enhanced access to income and resources;

e. Ensure that women do not bear a disproportionate burden of the transitional costs of such processes.

At the international level, we will:

f. Work to ensure that multilateral development banks and other donors complement adjustment lending with enhanced targeted social development investment lending;

g. Strive to ensure that structural adjustment programmes respond to the economic and social conditions, concerns and needs of each country;

h. Enlist the support and cooperation of regional and international organizations and the United Nations system, in particular the Bretton Woods Institutions, in the design, social management and assessment of structural adjustment policies, and in implementing social development goals of integrating them into their policies, programmes, and operations.

Commitment 9

We commit ourselves to increasing significantly and/or utilizing more efficiently the resources allocated to social development in order to achieve the goals of the Summit through national action and regional and international cooperation.

To this end, at the national level, we will:

a. Develop economic policies to promote and mobilize domestic savings and attract external resources for productive investment, and seek innovative sources of funding, both public and private, for social programmes, while ensuring their effective utilization;

b. Implement macroeconomic and micro-economic policies to ensure sustained economic growth and sustainable development to support social development;

c. Promote increased access to credit for small and micro-enterprises, including those in the informal sector, with particular emphasis on the disadvantages sectors of society;

d. Ensure that reliable statistics and statistical indicators are used to develop and assess social policies and programmes so that economic and social resources are used efficiently and effectively;

e. Ensure that, in accordance with national priorities and policies, taxation systems are fair, progressive and economically efficient, cognizant of sustainable development concerns and ensure effective collection of tax liabilities;

f. In the budgetary process, ensure transparency and accountability in the use of public resources, and give priority to providing and improving basic social services;

g. Undertake to explore new ways of generating new public and private financial resources, *inter alia*, through the appropriate reduction of excessive military expenditures, including global military expenditures and the arms trade, and investments for arms production and acquisition, taking into consideration national security requirements, so as to allow possible allocation of additional funds for social and economic development;

h. Utilize and develop fully the potential and contribution of cooperatives for the attainment of social development goals, in particular the eradication of poverty, the generation of full and productive employment, and the enhancement of social integration.

At the international level, we will:

i. Seek to mobilize new and additional financial resources that are both adequate and predictable and are mobilized in a way that maximizes the availability of such resources and uses all available funding sources and mechanisms, inter alia, multilateral, bilateral and private sources, including on concessional and grant terms;

j. Facilitate the flow to developing countries of international finance, technology and human skill in order to realize the objective of providing new and additional resources that are both adequate and predictable;

k. Facilitate the flow of international finance, technology and human skill towards the countries with economies in transition;

l. Strive for the fulfillment of the agreed target of 0.7 per cent of gross national product for overall official development assistance as soon as possible, and increase the share of funding for social development programmes, commensurate with the scope and scale of activities required to achieve the objectives and goals of the present Declaration and the Programme of Action of the Summit;

m. Increase the flow of international resources to meet the needs of countries facing problems rating to refugees and displaced persons;

n. Support South-South cooperation, which can take advantage of the experience of developing countries that have overcome similar difficulties;

o. Ensure the urgent implementation of existing debt-relief agreements and negotiate further initiative, in addition to existing ones, to alleviate the debts of the poorest and heavily indebted low-income country at an early date, especially through more favourable terms of debt for giveness, including application of the terms of debts forgiveness agreed upon in the Paris Club in December 1994, which encompass debt reduction, including cancellation or other debt-relief measures; where appropriate, these counties should be given a reduction of their bilateral official debt sufficient to enable them to exist from the rescheduling process and resume growth and development; invite the international financial institutions to examine innovative approaches to assist low-income countries with a high proportion of multilateral debt, with a view to alleviating their debt burdens; develop techniques of debt conversion applied to social development programmes and project in conformity with Summit priorities;

p. Fully implement the Final Act of the Uruguay Round of multilateral trade negotiations as scheduled, included the complementary provision specified in the Marrakesh Agreement establishing the World Trade Organization, in recognition of the fact that broadly based growth in incomes, employment trade are mutually reinforcing, taking into account the need to assist African counties and the least developed countries in evaluating the impact of the implementation of the Final Act so that they can benefit fully;

q. Monitor the impact of trade liberalization on the progress made in developing countries to meet basic human needs, giving particular attention to new initiatives to expand their access to international markets;

r. Give attention to the needs of countries with economies in transition with respect to international cooperation and financial and technical assistance, stressing the need for the full integration of economies in transition into the world economy, in particular to improve market access for exports in accordance with multilateral trade rules, taking into account the needs of developing countries;

s. Support United Nations development efforts by a substantial increase in resources for operational activities on a predictable, continuous and assured basis, commensurate with the increasing needs of developing countries and strengthen the capacity of the United Nations and the specialized agencies to fulfil their responsibilities in the implementation of the outcome of the World Summit for Social Development.

Commitment 10

We commit ourselves to an improved and strengthen framework for international, regional and subregional cooperation for social development, in a spirit of partnership, through the United Nations and other multilateral institutions.

To this end, at the national level, we will:

a. Adopt the appropriate measures and mechanisms for implementing and monitoring the outcome of the World Summit for Social Development, with the assistance, upon request, of the specialized agencies, programmes and regional commissions of the United Nations system, with broad participation of all sectors of civil society.

At the regional level, we will:

b. Pursue such mechanisms and measures as are necessary and appropriate in particular regions or subregions. The regional commissions, in cooperation with regional inter government organizations and banks, could convene, on a biennial basis, a meeting a high political level to evaluate progress made towards fulfilling the outcome of the Summit, exchange views on their respective experiences and adopt appropriate measures. The regional commissions should report, through the appropriate mechanisms, to the Economic and Social Council on the outcome of such meetings.

At the international level, we will:

c. Instruct our representatives to the organizations and bodies of the United Nations system, international development agencies and multilateral development banks to enlist the support and cooperation of these organizations and bodies to take appropriate and coordinated measures for continuous and sustained progress in attaining the goals and commitments agreed to by the Summit. The United Nations and the Bretton Woods institutions should establish regular and substantive dialogue, including at the field level, for more effective and efficient coordination of assistance for social development;

d. Refrain from any unilateral measure not in accordance with international law and the Charter of the United Nations that creates obstacles to trade relations among States;

c. Strengthen the structure, resources and processes of the Economic and Social Council and its subsidiary bodies, and other organizations within the United Nations system that are concerned with economic and social development;

f. Request the Economic and Social Council to review and asses, on the basis of reports of national Governments, the regional commissions, relevant functional commissions and specialized agencies, progress made by the international community towards implementing the outcome of the World Summit for Social Development, and to report to the General Assembly, accordingly, for its appropriate consideration and action;

g. Request the General Assembly to hold a special session in the year 2000 for an overall review and appraisal of the implementation of the outcome of the Summit and to consider further actions and initiatives.

2
Programme of Action of the World Summit for Social Development

Introduction

1. The present Programme of Action outlines, policies, actions and measures to implement the principles and fulfil the commitments enunciated in the Copenhagen Declaration on Social Development adopted by the World Summit for Social Development. Our success will be based on the results that we achieve.

2. Actions are recommended to create, in a framework of sustained economic growth and sustainable development, a national and international environment favourable to social development, to eradicate poverty, to enhance production employment and reduce unemployment, and to foster social integration. All the recommended actions are linked, either in the requirements for their design, including the participation of all concerned, or in their consequences for the various facets of the human condition. Policies to eradicate poverty, reduce disparities and combat social exclusion require the creation of employment opportunities, and would be incomplete and ineffective without measures to eliminate discrimination and promote participate on and harmonious social relationship among groups and nations. Enhancing

positive interaction between environmental, economic and social policies is also essential for success in the longer time. The well-being of people also requires the exercise of all human rights and fundamental freedom, access to the provision of good development of harmonious relations within communities. Social integration, or the capacity of people to live together with full respect for the dignity of each individual, the common good, pluralism and diversity, non-violent and solidarity, as well as their ability to participate in social, cultural, economic and political life, encompasses all aspects of social development and all policies. It requires the protection of the weak, as well as the right to differ, to create and to innovate. It calls for a sound economic environment, as well as for cultures based on freedom and responsibility. It also calls for the full involvement of both the State and the civil society.

3. Many of the issues mentioned in the present Programme of Action have been addressed in greater detail by previous world conferences concerned with questions closely related to the different aspects of social development. The Programme of Action was elaborated against the background of, and taking into account the commitments, principles and recommendations of, these other conferences, and is also based on the experience of many countries in promoting social objectives in the context of their particular conditions. The special importance of the Programme of Action lies in its integrated approach and its attempt to combine many different actions for poverty eradication, employment creation and social integration in coherent national and international strategies for social development. The implementation of the recombinations contained in the Programme of Action is the sovereign right of each country, consistent with national laws and development priorities, with full respect for the various religious and ethical values and cultural back grounds of its people, and in conformity with all human rights and fundamental freedoms. Each country will also take action in accordance with its evolving capacities. The outcome of relevant international conferences would also be duly taken into account in the implementation of the present Programme of Action.

1. An Enabling Environment for Social Development

Basis for Action and Objectives

4. Social development is inseparable from the cultural, ecological, economic, political and spiritual environment in which it takes place. It cannot be pursued as a sectoral initiative. Social development is also clearly linked to the development of peace, freedom, stability and security, both nationally and internationally. To promote social development requires an orientation of values, and objectives and priorities towards the well-being of all and the strengthening and promotion of conducive initiations and policies, Human dignity, all human rights and fundamental freedoms, equality, equity and social justice constitute the fundamental values of all societies. The pursuit, promotion and protection of these values, among others, provides the basic legitimacy of all institutions and and all exercise of authority and promotes an environment in which human beings are at the centre of concern for sustainable development. They are entitled to a healthy and productive life in harmony with nature.

5. The economies and societies of the world are becoming increasingly interdependent. Trade and capital flows, migration, scientific and technological innovations, communities and cultural exchanges are shaping the global community. The same global community is threatened by environmental degradation, severe food crises, epidemics, all forms of racial discrimination, xenophobia, various forms of intolerance, violence and criminality and risk of losing the richness of cultural diversity. Governments increasingly recognize that their response to changing circumstances and their desires to achieve sustainable development and social progresss will require programmes and strengthened international cooperation. Such cooperation is particularly crucial to ensure that countries in need of assistance, such as those in Africa and the least development countries, can benefit from the process of globalization.

6. Economic activities, through which individuals express their initiative and creativity and which enhance the wealth of communities, are a fundamental basis for social progress.

But social progress will not be realized simply through the free interaction of market forces. Public policies are necessary mechanisms, to maintain social stability and to create a national and international economic environment that promotes sustainable growth on a global scale. Such growth should promote equity and social justice, tolerance, responsibility and involvement.

7. The ultimate goal of social development is to improve and enhance the quality of life of all people. It requires democratic institutions, respect for all human rights and fundamental freedoms, increased and equal economic opportunities, the rule of law, the promotion of respect for cultural diversity and the rights of persons belonging to minorities, and an active involvement of civil society. Empowerment and participation are essential for democracy, harmony and social development. All members of society should have the opportunity and be able to exercise the right and responsibility to take an active part in the affairs of the community in which they life. Gender equality and equity and the full participation of women in all economic, social and political activities are essential. The obstacles that have limited the access of women to decision-making, education, health-care services and productive empowerment must be eliminated and an equitable partnership between men and women established, involving men's full responsibility in family life. It is necessary to change the prevailing social paradigm of gender to usher in a new generation of women and men working together to create a more humane world older.

8. Against this background, we will promote and enable environment based on a people-centered approach to sustainable development, with the following features;

- Broad-based participation and involvement of civil society in the formulation and implementation of decisions determining the functioning and well-being of our societies;
- Broad-based patterns of sustained economic growth and sustainable development the integration of population issues into economic and development strategies, which

will speed up the pace of sustainable development and poverty eradication and contribute to the achievement of population objectives and an improved quality of life of the population;

- Equitable and non-discriminatory distribution of the benefits of growth among social groups and countries and expanded access to productive resources for people living in poverty;
- An interaction of market forces conducive to efficiency and social development;
- Public policies that seek to overcome socially divisive disparities and that respect pluralism and diversity;
- A supportive and stable political and legal framework that promotes the mutually reinforcing relationship between democracy, development and all human rights and fundamental freedoms;
- Political and social process that avoid exclusion while respecting pluralism and diversity, including religious and cultural diversity;
- A strengthened role for the family in accordance with the principles, goals and commitments of the Copenhagen Declaration on Social Development and those of the International conference on Population and Development, as well as for community and civil society;
- Expanded access to knowledge, technology, education, health-care services and information;
- Increased solidarity, partnership and cooperation at all levels;
- Public policies that empower people to enjoy good health and productivity throughout their lives;
- Protection and conservation of the natural environment in the context of people-centered sustainable development.

Actions

A. A favourable national and international economic environment

9. The promotion of mutually reinforcing, broad-based, sus-

tained economic growth and sustainable development on a global scale, as well as growth in production, a non-discriminatory and multilateral rule-based international trading system, employment and incomes, as a basis for social development, requires the following actions:

a. Promoting the establishment of an open, equitable, co-operative and mutually beneficial international economic environment;

b. Implementing sound and stable macroeconomic and sectoral policies that encourage broad-based, sustained economic growth and development that is sustainable and equitable, that generate jobs, and that are geared towards eradicating poverty and reducing social and economic inequalities and exclusion;

c. Promoting enterprise, productive investment and expanded access to open and dynamic markets in the context of an open, equitable, secure, non-discriminatory, predictable, transparent and multilateral rule-based international trading system, and to technologies for all people, particularly those living in poverty and the disadvantaged, as well as for the least development countries;

d. Implementing fully and as scheduled the Final Act of the Uruguay Round of multilateral trade negotiations;

e. Refraining from any unilateral measure not in accordance with international law and Chapter of the United Nations that creates obstacles to trade relations among State, impedes the full realization of social and economic development and hinders the well-being of the population in the affected countries;

f. Increasing food production, through the sustainable development of the agricultural sector and improvement of market opportunities, and improving access to food by low-income people in developing countries, as a means of alleviating poverty, eliminating malnutrition and raising their standards of living;

g. Promoting the coordination of macro economic policies at the national, subregional, regional and international levels in order to promote an international financial system that is more conductive to stable and sustained economic growth and sustainable development through, *inter alia*, a higher degree of stability in financial markets, reducing the risk of financial crisis, improving the stability of exchange rates, stabilizing and striving for low real interest rates in the long run and reducing the uncertainties of financial flows;

h. Establishing, strengthening or rehabilitating, *inter alia*, through capacity-building where necessary, national and international structures, processes and resources available, to ensure appropriate consideration and coordination of economic policy, with special emphasis on social development;

i. Promoting or strengthening capacity-building in developing countries, particularly in Africa and the least developed countries, to develop social activities;

j. Ensuring that, in accordance with Agenda 21 and the various consensus agreements, conventions and programmes of action adoption within the framework of the follow-up to the outcome of the United Nations Conference on Environment and Development, broad-based, sustained economic growth and sustainable development respects the need to protect the environment and the interests of future generations;

k. Ensuring that the special needs and vulnerabilities of small island developing States are adequately addressed in order to enable them to achieve sustained economic growth and sustainable development with equity by implementing the Programme of Action for the Sustainable Development of Small Island Developing States.

10. To ensure that the benefits of global economic growth are equitably distributed among countries, the following actions are essential:

a. Continuing efforts to alleviate the onerous debt and debt-service burdens connected with the various types of debt of many developing countries, on the basis of an equitable and duration approach and, where appropriate, addressing the full stock of debt of the poorest and most indebted developing countries as a matter of priority, reducing trade barriers and promoting expanded access by all countries to markets, in the context of an open, equitable, secure, non-discriminatory, predictable, transparent and multilateral rule-based international trading system, as well as to productive investment, technologies and know-how;

b. Strengthening and improving technical and financial assistance to developing countries to promote sustainable development and overcome hindrances to their full and effective participation in the world economy;

c. Changing unsustainable consumption and production patterns, taking into account that the major cause of continued deterioration of the global environment is the unsustainable pattern of consumption and production, particularly in industrialized countries, which is a matter of grave concern, aggravating poverty and imbalances;

d. Elaborating police is to enable developing countries to take advantage of expanded international trading opportunities in the context of the full implementation of the Final Act of the Uruguay Round of multilateral trade negotiations; and assisting countries, particularly in Africa, that are not currently in a position to benefit fully from the liberalization of the world economy;

e. Supporting the efforts of developing countries, particularly those heavily dependent on commodity exports, to diversify their economies.

11. Within the framework of support to developing countries, giving priority to the needs of Africa and the least developed countries, the following actions are necessary at the national and international levels, as appropriate;

a. Implementing effective policies and development strategies that establish a more favourable climate for social development, trade and investments, giving priority to human resources development and promoting the further development of democratic institutions;

b. Supporting African countries and least developed countries in their efforts to create an enabling environment that attracts foreign and domestic direct investment, encourages savings, induces the return of flight capital and promotes the full participation of the private sector, including non-governmental organizations, in the growth and development process;

c. Supporting economic reforms to improve the functioning of commodity markets and commodity diversification efforts through appropriate mechanisms, bilateral and multilateral financing and technical cooperation, including South-South cooperation, as well as through trade and partnership;

d. Continuing to support the commodity diversification efforts of Africa and the least development countries, *inter alia*, by providing technical and financial assistance for the preparatory phase of their commodity diversification projects and programmes;

e. Finding effective, development-oriented and durable solutions to external debt problems, through the immediate implementation of the terms of debt forgiveness agreed upon in the Paris Club in December 1994, which encompass debt reducing, including cancellation or other debt relief measures; inviting the international financial institutions to examine innovative approaches to assist low-income countries with a high proportion of multilateral debt with a view to alleviating their debt burden; developing techniques of debt conversion applied to social development programmes and projects in conformity with Summit priorities. These actions should take into account the mid-term review of the United Nations New Agenda for the Development of Africa in the 1990s and the Programme of Action for the Least Development Countries for the 1990s and should be implemented as soon as possible;

f. Supporting the development of strategies adopted by these countries and working in partnership to ensure the implementation of measures for their development;

g. Taking appropriate actions, consistent with the Final Act of the Uruguay Round of multilateral trade negotiations, in particular the decision on measures in favour of the least developed countries the and the decision on measures concerning the possible negative effects of the reform programme on the least development countries and the net food importing developing countries, in order to give these countries special attention, with a view to enhancing their participation in the multilateral trading system and to mitigating any adverse effects of the implementation of the Uruguay Round, while stressing the need to support the African countries so that they can benefit fully from the results of the Uruguay Round;

h. Increasing official development assistance, both in total and for social programmes, and improving its impact, consistent with countries; economic circumstances and capabilities to assist, and consistent with commitments in international agreements, and striving to attain the agreed upon target of 0.7 per cent of gross national product for official development assistance and 0.15 per cent to the least development countries, as soon as possible.

12. Making economic growth and the interaction of market forces more conductive to social development requires the following actions:

a. Implementing measures to open market opportunities for all, especially people living in poverty and the disadvantaged, and to encourage individuals and communities to take economic initiatives, innovate and invest in activities that contribute to social development while promoting broad-based sustained economic growth and sustainable development;

b. Improving, broadening and regulating, to the extent necessary, the functioning of markets to promote sustained economic growth and sustainable development, stability and long-term investment, fair competition and ethical conduct; adopting and implementing policies to promote equitable distribution of the benefits of growth and protect crucial social services, *inter alia*, through complementing market mechanisms and mitigating any negative impacts posed by market forces; and implementing complementary policies to foster social development, while dismantling, consistent with the provisions of the Final Act of the Uruguay Round of multilateral trade negotiations, protectionist measures, and to integrate social and economic development;

c. Establishing an open market policy that reduces barriers to entry, promotes transparency of markets through, *inter alia*, better access to information and widens the choices available to consumers;

d. Promoting greater access to technology and technical assistance, as well as corresponding know-how, especially for micro-enterprises and small and medium-sized enterprises in all countries, particularly in developing countries;

e. Encouraging transnational and national corporations to operate in a framework of respect for the environments while copying with national laws and legislation, and in accordance with international agreements and conventions, and with proper consideration for the social and cultural impact of their activities;

f. Adopting and implementing long-term strategies to ensure substantial, well-directed public and private investment in the construction and renewal of basic infrastructure, which will benefit people living in poverty and generate employment;

g. Ensuring substantial public and private investment in human resource development and in capacity-building in health and education, as well as in empowerment and participation, especially for people living in poverty or suffering from social exclusion;

h. Supporting and paying special attention to the development of small-scale and micro-enterprises, particularly in rural areas, as well as subsistence economics, to secure their safe interaction with larger economies;

i. Supporting the economic activities of indigenous people, improving their conditions and development, and securing their safe interaction with larger economies;

j. Supporting institutions, programmes and system to disseminate practical information to promote social progress.

13. Ensuring that fiscal system and other public policies are geared towards poverty eradication and that they do not generate socially divisive disparities calls for:

a. Enacting rules and regulations and creating a moral and ethical climate that prevents all forms of corruption and exploitation of individuals, families and groups;

b. Promoting fair competition and ethical responsibility in business activities, and enhancing cooperation and interaction among Governments, the private sector and civil society;

c. Ensuring that fiscal and monetary policies promote savings and long-term investment in productive activities in accordance with national priorities and policies;

d. Considering measures to address inequities arising from accumulation of wealth through, *inter alia*, the use of appropriate taxation at the national level, and to reduce inefficiencies and improve stability in financial markets in accordance with national priorities and policies;

e. Re-examining the distribution of subsidies, *inter alia*, between industry and agriculture, urban and rural areas, and private and pubic consumption, to ensure that subsidy systems benefit people living in poverty, especially the vulnerable, and reduce disparities;

f. Promoting international agreements that address effectively issues of double taxation, as well as cross-border tax evasion, in accordance with the priorities and policies of State concerned, while improving the efficiency and fairness of tax collection;

g. Assisting developing countries, upon their request, to establish efficient and fair systems by strengthening the administrative capacity for tax assessment and collection and tax evader prosecution, and to support a more progressive tax system;

h. Assisting countries with economies in transition to establish fair and effective systems of taxation on a solid legal basis, contribution to the socio-economic reforms under way in those countries;

B. A favourable national and international political and legal environment

14. To ensure that the political framework supports the objectives of social development, the following actions are essential:

a. Ensuring the governmental institutions and agencies reasonable for the planning and implementation of social policies have the status, resources and information necessary to give high priority to social development in policy-making;

b. Ensuring the rule of law and democracy and the existence of rules and processes to create transparency and accountability for all public and private institutions and to prevent and combat all forms of corruption, sustained through education and development of attitudes and values promoting responsibility, solidarity and a strengthened civil society;

c. Eliminating all forms of discrimination, while developing and encouraging educational programmes and media campaigns to that end;

d. Encouraging decentralization of public institutions and services to a level that, compatible with the overall responsibility, priorities and objectives of Governments, responds properly to local needs and facilitates local participation;

e. Establishing conditions for the social partners to organize and function with guaranteed freedom of expression and association and the right to engage in collective bargaining and to promote mutual interests, taking due account of national laws and regulations;

f. Establishing similar conditions for professional organizations and organizations of independent workers;

g. Promoting political and social process inclusive of all members of society and respectful of political pluralism and cultural diversity;

h. Strengthening the capacities and opportunities of all, people especially those who are disadvantaged or vulnerable, to enhance their own economic and social development, to establish and maintain organizations representing their interests and to be involved in the planning and implementation of government policies and programmes by which they will be directly affected;

i. Ensuring full involvement and participation of women at all levels in the decision-making and implementation process and in the economic and political mechanisms through which policies are formulated and implemented;

j. Removing all legal impediments to the ownership of all means of production and property by men and women;

k. Taking measures, in cooperation with the international community, as appropriate, in accordance with the Charter of the United Nations, the Universal Declaration of Human Rights, other international instruments and relevant United Nations resolutions, to create the appropriate political and legal environment to address the root cause of movements of refugees, to allow their voluntary return in safety and dignity. Measures should also be taken at the national level, with international cooperation, as appropriate, in accordance with the Charter of the United Nations, to create conditions for internally displaced persons to voluntarily return to their places of origin.

15. It is essential for social development that all human rights and fundamental freedoms, including the right to development as an integral part of fundamental human rights, be promoted and protected through the following actions:

a. Encouraging ratification of existing international human rights conventions that have not been ratified; and implementing the provisions of conventions and covenants that have been ratified;

b. Reaffirming and promoting all human rights and fundamental freedoms, which are universal, indivisible, interdependent and interrelated, including the right to development, and striving to ensure that they are respected, protected and observed through appropriate legislation, dissemination of information, education and training and the provision of effective mechanisms and remedies for enforcement, *inter alia*, through the establishment or strengthening of national institutions responsible for monitoring and enforcement;

c. Taking measures to ensure that every human person and all peoples are entitled to participate, to contribute to and to enjoy economic, social, cultural and political development; encouraging all human persons to take responsibility for development, individually and collectively; and recognizing that State have the primary responsibility for the creation of national and international conditions favourable for the realization of the right to development, taking into account the relevant provisions of the Vienna Declaration and Programme of Action;

d. Promoting the realization of the right to development through strenghtening democracy, development and respect for human rights and fundamental freedoms and through effective development policies at the national level, as well as equitable economic relations and a favourable economic environment at the international level, since sustained action is indispensable for fostering a more rapid development of developing countries;

e. Removing obstacles to the realization of the right of peoples to self-determination, in particular of peoples living under colonial or other forms of alien domination or foreign occupation, which adversely affect their social and economic development;

f. Promoting and protecting the human rights of women and removing all obstacles to full equality and equity between women and men in political, civil, economic, social and cultural life;

g. Giving special attention to promoting and protecting the rights of the child, with particular attention to the rights of the girl child, by, *inter alia*, encouraging the ratification and implementation of the Convention on the Rights of the Child and the Plan of Action for Implementing the World Declaration on the Survival, Protection and Development of Children in the 1990s adopted at the World Summit for Children;

h. Providing all people, in particular the vulnerable and disadvantaged in society, with the benefit of an independent, fair and effective system of justice, and ensuring access by all to competent sources of advice about legal rights and obligations;

i. Taking effective measures to bring to an end all *de jure* and de facto discrimination against persons with disabilities;

j. Strengthening the ability of civil society and the community to participate actively in the planning, decision-making and implementation of social development programmes, by education and access to resources;

k. Promoting and protecting the rights of individuals in order to prevent and eliminate situations of domestic discrimination and violence.

16. An open political and economic system requires access by all to knowledge, education and information by:

a. Strengthening the educational system at all levels; as well as other means of acquiring skills and knowledge, and ensuring universal access to basic education and lifelong educational opportunities, while removing economic and socio-cultural barriers to the exercise of the right to education;

b. Raising public awareness and promoting gender-sensitivity education to eliminate all obstacles to full gender equality and equity;

c. Enabling and encouraging access by all to a wide range of information and opinion on matters of general interest through the mass media and other means;

d. Encouraging education system and, to the extent consistent with freedom of expression, communication media to raise people's understanding and awareness of all aspects of social integration, including gender sensitivity, non-violence, tolerance and solidarity and respect for the diversity of cultures and interests, and to discourage the exhibition of pornography and the gratuitous depiction of explicit violence and cruelty in the media;

e. Improving the reliability, validity, utility and public availability of statistical and other information on social development gender issues, including the effective use of gender-disaggregated statistics collected at the national, regional and international levels, including through support to academic and research institutions.

17. International support for national efforts to promote a favourable political and legal environment must be in conformity with the Charter of the United Nations and principles of international law and consistent with the Declaration on Principles of International Law concerning Friendly Relations and Cooperation among States in accordance with the Charter of the United Nations. Support calls for the following actions:

a. Making use, as appropriate, of the capacity of the United Nations and other relevant international, regional and subregional organizations to prevent and resolve armed conflicts and promote social progress and better standards of life in larger freedom;

b. Coordinating policies, actions and legal instruments and/or measures to combat terrorism, all forms of extremist violence, illicit arms trafficking, organized crime and illicit drug problems, money laundering and related crimes, trafficking in women, adolescents, children, migrants, and human organs, and other activities contrary to human rights and human dignity;

c. States cooperating with one another in ensuring development and eliminating obstacles to development. The international community should promote effective international cooperation, supporting the efforts of developing countries, for the realization of the right to development and the elimination of obstacles to development, through, *inter alia*, the implementation of the provisions of the Declaration on the Right to Development as reaffirmed by the Vienna Declaration and Programme of Action. Lasting progress towards the implementation of the right to development requires effective development policies at the national level, as well as equitable economic relations and a favourable economic environment at the international level. The right to development should be fulfilled so as to equitably meet the social development and environment needs of present and future generations;

d. Ensuring that human persons are at the center of social development and that is fully reflected in the programmes and activities of subregional, regional and international organizations;

e. Reinforcing the capacity of relevant national, regional and international organization, within their mandates, to promote the implementation of all human rights and fundamental freedoms and the elimination of all forms of discrimination;

f. Elaborating policies, within the mandates and functions of the various international institutions, that will support the objectives of social development and contribute to institutional development through capacity-building and other forms of cooperation;

g. Strengthening the capacities of Governments, the private sector and civil society, especially in Africa and the least developed countries, to enable them to meet their specific and global responsibilities;

h. Reinforcing the capacities of Governments, the private sector and civil society in the countries with economies in transition, with a view to helping them in the process of transforming their economies from centrally planned to market-oriented ones.

2. Eradication of Poverty

Basis for action and objectives

18. Over 1 billion people in the world today live under unacceptable conditions of poverty, mostly in developing coun-

tries, and particularly in rural areas of low-income Asia and the Pacific, Africa, Latin America and Caribbean, and the least developed countries.

19. Poverty has various manifestations, including lack of income and productive resources sufficient to ensure sustainable livelihoods; hunger and malnutrition; ill health; limited or lack of access to education and other basic services; increased morbidity and mortality from illness; hopelessness and inadequate housing; unsafe environments; and social discrimination and exclusion. It is also characterized by a lack of participation in decision-making and in civil, social and cultural life. It occurs in all countries: as mass poverty in many developing countries, pockets of poverty amid wealth in developed countries, loss of livelihoods as a results of economic recession, sudden poverty as a result of disaster or conflict, the poverty of low-wage workers, and the utter destitution of people who fall outside family support systems, social institutions and safety nets. Women bear a disproportionate burden of poverty, and children growing up in poverty are often permanently disadvantaged. Older people, people with disabilities, indigenous people, refugees and internally displaced persons are also particularly vulnerable to poverty. Furthermore, poverty in its various forms represents a barrier to communication and access to services, as well as a major health risk, and people living in poverty are particularly vulnerable to the consequences of disasters and conflicts. Absolute poverty is a condition characterized by severe deprivation of basic human needs, including food, safe drinking water, sanitation facilities, health, shelter, education and information. It depends not only on income but also on access to social services.

20. There is general agreement that persistent widespread poverty, as well as serious social and gender inequities, have significant influences on and are in turn influenced by demographic parameters, such as population growth, structure and distribution and production patterns are contributing to the unsustainable use of natural resources and environmental degradation, as well as to the reinforcement of social inequities and poverty, with the above-mentioned

consequences for demographic parameters.

21. Urban poverty is rapidly increasing in pace with overall urbanization. It is a growing phenomenon in all countries and regions, and often poses special problems, such as overcrowding, contaminated water and bad sanitation, unsafe shelter, crime and additional social problems. An increasing number of low-income urban households are female-maintained.

22. Among people living in poverty, gender disparities are marked, especially in the increase in female-maintained households. With increasing population, the numbers of youth living in poverty will increase significantly. Therefore, specific measures are needed to address the juvenilization and feminization of poverty.

23. Poverty has various causes, including structural ones. Poverty is a complex multidimensional problem with origins in both the national and international domains. No uniform solution can be found for global application. Rather, country-specific programmes to tackle poverty and international efforts supporting national efforts, as well as the parallel processes of creating a supportive international environment, are crucial for a solution to this problem. Poverty is inseparably linked to lack of control over resources, including land, skills, knowledge, capital and social connections. Without those resources, people are easily neglected by policy makers and have limited access to institutions, markets, employment and public services. The eradication to poverty cannot be accomplished through anti-poverty programmes alone but will require democratic participation and changes in economic structures in order to ensure access for all to resources, opportunities and public services, to undertake policies geared to more equitable distribution of wealth and income, to provide social protection for those who cannot support themselves, and to assist people confronted by unforeseen catastrophe, whether individual or collective, natural, social or technological.

24. The eradication of poverty requires universal access to economic opportunities that will promote sustainable livelihood and basic social services, as well as special efforts to facilitate

access to opportunities and services for the disadvantaged. People living in poverty and vulnerable groups must be empowered through organization and participation in all aspects of political, economic and social life, in particular in the planning and implementation of policies that affect them, thus enabling them to become genuine partners in development.

25. There is therefore an urgent need for:

- National strategies to reduce overall poverty substantially, including measures to remove the structural barriers that prevent people from escaping poverty, with specific time-bound commitments to eradicate absolute poverty by a target date to be specified by each country in its national context;
- Stronger international cooperation and the support of international institutions to assist countries in their efforts to eradicate poverty and to provide basic social protection and services;
- Development of methods to measures all forms of poverty, especially absolute poverty, and to assess and monitor the circumstances of those at risk, within the national context;
- Regular national reviews of economic policies and national budgets to orient them towards eradicating poverty and reducing inequalities;
- Expanded opportunities to enable people living in poverty to enhance their overall capacities and improve their economic and social conditions, while managing resources sustainably;
- Human resources development and improved infrastructural facilities;
- Comprehensive provision for the basic needs of all;
- Policies ensuring that all people have adequate economic and social protection during unemployment, ill health, maternity, disability and old age;
- Policies that strengthen the family and contribute to its

stability in accordance with the principles, goals and commitments contained in the Copenhagen Declaration on Social Development and in the Programme of Action of the International Conference on Population and Development;

- Mobilization of both the public and the private sectors, more developed areas, educational and academic institutions and non-governmental organizations to assist poverty-stricken areas.

Actions

A. Formulation of Integrated Strategies

26. Governments should give greater focus to public efforts to eradicate absolute poverty and to reduce overall poverty substantially by:

a. Promoting sustained economic growth, in the context of sustainable development, and social progress, requiring that growth be broadly based, offering equal opportunities to all people. All countries should recognize their common but differentiated responsibility. The developed countries acknowledge the responsibility they bear in the international pursuit of sustainable development, and should continue to improve their efforts to promote sustained economic growth and to narrow imbalances in a manner that can benefit all countries, particularly the developing countries;

b. Formulating or strengthening, preferably by 1996, and implementing national poverty eradication plans to address the structural causes of poverty, encompassing action on the local, national subregional, regional and international levels. These plans should establish, within each national context, strategies and affordable time-bound goals and targets for the substantial reduction of overall poverty and the eradication of absolute poverty. In the context of national plans, particular attention should be given to employment creation as a means of eradicating poverty, giving appropriate consideration to health and education, assigning a higher priority to basic social services, generating household income, and promoting access to productive assets and economic opportunities;

c. Identifying the livelihood systems, survival strategies and self-help organizations of people living in poverty and working with such organizations to develop programmes for combating poverty that build on their efforts, ensuring the full participation of the people concerned and responding to their actual needs;

d. Elaborating, at the national level, the measurements, criteria and indicators for determining the extend and distribution of absolute poverty. Each country should develop a precise definition and assessment of absolute poverty, preferably by 1996, the International Year for the Eradication of Poverty;

e. Establishing policies, objectives and measurable targets to enhance and broaden women's economic opportunities and their access to productive resources, particularly women who have no source of income;

f. Promoting effective enjoyment by all people of civil, cultural, economic, political and social rights, and access to existing social protecting and public services, in particular through encouraging the ratification and ensuring the full implementation of relevant human rights instruments, such as the international of relevant human rights instruments, such as the International Covenant on Economic, Social and Cultural Rights and the International Covenant on Civil and Political Rights;

g. Eliminating the injustice and obstacles that women are faced with, and encouraging the strengthening the participation of women of taking decisions and in implementing them, as well as their access to productive resources and land ownership and their right to inherit goods;

h. Encouraging and supporting local community development projects that foster the skill, self-reliance and self-confidence of people living in poverty and that facilitate their active participate in efforts to eradicate poverty.

27. Governments are urged to integrate goals and targets for combating poverty into overall economic and social policies and planning at the local, national and, where appropriate, regional levels by:

a. Analysing polices and programmes, including those relating to macroeconomic stability, structural adjustment programmes, taxation, investments, employment, markets and all relevant sectors of the economy, with respect to their impact on poverty and inequality, assessing their impact on family well-being and conditions, as well as their gender implications, and adjusting them, as appropriate, to promote a more equitable distribution of productive assets, wealth, opportunities income and services;

b. Redesigning public investment policies that relate to infrastructure development, the management of natural resources and human resource development to benefit people living in poverty and to promote their compatibility with the long-term improvement of livelihoods;

c. Ensuring that development policies benefit low-income communities and rural and agricultural development;

d. Selecting, wherever possible, development schemes that do not displace local populations, and designing an appropriate policy and legal framework to compensate the displaced for their losses, to help them to re-establish their livelihoods and to promote their recovery from social and cultural disruption;

e. Designing and implementing environmental protection and resources management measures that take into account the needs of people living in poverty and vulnerable groups in accordance with Agenda 21 and the various consensus agreements, conventions and programmes of action adopted in the framework of the follow-up to the United Nations Conference on Environment and Development;

f. Establishing and strengthening, as appropriate, mechanisms for the coordinations of efforts to combat poverty, in collaboration with civil society, including the private sector, and developing integrated intersectoral and intragovernmental responses for such purposes.

28. People living in poverty and their organizations should be empowered by:

a. Involving them fully in the setting of targets and in the design, implementation, monitoring and assessment of national strategies and programmes for poverty eradication and community-based development, and ensuring that such programmes reflect their priorities;

b. Integrating gender concerns in the planning and implementation of policies and programmes for the empowerment of women;

c. Ensuring that policies and programmes affecting people living in poverty respect their dignity and culture and make full use of the knowledge, skills and resourcefulness;

d. Strengthening education at all levels and ensuring the access to education of people living in poverty, in particular their access to primary education and other basic education opportunities;

e. Encouraging and assisting people living in poverty to organize so that their representative can participate in economic and social policy-making and work more effectively with government, non-governmental and other relevant institutions to obtain the services and opportunities they need;

f. Placing special emphasis on capacity-building and community-based management.

g. Educating people about their rights, the political system and the availability of programmes.

29. There is a need to periodically monitor, assess and share information on the performance of poverty eradication plans, evaluate policies to combat poverty, and promote an understanding and awareness of poverty and its causes and consequences. This could be done, by Government, *inter alia*, through:

a. Developing, updating and disseminating specific and agreed gender-disaggregated indicators of poverty and vulnerability, including income, wealth, nutrition, physical and mental health, education, literacy, family conditions, unemployment, social exclusion and isolation, homelessness, landlessness and factors, as well as indicators of the national and international causes underlying poverty; for this purpose, gathering comprehensive and comparable data, disaggregated by ethnicity, gender disability, family status, language groupings, regions and economic and social sectors;

b. Monitoring and assessing the achievement of goals and targets agreed to in international forums in the area of social development; evaluating, quantitatively and qualitatively, changes in poverty levels, the persistence of poverty, and vulnerability to poverty, particularly concerning household income levels and access to resources and services; and assessing the effectiveness of poverty eradication strategies, based on the priorities and perceptions of households living in poverty and low-income communities;

c. Strengthening international data collection and statistical systems to support countries in monitoring social development goals, and encouraging the expansion of international databases to incorporate socially beneficial activities that are not included in available data, such as women's unremunerated work and contributions to society, the informal economy and sustainable livelihoods;

d. Mobilizing public awareness, in particular through educational institutions, non-governmental organizations and the media, to enable society to prioritize the struggle against poverty, while focusing attention on progress or failure in the pursuit of defined goals and targets;

e. Mobilizing the resources of universities and research institutions to improve the understanding of the causes of poverty and their solutions, as well as the impact of structural adjustment measures on people living in poverty and the effectiveness of anti-poverty strategies and programmes, strengthening the capacity for social science research in developing countries and integrating, as appropriate, the results of research into decision-making processes;

f. Facilitating and promoting the exchange of knowledge and experience, especially among developing countries; through, *inter alia*, sub-regional and regional organizations.

30. Members of the international community should, bilaterally or through multilateral organization, foster an enabling environment for poverty eradication by:

a. Coordinating policies and programmes to support the measures being taken in the developing countries, particularly in Africa and the least developed countries, to eradicate poverty, provide remunerative work and strengthen social integration in order to meet basic social development goals and targets;

b. Promoting international cooperation to assist developing countries, at their request, in their efforts, in particular at the community level, towards achieving gender equality and the empowerment of women;

c. Strengthening the capacities of developing countries to monitor the progress of national poverty eradication plans and to assess the impact of national and international policies and programmes on people living in poverty and address their negative impacts;

d. Strengthening the capacity of countries with economies in transition to develop their social protection systems and social policies, for *inter alia*, the reduction of poverty.

e. Addressing the special needs of small island developing States with respect to eradicating poverty and meeting poverty eradication goals and targets within the context of social development programmes that reflect that national priorities;

f. Addressing the problems faced by the land-locked developing countries in eradicating poverty and supporting their efforts aimed at social development.

g. Supporting societies disrupted by conflict in their efforts to rebuild their social protection systems and eradicate poverty.

B. Improved Access to Productive Resources and Infrastructure

31. The opportunities for income generation, diversification of activities and increase of productivity in low-income and poor communities should be enhanced by:

    a. Improving the availability and accessibility of transportation, communication, power and energy services at the local or community level, in particular for isolated, remote and marginalized communities;

    b. Ensuring that investments in infrastructure support sustainable development at the local or community levels;

    c. Emphasizing the need for developing countries that are heavily dependent on primary commodities to continue to promote a domestic policy and an institutional environment that encourage diversification and enhance competitiveness;

    d. Supporting the importance of commodity diversification as a means to increase the export revenues of developing countries and to improve their competitiveness in the face of the persistent instability in the price of some primary commodities and the general deterioration in the terms of trade;

    e. Promoting, including by micro-enterprises, rural non-farm production and service activities, and such as agro-processing, sales and services of agricultural equipment and inputs, irrigation, credit services and other income-generating activities through, *inter alia*, supportive laws and administrative measures, credit policies, and technical and administrative training;

    f. Strengthening and improving financial and technical assistance for community-based development and self-help programmes, and strengthening cooperation among Governments, community organizations, cooperatives, formal and informal banking institutions, private enterprise and international agencies, with the aim of mobilizing local savings, promoting the creation of local financial networks, and increasing the availability of credit and market information to small entrepreneurs, small farmers and other low-income self-employed workers, and particular efforts to ensure the availability of such services to women;

g. Strengthening organizations of small farmers, landless tenants and labourers, other small producers, fisherfolk, community-based and workers' cooperatives, especially those run by women, in order to, *inter alia*, improve market access and increase productivity, provide inputs and technical advice, promote cooperation in production and marketing operations, and strengthen participation in the planning and implementation of rural development.

h. Promoting national and international assistance in providing economically viable alternatives for social groups, especially farmers involved in the cultivation and processing of crops used for the illegal drug trade;

i. Improving the competitiveness of natural products with environmental advantages and straightening the impact that this could have on promoting sustainable consumption and production patterns, and strengthening and improving financial and technical assistance to the developing countries for research and development of such products;

j. Promoting comprehensive rural development, including by land reform, land improvement and economic diversification;

k. Improving economic opportunities for rural women through the elimination of legal, social cultural and practical obstacles to women's participation in economic activities and ensuring that women have equal access to productive resources.

32. Rural poverty should be addressed by:

a. Expanding and improving land ownership through such measures as land reform and improving the security of land tenure, and ensuring the rights of women and men in this respect, developing new agricultural land, promoting fair land rents, making land transfers more efficient and fair, and adjudicating land disputes;

b. Promoting fair wages and improving the conditions of

agricultural labour, and increasing the access of small farmers to water, credit, extension services and appropriate technology, including for women, persons with disabilities and vulnerable groups on the basis of equality;

c. Strengthening measures and actions designed to improve the social, economic and living conditions in rural areas and thereby discouraging rural exodus;

d. Promoting opportunities for small farmers and other agricultural, forestry and fishery workers on terms that respect sustainable development;

e. Improving access to markets and market information in order to enable small producers to obtain better prices for their products and pay better prices for the materials they need;

f. Protecting, within the national context, the traditional rights to land and other resources of pastoralists, fishery workers and nomadic and indigenous people, and strengthening land management in the areas of pastoral or nomadic activity, building on traditional communal practices, controlling encroachment by others, and developing improved systems of range management and access to water, markes, credit, animal production, veterinary services, health including health services, education and information;

g. Promoting education, research and development on farming systems and small-holder cultivation and animal husbandry techniques, particularly in environmentally fragile areas, building on local and traditional practices of sustainable agriculture and taking particular advantages of women's knowledge;

h. Strengthening agricultural training and extension services to promote a more effective use of existing technologies and indigenous knowledge systems and to disseminate new technologies in order to reach both men and women farmers and other agricultural workers, including through the hiring of more women as extension workers;

i. Promoting infrastructural and institutional investment in small-scale farming in resource-poor regions so that small-scale farmers can fully explore market opportunities, within the context of liberalization.

33. Access to credit by small rural or urban producers, landless farmers and other people with low or no income should be substantially improved, with special attention to the needs of women and disadvantaged and vulnerable groups, by:

a. Reviewing national legal, regulatory and institutional frameworks that restrict the access of people living in poverty, especially women, to credit on reasonable terms;

b. Promoting realistic targets for access to affordable credit, where appropriate;

c. Providing incentives for improving access to and strengthening the capacities of the organized credit system to deliver credit and related services to people living in poverty and vulnerable groups;

d. Expanding financial networks, building on existing community networks, promoting attractive opportunities for savings and ensuring equitable access to credit at the local level.

34. Urban poverty should further be addressed by:

a. Promoting and strengthening micro-enterprises, new small businesses, cooperative enterprises, and expanded market and other employment opportunities and, where appropriate, facilitating the transition from the informal to the formal sector;

b. Promoting sustainable livelihoods for people living in urban poverty through the provision or expansion of access to training, education and other employment assistance services, in particular for women, youth, the unemployed and the under employed;

c. Promoting public and private investments to improve for the deprived the overall human environment and infrastructure, in particular housing, water and sanitation, and public transportation;

d. Ensuring that strategies for shelter give special attention to women and children, bearing in mind the perspectives of women in the development of such strategies;

e. Promoting social and other essential services, including, where necessary, assistance for people to move to areas that offer better employment opportunities, housing, educations health and other social services;

f. Ensuring safety through effective criminal justice administration and protective measures that are responsive to the needs and concerns of the community;

g. Strengthening the role and expanding the means of municipal authorities, non-governmental organizations, universities and other educational institutions, business and community organizations, enabling them to be more actively involved in urban planning, policy development and implementation;

h. Ensuring that special measures are taken to protect the displaced, the homeless, street children, unaccompanied minors and children in special and difficult circumstances, orphans, adolescents and single mothers, people with disabilities, and older persons, and to ensure that they are integrated into their communities.

C. Meeting the Basic Human Needs of All

35. Governments, in partnership with all other development actors, in particular with people living in poverty and their organizations, should cooperate to meet the basic human needs of all, including people living in poverty and vulnerable groups by:

a. Ensuring universal access to basic social services, with particular efforts to facilitate access by people living poverty and vulnerable groups;

b. Creating public awareness that the satisfaction of basic human needs is an essential element of poverty reduction; these needs are closely interrelated and comprise nutrition, health, water and sanitation, education, employment, housing and participation in cultural and social life;

c. Ensuring full and equal access to social services, especially education, legal services and health-care services for women of all ages and children, recognizing the rights, duties and responsibilities of parents and other persons legally responsible for children, consistent with the Convention on the Rights of the Child;

d. Ensuring that due priority is given and adequate resources made available, at the national, regional and international levels, to combat the threat to individual and public health posed by the rapid spread of HIV/AIDS globally and by the re-emergence of major disease, such as tuberculosis, malaria, onchocerciasis (river blindness) and diarrhoeal diseases, in particular cholera;

e. Taking particular actions to enhance the productive capacities of indigenous people, ensuring their full and equal access to social services and their participation in the elaboration and implementation of policies that affect their development, with full respect for their cultures, languages, traditions and forms of social organizations, as well as their own initiatives;

f. Providing appropriate social services to enable vulnerable people and people living in poverty to improve their lives, to exercise their rights and to participate fully in all social, economic and political activities and to contribute to social and economic development;

g. Recognizing that improving people's health is inseparably linked to a sound environment;

h. Ensuring physical access to all basic social services for persons who are holder, disabled or home-bound;

i. Ensuring that people living in poverty have full and equal access to justice, including knowledge of their rights and, as appropriate, through the provision of free legal assistance. The legal system should be made more sensitive and responsive to the needs and special circumstances of vulnerable and disadvantaged groups in order to ensure a strong and independent administration of justice;

j. Promoting full restorative services, in particular for those who require institutional care or are home-bound, and a comprehensive array of community-based, long-term care services for those facing loss of independence.

36. Governments should implement the commitments that have been made to meet the basic needs of all, with assistance from the international community consistant with chapter 5 of the present Programme of Action, including, *inter alia*, the following:

a. By the year, 2000, universal access to basic education and completion of primary education by at least 80 per cent of primary school-age children; closing the gender gap in primary and secondary school education by the year 2005; universal; primary education in all countries before the year 2015;

b. By the year 2000, life expectancy of not less than 60 years in any country;

c. By the year 2000, reduction of mortality rates of infants and children under five years of age by one third of the 1990 level, or 50 to 70 per 1,000 live births, whichever is less; by the year 2015, achievement of an infant mortality rate below 35 per 1,000 live births and an under five mortality rate below 45 per 1,000;

d. By the year 2000, a reduction in maternal mortality by one half of the 1990 level; by the year 2015, a further reduction by one half;

e. Achieving food security by ensuring a safe and nutritionally adequate food supply, at both the national and international levels, a reasonable degree of stability in the supply of food, as well as physical, social and economic access to enough food for all, while reaffirming that food should not be used as a tool for political pressure;

f. By the year 2000, a reduction of severe and moderate malnutrition among children under five years of age by half of the 1990 level;

g. By the year 2000, attainment by all peoples of the world of a level of health that will permit them to lead a socially and economically productive life, and to this end, ensuring primary health care for all;

h. Making accessible through the primary health-care system reproductive health to all individuals of appropriate ages as soon as possible and no later than the year 2015, in accordance with the Programme of Action of the International Conference on Population and Development, and taking into account the reservations and declarations made at that Conference, especially those concerning the need for parental guidance and parental responsibility;

i. Strengthening efforts and increasing commitments with the aim, by the year 2000, of reducing malaria mortality and morbidity by at least 20 per cent compared to 1995 levels in at least 75 per cent of affected countries, as well as reducing social and economic losses due to malaria in the developing countries, especially in Africa, where the overwhelming majority of both cases and deaths occur;

j. By the year 2000, eradicating, eliminating or controlling major diseases constituting global health problems;

k. Reducing the adult illiteracy rate-the appropriate age group to be determined in each country-to at least half its 1990 level, with an emphasis on female literacy; achieving universal access to quality education, with particular priority being given to primary and technical education and job training, combating illiteracy, and eliminating gender disparities in access to, retention in and support for education;

l. Providing, on a sustainable basis, access to safe drinking water in sufficient quantities, and proper sanitation for all;

m. Improving the availability of affordable and adequate shelter for all, in accordance with the Global Strategy for Shelter to the year 2000;

n. Monitoring the implementation of those commitments at the highest appropriate level and considering the possibility of expediting their implementation through the dissemination of sufficient and accurate statistical data and appropriate indicators;

37. Access to social services for people living in poverty and vulnerable groups should be improved through:

a. Facilitating access and improving the quality of education for people living in poverty by establishing schools in unserved areas, providing social services, such as meals and health care, as incentives for families in poverty to keep children in school, and improving the quality of schools in low-income communities;

b. Expanding and improving opportunities for continuing education and training by means of public and private intiatives and non-formal education in order to improve opportunities for people living in poverty, including people with disabilities, and in order to develop the skills and knowledge that they need to better their conditions and livelihoods;

c. Expanding and improving preschool education, both formal and non-formal, including through new learning technologies, radio and television, to overcome some of the disadvantages faced by young children growing up in poverty;

d. Ensuring that people living in poverty and low-income communities have access to quality health care that provides primary health-care services, consistent with the Programme of Action of the International Conference on Population and Development, free of charge or at affordable rates;

e. Promoting cooperation among government agencies, health-care workers, non-governmental organizations, women's organizations and other institutions of civil society in order to develop a comprehensive national strategy for improving reproductive health care and child health-care services and ensuring that living in poverty have full access to those services, including, *inter alia*, education and services on family planning, safe motherhood and prenatal and postnatal care, and the benefits of breast-feeding, consistent with the Programme of Action of the International Conference on Population and Development;

f. Encouraging health-care workers to work in low-income communities and rural areas, and providing outreach services to make health care available to otherwise unserved areas, recognizing that investing in a primary health-care system that ensure prevention, treatment and rehabilitation for all individuals is an effective means of promoting social and economic development as well as broad participation in society.

D. Enhanced Social Protection and Reduced Vulnerability

38. Social protection systems should be based on legislation and, as appropriate, strengthened and expanded, as necessary, in order to protect from poverty people who cannot find work; people who cannot due to sickness, disability, old age or maternity, or to their caring for children and sick or older relatives; families that have lost a breadwinner through death or martial breakup; and people who have lost their livelihoods due to natural disasters or civil violence, wars or forced displacement. Due attention should be given to people affected by the human immunodeficiency virus/acquired imunodeficiency syndrome (HIV/AIDS) pandemic. Actions to this end should include;

   a. Strengthening and expanding programmes targeted to those in need, programmes providing universal basic protection, and social security insurance programmes, with the choice of programmes depending on national financial and administrative capacities;

   b. Developing, where necessary, a strategy for a gradual expansion of social protection programmes that provide social security for all, according to a schedule and terms and conditions, related to national contexts;

   c. Ensuring that social safety nets associated with economic restructuring are considered as complementary strategies to overall poverty reduction and an increase in productive employment. Short term by nature, safety nets must protect people living in poverty and enable them to find productive employment;

   d. Designing social protection and support programmes to help people become self-sufficient as fully and quickly as possible, to assist and protect families, to reintegrate people excluded from economic activity and to prevent the social isolation or stigmatization of those who need protection;

e. Exploring a variety of means for raising revenues to strengthen social protection programmes, and promoting efforts by the private sector and voluntary associations to provide social protection and support;

f. Promoting the innovative efforts of self-help organizations, professional associations and other organizations of civil society in this sphere;

g. Expanding and strengthening social protection programmes to protect working people, including the self—employed and their families, from the risk of falling into poverty, by extending coverage to as many as possible, providing benefits quickly and ensuring that entitlements continue when workers change jobs;

h. Ensuring, through appropriate regulation, that contributory social protection plans are efficient and transparent so that the contributions of workers, employers and the State and accumulation of resources can be monitored by the participants;

i. Ensuring an adequate social safety net under structural adjustment programmes;

j. Ensuring that social protection and social support programmes and the needs of women, and especially that they take into account women's multiple roles and concerns, in particular the reintegration of women into formal work after periods of absence, support for older women, and the promotion of acceptance of women's multiple roles and responsibilities;

39. Particular efforts should be made to protect children and youth by:

a. Promoting family stability and supporting families in providing mutual support, including in their role as nurturers and educators of children;

b. Promoting social support, including, good quality child care and working conditions that allow both parents to reconcile parenthood with working life;

c. Supporting and involving family organizations and networks in community activities;

d. Taking the necessary legislative, administrative, social and education measures to protect and promote the rights of the child, with particular attention to the girl child;

e. Improving the situation and protecting the rights of children in especially difficult circumstances, including children in areas of armed conflict, children who lack adequate family support, urban streed children, abandoned children, children with disabilities, children addicted to narcotic drugs, children affected by war or natural and man-made disasters, unaccompanied minor refugee children, working children, and children who are economically and sexually exploited or abused, including the victims of the sale and trafficking of children; ensuring that they have access to food, shelter, education and health care and are protected from abuse and violence, as well as provided with the necessary social and psychological assistance for their healthy reintegration into society and for family reunification consistent with the Convention on the Rights of the Child; and substituting education for child work;

f. Developing and strengthening programmes targeted at youth living in poverty in order to enhance their economic, educational, social and cultural opportunities, to promote constructive social relations among them and to provide them with connections outside their communities to break the intergenerational cycle of poverty;

g. Addressing the special needs of indigenous children and their families, particularly those living in poor areas, enabling them to benefit adequately from economic and social development programmes, with full respect for their cultures, languages and traditions;

h. Improving the condition of the single parent in society and ensuring that single-parent families and female-headed or female-maintained households receive the social support they need, including support for adequate housing and child care.

40. Particular efforts should be made to protect older persons, including those with disabilities, by:

a. Strengthening family support systems;

b. Improving the situation of older persons, in particular in cases where they lack adequate family support, including rural older persons, working older persons, those affected by armed conflicts and natural or man-made disasters, and those who are exploited, physically or psychologically neglected, or abused;

c. Ensuring that older persons are able to meet their basic human needs through access to social services and social security, that those in need are assisted, and that older persons are protected from abuse and violence and are treated as a resource and not a burden;

d. Providing assistance to grandparents who have been required to assume responsibility for children, particularly of parents who are affected by serious diseases, including AIDS or leprosy, or others who are unable to care for their dependents;

e. Creating a financial environment that encourages people to save for their old age;

f. Strengthening measures and mechanisms to ensure that retired workers do not fall into poverty, taking into account their contribution to the development of their countries;

g. Encouraging and supporting cross-generational participation in policy and programme development and in decision-making bodies at all levels.

41. People and communities should be protected by impoverishment and long-term displacement and exclusion resulting from disasters through the following actions at the national and international levels, as appropriate:

a. Designing effective mechanisms to reduce the impact and to mitigate the effects of natural disasters, such as droughts, earthquakes, cyclones and floods;

b. Developing long-term strategies and contingency plans for the effective mitigation of natural disasters and for famine, including early warning, assessment, information dissemination and management, as well as rapid response strategies, that ensure the quick evolution of relief activities into rehabilitation and development;

c. Developing complementary mechanisms that integrate governmental, intergovernmental and non-governmental efforts, including the establishment of national volunteer corps to support United Nations activities in the areas of humanitarian emergency assistance, as well as mechanisms to promote a smooth transition from relief to rehabilitation, reconstruction and development;

d. Developing and strengthening emergency food reserves as a means to prevent acute food shortages and stabilize prices, with facilities for food storage, transportation and distribution during emergencies, making full use of traditional and market mechanisms;

e. In disaster-prone areas and in cooperation with community-based organizations, developing drought and flood mitigation agronomic practices and resources conservation and infrastructure-building programmes, using food-for-work, where appropriate, and incorporating traditional disaster-response practices that can be rapidly expanded into emergency employment and rebuilding programmes in disaster situations;

f. Establishing the necessary planning and logistical mechanisms to enable quick and effective response in disaster situations in provide food, psychological and social care, medicines, medical supplies and other relief to victims, especially women and children, and ensuring that the relief is effectively targeted to those who need it; and channelling and organization disaster assistance so as to regenerate the local economy and support resource protection and development efforts;

g. Mobilizing and coordinating regional and international assistance, including assistance from the United Nations system, and from non-governmental organizations, to support the actions of Governments and communities confronting disaster situations;

h. Reducing vulnerability to natural disasters through the development of early warning systems;

3. Expansion of Productive Employment and Reduction of Unemployment

Basis for Aaction and Objectives

42. Productive work and employment are central elements of development as well as decisive elements of human identity. Sustained economic growth and sustainable development as well as the expansion of productive employment should go hand in hand. Full and adequately and appropriately remunerated employment is an effective method of combating poverty and promoting social integration. The goal of full employment requires that the State, the social partners and all the other parts of civil society at all levels cooperate to create conditions that enable everyone to participate in and benefit from productive work. In a world of increasing globalization and interdependence among countries, national efforts need to be buttressed by initernational cooperation.

43. Globalization and rapid technological development give rise to increased labour mobility, bringing new employment opportunities as well as new uncertainties. There has been an increase in part-time, casual and other forms of atypical employment. In addition to requiring the creation of new employment opportunities on an unprecedented scale, such an environment calls for expanded efforts to enhance human resource development for sustainable development by, *inter alia*, enhancing the knowledge and skills necessary for people, particularly for women and youth, to work productively and adapt to changing requirements.

44. In many developed countries, growth in employment is currently great in small and medium-sized enterprises and in self-employment. In many developing countries, informal sector activities with limited access to formal-sector wage employment, in particular for women. The removal of obstacles to the operation of such enterprises and the provision of support for their creation and expansion must be accompanied by protection of the basic rights, health and safety of workers and the progressive improvement of overall working conditions, together with the strengthening of efforts to make some enterprises part of the formal sector.

45. While all groups can benefit from more employment opportunities, specific needs and changings demographic patterns and trends call for appropriate measures. Particular efforts by the public and private sectors are required in all spheres of employment policy to ensure gender equality, equal opportunity and non-discrimination on the basis of race/ethnic group, religion, age, health and disability, and with full respect for applicable international instruments. Special attention must also be paid to the needs of groups who face particular disadvantages in their access to the labour market so as to the ensure their integration into productive activities, including through the promotion of effective support mechanisms.

46. Much unremunerated productive work, such as caring for children and older persons, producing and preparing food for the family, protecting the environment and providing voluntary assistance to volunerable and disadvantaged individuals and groups, is of great social importance. Worldwide, most of this work is done by women who often face the double burden of remunerated and unremunerated work. Efforts are needs to acknowledge the social and economic importance and value of unremunerated work, to facilitate labour-force participation in combination with such work through flexible working arrangements, encouraging voluntary social activities as well as broadening the very conception of productive work, and to accord social recognition for such work, including by developing methods for reflecting its value in quantitative terms for possible reflection in accounts that may be produced separately from, but consistent with, core national accounts.

47. There is therefore an urgent need, in the overall context of promoting sustained economic growth and sustainable development, for:

- Placing the creating of employment at the center of national strategies and policies, with the full participation of employers and trade unions and others parts of civil society;
- Policies to expand work opportunities and increase pro-

ductivity in both rural and urban sectors;

- Education and training that enable workers and entrepreneurs to adapt to changing technologies and economic conditions;
- Quality jobs, with full respect for the basis rights of workers as defined by relevant International Labour Organization and other international instruments;
- Giving special priority, in the design of policies, to the problems of structural, long-term unemployment and underemployment of youth, women, persons with disabilities and all other disadvantaged groups and individuals;
- Empowerment of women, gender balance in decision-making process at all levels and gender analysis in policy development to ensure equal employment opportunities and wage rates for women and to enhance harmonious and mutually beneficial partnerships between women and men in sharing family and employment responsibilities;
- Empowerment of members of vulnerable and disadvantaged groups, and including through the provision of education and training;
- A broader recognition and understanding of work and employment and greater flexibility in working time arrangements for both men and women.

Actions

A. The Centrality of Employment in Policy Formulation

48. Placing the expansion of productive employment at the center of sustainable development strategies and economic and social policies requires:

    a. Promoting and pursuing active policies for full, productive, appropriately remunerated and freely chosen employment;

    b. Giving priority at the national and intentional levels to the policies that can address the problems of unemployment and under-employment.

49. Minimizing the negative impact on jobs of measures for macroeconomic stability requires:

a. Pursuing the coordination of macroeconomic policies so that they are mutually reinforcing and conducive to broad-based and sustained economic growth and sustainable development, as well as to substantial increases in productive employment expansion and a decline in unemployment worldwide;

b. Giving priority to programmes that most directly promote viable and long-term growth when budgetary adjustments are required;

c. Removing structural constraints to economic growth and employment creation as a part of stabilization policies;

d. Enabling competing claims on resources to be resolved in a non-inflationary manner through the development and use of sound industrial relations systems;

e. Monitoring, analysing and disseminating information on the impact of trade and investment liberalization on the economy, especially on employment;

f. Exchanging information on different employment promotion measures and their consequences, and monitoring the development of global employment trends;

g. Establishing appropriate social safety mechanism to minimize be adverse effects of structural adjustment, stabilization or reform programmes on the workforce, especially the vulnerable, and for those who lose their jobs, creating conditions for their re-entry through, *inter alia*, continuing education and retraining.

50. Promoting patterns of economic growth that maximize employment creation requires:

a. Encouraging, as appropriate, labour-intensive investment in economic and social infrastructure that use local resources and create, maintain and rehabilitate community assets in both rural and urban areas;

b. Promoting technological innovations and industrial polices that have the potential to simulate short and long-term employment creation, and considering their impact on vulnerable and disadvantaged groups;

c. Giving developing countries the capacity to select specific and suitable technologies;

d. Providing technical assistance and expanded transfer of technology to developing countries to integrate technology and employment policies with other social objectives, and to establish and strengthen national and local technology institutions;

e. Encouraging the realization in the countries with economies in transition of programmes for one-the-job personnel training, facilitating their adaptation to market-oriented reforms and reducing mass unemployment;

f. Promoting mutually supportive improvements in rural farm and non-farm production, including and animal husbandry, forestry, fisheries and agro-processing industries, aiming to expand and diversify environmentally sound, sustained economic activity and productive employment in the rural sector;

g. Encouraging community economic development strategies that build on partnerships among Governments and members of civil society to create jobs and address the social circumstances of individuals, families and communities;

h. Introducing sound policies to mobilize savings and stimulate investment in capital-short areas;

i. Maximizing the job creation potential inherent in Agenda 21 through the conservation and management of natural resources, the promotion of alternative livelihoods in fragile ecosystems, and the rehabilitation and regeneration of critically affected and vulnerable land areas and natural resources;

j. Encouraging the utilization of renewable energy, based on local employment-intensive resources, in particular in rural areas.

51. Enhancing opportunities for the creation and growth of private-sector enterprises that would generate additional employment requires:

a. Removing obstacles faced by small and medium-sized enterprises and easing regulations that discourage private initiative;

b. Facilitating access by small and medium-sized enterprises to credit, national and international markets, management training and technological information;

c. Facilitating arrangements between large and small enterprises, such as subcontracting programmes, with full respect for workers' rights;

d. Improving opportunities and workers conditions for women and youth entrepreneurs by eliminating discrimination in access to credit, productive resources and social security protection, and providing and increasing, as appropriate, family benefits and social support, such as health care and child care;

e. Promoting, supporting and establishing legal frameworks to foster the development of cooperative enterprises, and encouraging them to mobilize capital, develop innovative lending programmes and promote entrepreneurship;

f. Assisting informal sectors and local enterprises to become more productive and progressively integrated into the formal economy through access to affordable credit, information, wider markets, new technology and appropriate technological and management skills, opportunities to upgrade technical and management skills,and improved premises and other physical infrastructure, as well as by progressively extending labour standards and social protection without destroying the ability of informal sectors to generate employment;

g. Promoting the creation and development of independent organizations, such as chambers of commerce and other associations or self-help institutions of small formal and informal enterprises;

h. Facilitating the expansion of training and employment-generating opportunities of industries.

B. Education, Training and Labour Policies

52. Facilitating people's access to productive employment in today's rapidly changing global environment and developing better quality jobs requires:

a. Establishing well-defined educational priorities and investing effectively in education and training systems;

b. Introducing new and revitalized partnerships between education and other government departments, including labour, and communications and partnerships, between Governments and non-governmental organizations, the private sector, local communities, religious groups and families;

c. Ensuring broad basic education, especially literacy, and promoting general education, including the analytical and critical thinking that is essential to improve learning skills. This is the foundation for acquiring specialized skills and for renewing, adapting and upgrading them rapidly to facilitate horizontal and vertical occupational mobility;

d. Promoting the active participation of youth and adults learners in the design of literacy campaigns, education and training programmes to ensure that the labour force and social realities of diverse groups are taken into account;

e. Promoting lifelong learning to ensure that education and training programmes respond to changes in the economy, provide full and equal access to training opportunities, secure the access of women to training programmes, offer incentives for public and private sectors to provide and for workers to acquire training on a continuous basis, and stimulate entrepreneurial skills;

f. Encouraging and supporting through technical assistance programmes, including those of the United Nations system, well-designed and adaptable vocational training and apprenticeship programmes to enhance productivity and productive employment;

g. Promoting and strengthening training programmes for the employment of new entrants to the job market and retraining programmes for displaced and retrenched workers;

h. Developing an enhanced capacity for research and knowledge dissemination by encouraging national and international exchanges for informing on innovative models and best practices;

i. Developing in the area of vocational and continuing education, innovative methods of teaching and learning, including interactive technologies and inductive methods involving close coordination between working experience and training.

53. Helping workers to adapt and to enhance their employment opportunities under changing economic conditions requires:

a. Designing, developing, implementing, analysis and monitoring active labour policies to stimulate the demand for labour in order to ensure that the burden of indirect labour costs on employers does not constituent a disincentive to hiring workers, identifying skill shortages and surpluses, providing vocational guidance and counselling services and active help in job searches, promoting occupational choice and mobility, offering advisory services and support to enterprises, particularly small enterprises, for the more effective use and development of their workforce, and establishing institutions and processes that prevent all forms of discriminatioin and improve the employment opportunities of groups that are vulnerable and disadvantaged;

b. Improving employment opportunities and increasing ways and means of helping youth and persons with disabilities to develop the skills they need to enable them to find employment;

c. Promoting access by women and girls to traditionally male-dominated occupations;

d. Developing strategies to address the needs of people engaged in various forms of atypical employment;

e. Promoting labour mobility, retraining and maitenance of adequate levels of social protection to facilitate worker redevelopment when there is phasing out of production or closure of an enterprise, giving special attention of vulnerable and disadvantaged groups;

f. Facilitating the integration or reintegration of women

into the work force by developing adequate child care, care for older persons and other support services and facilities;

g. Encouraging cooperation between employers and workers to prepare for the introduction of new technologies, and to plan for their employment effects as far in advance as possible, while ensuring adequate protection and adjustment;

h. Strengthening public and private employment services to assist workers to adapt to changing job markets and provide social safety mechanisms, occupational guidance, employment and jobs search counselling, training, placement, apprenticeship and the sharing of information;

i. Strengthening labour market information systems, particularly through development of appropriate data and indicators on employment, underemployment, unemployment and earnings, as well as dissemination of information concerning labour markets, including, as far as possible, work situations outside formal markets. All such data should be disaggrevated by gender in order to monitor the status of women relative to men.

C. Enhanced Quality of Work and Employment

54. Governments should enhance the quality of work and employment by:

a. Observing and fully implementing the human rights obligations that that have assumed;

b. Safegaurding and promoting respect for basic workers' rights, including the prohibition of forced labour and child labour, freedom of association and the right to organize and bargain collectively, equal remuneration for men and women for work of equal value, and non discrimination in employment, fully implementing the conventions of the International Labour Organization (ILO) in the case of States parties to those conventions in the case of those countries that are not States parties to thus achieves truly sustained economic growth and sustainable development;

c. Strongly considering ratification and full implementation of ILO conventions in these areas, as well as those relating to the employment rights of minors, women, youth, persons with disabilities and indigenous people;

d. Using existing international labour standards to guide the formulation of national labour legislation and policies;

e. Promoting the rule of ILO, particularly as regards improving the level of employment and the quality of work;

f. Encouraging, where appropriate, employers and workers to consider ways and means for enhancing the sharing of workers in the profits of enterprises and promoting cooperation between workers and employers in the decisions of enterprises.

55. To achieve a healthy and safe working environment, remove exploitation, abolish child labour, raise productivity and enhance the quality of life requires;

a. Developing and implementing policies designed to promote improved working conditions, including health and safety condition;

b. Improving health policies that reduce, with a view to eliminating, environmental health hazards and provides for occupational health and safety, in conformity with the relevant conventions, and providing informal sector enterprises and all workers and accessible information and guidance on how to enhance occupational safety and reduce health risks;

c. Promoting, in accordance with national laws and regulations, sound labour relations based on tripartite cooperation and full respect for freedom of association and the right to organize and bargain collectively;

d. Setting specific target dates for eliminating all forms of child labour that contrary to accepted international standard and ensuring the full enforcement of relevant existing laws, and, where appropriate, enacting the legislation necessary to implementing the Convention on the Rights of the Child and ILO Standards, ensuring the protection of working children, in particular of street children, through the provision of appropriate health, education and other social services;

e. Designing labour policies and programmes to help eradicate family poverty, which is a main cause of child labour, eliminating child labour and encouraging parents to send their children to school through, *inter alia,* the provision of social services and other incentives;

f. Establishing policies and programmes to protect workers, especially workers, from sexual harassment and violence;

g. Encouraging incentives to public and private enterprises to develop, transfer and adopt technologies and know-how that improve the working environment, enhance occupational safety and reduce, with a view to eliminating, health risks.

56. The full participation of women in the labour market and their equal access to employment opportunities require:

a. Establishing the principle of equality between men and women as a basis for employment policy and promoting gender-sensitivity training to eliminate prejudice against the employment of women;

b. Eliminating gender discrimination, including by taking positive action, where appropriate, in hiring, wages, access to credit, benefits, promotion, training, career developing, job assignment, working conditions, job security and social security benefits;

c. Improving women's access to technologies that facilitate their occupational and domestic work, encourage self-support, generate income, transform gender-prescribed roles within the productive process and enable them to move out of stereotyped, low-paying jobs;

d. Changing those polices and attitudes that reinforce the division of labour based on gender, and providing institutional support, such as social protection for maternity, parental leave, technologies that facilitate the sharing and reduce the burden of domestic chores, and flexible working arrangements, including parental voluntary part time employment and work-sharing, as well as accessible and affordable quality child-care facilities, to enable working parents to reconcile work with family responsibilities, paying particular attention to the needs of single-parent households;

e. Encouraging men to take an active part in all areas of family and household responsibilities, including the sharing of child-rearing and housework.

D. Enhanced Employment Opportunities for Groups with Specific Needs

57. The improvement of the design of policies and programmes requires:

a. Identifying and reflecting the specific needs of particular groups, and ensuring the programmes are equatable and non-discriminatory, efficient and effective in meeting the needs of those groups;

b. Activity involving representatives of these groups in planning, design and management, and monitoring, evaluating and reorienting these programmes by providing access to accurate information and sufficient resources to ensure that they reach their intended beneficiaries.

58. Employment policies can better address the problem of short-and long-term unemployment by:

a. Incorporating, with the involvement of the unemployed and/or their associations, a comprehensive set of measures including employment planning, re-education and training programmes, literacy, skills upgrading, counselling and job-search assistance, temporary work schemes, frequent contact with employment service offices and preparing for entry and re-entry into the labour market;

b. Analysing the underlying causes of long-term unemployment and their effect on different groups, including older workers and single parents, and designing employment and other supporting policies that address specific situations and needs;

c. Promoting social security schemes that the reduced barriers and disincentives to employment so as to enable the unemployed to improve their capacity to participate actively in society, to maintain an adequate standard of living and to be able to take advantage of employment opportunities.

59. Programmes for entry or re-entry into the labour market aimed at vulnerable and disadvantaged groups can effectively combat the causes of exclusion on the labour market by:

    a. Complementing literacy actions, general education or vocational training by work experience that may include support and instruction on business management and training so as to give better knowledge of the value of entrepreneurship and other private-sector contributions to society;

    b. Increasing the level of skills, and also improving the ability to get a job through improvements in housing, health and family life.

60. Policies should seek to guarantee all youth constructive options for their future by:

    a. Providing equal access to education at the primary and secondary levels, with literacy as a priority and with special attention to girls;

    b. Encouraging the struggle against illiteracy and promoting literacy training in national languages in developing countries, in particular in Africa;

    c. Encouraging various actors to join forces in designing and carrying out comprehensive and coordinated programmes that stimulate the resourcefulness of youth, preparing them for durable employment or self-employment, and providing them with guidance, vocational and managerial training, social skills, work experience and education in social values;

    d. Ensuring the participation of youth, commensurate with their age and responsibility, in planning and decision-making with regard to their future.

61. The full participation of indigenous people in the labour market and their equal access to employment opportunities requires developing comprehensive employment, education and training programmes that take account of the particular needs of indigenous people.

62. Broadening the range of employment opportunities for persons with disabilities requires:

a. Ensuring that laws and regulations do not discriminate against persons with disabilities;

b. Taking proactive measures, such as organizing support services, devising incentive schemes and supporting self-help schemes and small business;

c. Making appropriate adjustments in the workplace to accommodate persons with disabilities, including in that respect the promotion of innovative technologies;

d. Developing alternative forms of employment, such as supported employment, for persons with disabilities who need these services;

e. Promoting public awareness within society regarding the impact of the negative stereotyping of persons with disabilities on their participation in the labour market.

63. There is need for intensified international cooperation and national attention to the situation of migrant workers and their families. To that end:

a. Governments are invited to consider ratyfing existing insturments pertaining to migrant workers, particularly the International Convention on the Protection of the Rights of All Migrant Workers and Members of Their Families:

b. In accordance with national legislation, Governments of receiving countries are urged to consider extending to documented migrants who meet appropriate length-of-say requirements and to members of their families whose stay in the receiving country is regular, treatment equal to that accorded their own nationals with regards to the enjoyment of basic human rights, including equality of opportunity and treatment in respect of religious practices, working conditions, social security, participation in trade unions and access to health, education, cultural and other social services, as well as equal access to the judicial system and equal treatment before the law;

c. Governments of countries of origin, transit countries and countries of destination are urged to cooperate in reducing the causes of undocumented migration, safeguarding the basic human rights of undocumented migrants and preventing their exploitation;

d. Governments of both receiving countries and countries of origin should adopt effective sanctions against those who organise undocumented migration, exploit undocumented migrants or engate in trafficking in undocumented migrants;

e. Government of countries of origin are urged to facilitate the return of migrants and reintegration into their home communities and to devise ways of using their skills. Governments of countries of origin should consider collaborating with countries of destination and engaging the support of appropriate international organizations in promoting the return on a voluntary basis of qualified migrants who can play in a crucial role in the transfer of knowledge, skills and technology. Countries of destination are encouraged to facilitate return migration on a voluntary basis by adopting flexible policies, such as the transferability of pensions and other work benefits.

E. A Broader Recognition and Understanding of Work and Employment

64. A broader recognition and understanding of work and employment requires:

a. Acknowledging the important contribution of unremunerated work to societal well-being and bringing respect, dignity and value to societal perceptions of such work and the people who do it;

b. Developing a more comprehensive knowledge of work and employment through, *inter alia*, efforts to measure and better understand the type, extent and distribution of unremunerated work, particularly work in caring for dependents and unremunerated work done for family farms or business, and encouraging, sharing and disseminating information, studies and experience in this field, including on the development of methods for assessing its values in quantiative terms, for possible reflection in accounts that may be produced separately from, but are consistent with, core national accounts;

c. Recognizing the relationship between remunerated employment and unremunerated work in developing strategies to expand productive employment, to ensure equal access by women and men to employment, and to ensure the care and well-being of children and other dependents, as well as to combat poverty and promote social integration;

d. Encouraging an open dialogue on the possibilities and institutional requirements for a broader understand of various forms of work and employment;

e. Examining a range of policies and programmes, including social security legislation, and taxation systems, in accordance with national priorities and policies, to ascertain how to facilitate flexibility in the way people divide their time between education and training, paid employment, family responsibilitis, volunteer activity and other socially useful forms of work, leisure and retirement, giving particular attention to the situation of women, especially in female-maintained households;

f. Promoting socially useful volunteer work and allocating appropriate resources to support such work without diluting the objectives regarding employment expansion;

g. Intensifying international exchange of experience on various aspects of change in the recognition and understanding of work and employment and on new forms of flexible working time arrangements over the life time.

65. The development of additional socially useful new types of employment and work requires, *inter alia*:

a. Helping vulnerable and disadvantaged groups to integrate better into society and thus participate more effectively in economic and social development;

b. Helping older persons who are dependent or providing support for families in need of educational assistance or social support;

c. Strengthening social ties through these forms of employment and work, which represents an important achievement of social development policy.

4. Social Integration

Basis for Action and Objectives

66. The aim of social integration is to create "a society for all", in which every individual, each with rights and responsibilities, has an active role to play. Such as inclusive society must be based on respect for all human rights and fundamental freedoms, cultural and religious diversity, social justice and the special needs of vulnerable and disadvantaged groups, democratic participation and the rule of law. The pluralistic nature of most societies has at times resulted inproblmes for the different groups to achieve and maintain harmony and cooperation, and to have equal access to all resources in society. Full recognition of each individual's right sin the context of the rule of law has not always been fully guaranteed. Since the founding of the United Nations, this quest for humane, stable, safe tolerant and just societies has shown a mixed record at best.

67. Nevertheless, progress has been noted, as shown in the continuation of the ongoing process of deconlonization; the elimination of apartheid; the spread of democracy; wider recognition of the need to respect human dignity, all human rights and fundamental freedoms and cultural diversity; the unacceptability of discrimination; increasing recognition of the unique concerns of indigenous people in the world; an expanded notion of collective responsibility for all members of a society; expanded economic and educational opportunities and the globalization of communication; and greater possibilities for social mobility, choice and autonomy of action;

68. Notwithstanding the instances of progress, there are negative developments that include social polarization and fragmentation; widening disparities and inequalities of income and wealth within and among nations; problems arising from uncontrolled urban development and the degradation of the environment; marginalization of people, families, social groups, communities and even entire countries; and strains on in-

dividuals, families, communities and institutions as a result of the rapid pace of social change, economic transformation, migration and major dislocations of population, particularly in the areas of armed conflict.

69. Furthermore, violence, in its many manifestations, including domestic violence, especially against women, children, older persons and people with disabilities, is a growing threat to the security of individuals, families and communities everywhere. Total social breakdown is an all too real contemporary experience. Organized crime, illegal drugs, the illicit arms trade, trafficking in women and children, ethnic and religious conflict, civil war, terrorism, all forms of extremist violence, xenophobia, and politically motivated killing and even genocide present fundamental threats to societies and the global social order. These are compelling and urgent reasons for action by Governments individually and, as appropriate, jointly to foster social cohesion while recognizing, protecting and valuing diversity.

70. There is therefore an urgent need for :

- Transparent and accountable public institutions that are accessible to people on an equal basis and are responsive to their needs;
- Opportunities for all to participate in all spheres of public life;
- Strengthened participation and involvement of civil society in the formulation, implemention and evaluation of decisions determining the functioning and well-being of societies;
- Publicly available objective data to enable people to make informed decisions;
- Maintenance of social stability and promotion of social justice and progress;
- Promotion of non-discriminatioin, tolerance and mutual respect for an the value of diversity;
- Equity and equality of opportunity and social mobility;
- Gender equality and equity and empowerment of women;
- Elimination of physical and social barriers with the aim

of creating a society accessible for all, with special emphasis on measures to meet the needs and interests of those who face obstacles in participating fully in society;

- Giving special attention to the right to the enjoyment of the highest attainable standard of physical and mental health, and to health as a factor of development;
- Promoting the principle of caring for one another's well-being and fostering the spirit of mutual support, within the context of human rights education;
- While acknowledging legitimate national defence needs, recognizing and addressing the dangers to society of armed conflict, and the negative effect of excessive military expenditures, trade in arms, especially of those arms that are particularly injurious or have indiscriminate effects, and excessive investment for arms producing and acquisition. Similarly, the need to combat illicit arms acqui-
- sition. Similarly, the need to combat illicit arms trafficking, violence, crime, the production, use and trafficking of illicit drugs, and trafficking in women and children should be recognized and addressed;
- The elimination of all forms of violence and the full implementation of the Declaration on the Elimination of Violence against Women.

Actions

A. Responsive Government and Full Participation in Society

71. Governments should promote and protect all human rights and fundamental freedoms, including the right to development, bearing in mind the interdependent and mutually reinforcing relationship between democracy, development and respect for human rights, and should make public institutions more responsive to people's needs by:

a. Ensuring that decisions are based on accurate data and are taken with the participation of those who will be affected, keeping under review, with each country's constitutional framework, the responsibilities of the different levels of government and the administrative arrangements for organizing and delivering services;

b. Keeping under review, within each country's constitutional framework, the national, provincial, municipal and local capacity and capability in raising revenue, and allocating resources to promote local intiatives in maintaining and increasing community cohesion;

c. Simplifying administrative regulations, disseminating information about public policy issues and initiatives for collective interests, and facilitating maximum access to information;

d. Opening channels and promoting full confidence between citizens and government agencies, and developing affordable recourse procedures accessible to all people, especially those who have no access to channels and agencies of communications to seek redress of grievances;

e. Encouraging the production of relevant studies/research to assess the consequences of global and technological changes on social integration and the production of evaluations of the policies and programmes put in place to achieve the various components of social integration; and encouraging national and international exchanges and dissemnination of information on innovative models and successful practices;

f. Requiring accountability for the honest, just and equitable delivery of pubic services to the people from all public officials;

g. Making their services accessible to all citizens and taking special care to ensure that the services are providing to all persons in need;

h. Strengthening popular political participation, and promoting the transparency and accountability of political groupings at the local and national levels;

i. Encouraging the ratification of, the avoidance as far as possible of the resort of reservations to and the implementation of international human rights instruments aiming to eliminate barriers to the full enjoyment of all human rights.

72. Encouraging the fullest participation in society requires;

a. Strengthening the capacities and opportunities for all people, especially those who are vulnerable and disadvantaged, to establish and maintain independent organizations representing their interests, within each country; constitutional framework;

b. Enabling institutions of civil society, with special attention to those representing vulnerable and disadvantaged groups, to participate in the formulation, on a consultative basis, implementation and evaluation of policies related to social development;

c. Giving community organizations greater involvement in the design and implementation of local projects, particularly in the areas of education, health care, resource management and social protection;

d. Ensuring a legal framework and a support structure that encourage the formation of and constructive contributions from community organizations and voluntary associations of individuals;

e. Encouraging all members of society to exercise their rights, fulfil their responsibilities and participate fully in their societies, recognizing that Governments alone cannot meet all needs in society;

f. Establishing a universal and flexible social safety net that takes into account available economic resources and encourages rehabilitation and active participation in society;

g. Facilitating the access of disadvantaged and marginalized people to education and information, as well as their participation in social and cultural life;

h. Promoting equality and social integration through sports and cultural activity;

B. Non-discrimination, tolerance and mutual respect for and value of diversity

73. Eliminating discrimination and promoting tolerance and mutual respect for and the value of diversity at the national and international levels requires:

a. Enacting and implementing appropriate laws and other

regulations to combat racism, racial discrimination, religious intolgrance in all its various forms, xenophobia and all forms of discrimination in all walks of life in societies;

b. Encouraging the ratification of, the avoidance, as far as possible of the resort to reservations, and the implementation of international instruments, including the International Convention on the Elimination of All Forms of Racial Discrimination and the Convention on the Elimination of All Forms of Discrimination against Women;

c. Taking specific measures, in the context of the implementation of the Nairobi Forward-looking Strategies for the Advancement of Women, to remove long-sanding legal and social barriers to employment, education, productive resources and public services; assist women in becoming aware of and realizing their rights, and ensure the elimination of intra-family discrimination for the girl child, especially in regard to health, nutrition and education;

d. Ensuring gender equality and equity through changes in attitudes, policies and practices, encouraging the full participation and empowerment of women in social, economic and political life, and enhancing gender balance in decision-making process at all levels;

e. Reviewing with a view to changing legislation, public and codes and practices that perpetuate discriminatory practices;

f. Disseminating information in plain language to all groups in society about people's rights and the means available to redress complaints;

g. Strengthening or establishing machinery for monitoring and resolving disputes and conflicts related to discriminatory practices, and developing arbitration and conciliation procedures at the local and national levels;

h. Setting an example through State institutions and the educational system to promote and protect respect for freedom of expression; democracy, political pluralism; diversity of heritage, cultures and values; religious tolerance and principles; and the the national traditions on which a country has been built;

i. Recognizing that the languages spoken or used in the world should be respected and protected;

j. Recognizing that it is of utmost importance for all people to live in cooperation and harmony, and ensuring that the traditions and cultural heritage of nations are fully protected;

k. Encouraging independent communications media that promote people's understanding and awareness of all aspects of social integration, with full respect for freedom of information and expression.

C. Equality and Social Justice

74. Governments should promote equality and social justice by:

a. Ensuring that all people are equal before the law;

b. Carrying out a regular review of public policy, including health and education policies, and public spending from a social and gender equality and equity perspective, and promoting their positive contribution to equalizing opportunities;

c. Expanding and improving access to basic services with the aim of ensuring universal coverage;

d. Providing equal opportunities in public-sector employment and providing guidance, information and, as appropriate, incentives to private employees to do the same;

e. Encouraging the free formations of cooperatives, community and other grass-roots organizations, mutual support groups, recreational/sports associations and similar institutions that tend to strengthen social integration, paying particular attention to policies that assist families in their support, educational, socializing and nurturing roles;

f. Ensuring that structural adjustment programmes are so designed as to minimize that negative effects on vulnerable and disadvantaged groups and communities while ensuring their positive effects on them by preventing their marginalization in economic and social activities, and devising measures to ensure such groups and communities gain access to and control over economic resources and economic and social activities. Actions should be taken to reduce inequality and economic disparity;

g. Promoting full access to preventive and curative health care to improve the quality of life, especially by the vulnerable and disadvantaged groups, in particular women and children;

h. Expanding basic education by developing special measures to provide schooling for children and youth living in sparsely populated and remote areas, for children and youth of nomadic, pastoral, migrant or indigenous parents, and for street children, children and youth working or looking after younger siblings and disabled or aged parents, and disabled children and youth; establishing, in partnership with indigenous people, educational systems that will meet the unique need of their cultures;

i. Ensuring that the expansion of basic education is accompanied by improved quality, appropriate attention to children of different abilities, cooperation between family and school and close link between the school curriculum and the needs of the workplace;

j. Evaluating school systems on a regular basis by results achieved, and disseminating research findings regarding the appropriateness of different methods of evaluation;

k. Ensuring that all people can have access to variety of formal and non-formal learning activities throughout their lives that allows them to contribute to and benefit from full participation in society; making use of all forms of education, including non-conventional and experimental means of education, such as tele-courses and correspondence courses, through public institutions, the institutions of civil society and the private sector, to provide educational opportunities for those who in childhood missed necessary schooling, for youth in the transition from school to work, and for those for wish to continue education and upgrade skills throughout their lives;

l. Providing equal access for girls to all levels of education, including non-traditional and vocational training, and ensuring that measures are taken to address the various cultural and practical bearriers that impede their access to education through such measures as the hiring of female teachers, adoption of flexible hours, care of dependents and siblings, and provision of appropriate facilities;

D. Responses to Special Social Needs

75. Governmental responses to special needs of social groups should include:

a. Identifying specific means to encourage institutions and services to adapt to the special needs of vulnerable and disadvantaged groups;

b. Recognizing and promoting the abilities, talents and experience of groups that are vulnerable and disadvantaged, identifying ways to prevent isolation and alienation, and enabling them to make a positive contribution to society;

c. Ensuring access to work and social services through such measures as education, language training and technical assistance for people adversely affected by language barriers;

d. Supporting by legislation, incentives and other means, where appropriate, organizations, of the vulnerable and disadvantaged groups so that they may promote the interests of the groups concerned and become involved in local and national, economic, social and political decision-making that guides society as a whole;

e. Improving the opportunities for people who are disadvantaged or vulnerable to seek positions in legislatures, Governments, judiciaries and other positions of public authority or influence;

f. Taking measures to integrate into economic and social life demobilized persons and persons displaced by civil conflict and disasters;

g. Promoting and protecting the rights of indigenous people, and empowering them to make choices that enable them to retrain cultural identity while participating in national, economic and social life, with full respect for their cultural values, languages, traditions and forms of social organizations;

h. Implementing the Plan of Action adopted by the World Summit for Children in 1990 and ratifying, as appropriate, and implementing the provisions of the Convention on the Rights of the Child;

i. Encouraging youth to participate in discussions and decisions affecting them and in the design, implementation and evaluation of policies and programmes; ensuring that youth acquire the skills to participate in all aspects of life in society and lead self-sufficient lives through the provision of relevant and innovative educational programmes; and establishing laws and measures that ensure the protection of youth against physical and mental abuse and economic exploitation;

j. Adopting specific measures to equip young people for responsible adulthood, particularly out-of-school youth and street children;

k. Promoting the United Nations Standard Rules on the Equalization of Opportunities for Persons with Disabilities and developing strategies for implementing the Rules. Governments, in collaboration with organizations of people with disabilities and the private sector, should work towards the equalization of opportunities so that people with disabilities can contribute to and benefit from full participation in society. Policies concerning people with disabilities should focus on their abilities rather than their disabilities and should ensure their dignity as citizens;

l. Within the context of the United Nations Principles for Older Persons and the global targets on ageing on the Year 2001, reviewing or developing strategies for implementing the International Plan of Action on Ageing so that older persons can maximize their contribution o society and lay their full part in the community;

m. Facilitating the implementation of the guidelines for further planning and suitable follow-up in the field of youth with a view to promoting the integration of youth into societies;

n. Taking measures to enable persons belonging to minorities to participate fully and contribute to the development of their society.

E. Responses to Specific Social Needs of Refugees, Displaced Persons and Asylum-seekers, Documented Migrants and Undocumented Migrants

76. In order to address the special needs of refugees, displaced persons and asylum-seekers;

   a. Governments are urged to address the root causes of movements of refugees and displaced persons by taking appropriate measurs, particularly with respect to conflict resolution; the promotion of peace and reconciliation; respect for human rights, incluidng those of persons belonging to minorities; and respect for the independent, territorial integrity and sovereignty of States. Governments and all other entities should respect and safeguard the right of people of remain in safety in their homes and should refrain from policies or practices that forces people to flee;

   b. Government are urged to strengthen their support for international protection and assistance activities on behalf of refugees and, as appropriate, displaced persons, and to promote the search for durable solutions to their plight. In so doing, Governments are encouraged to enhance regional and international mechanisms that promote appropriate shared responsibility for the protectioin and assistance needs of refugees. All necessary measures should be taken to ensure the physical protection of refugees, in particular that of refugee women and refugee children and especially against exploitation, abuse and all forms of violence;

   c. Adequate international support should be extended to countries to asylum to meet the basic needs of refugees and to assist in the search for durable solutions. Refugees, particularly refugee women, should be involved in the planning of refugee assistance activities and in their implementation. In planning and implementing refugee assistance activities, special attention should be given to the specific needs of refugees and displaced women and children. Refugees should be provided with access to adequate accomodation, education, health services, including family planning, and other necessary social services. Refugees should respect the laws and regulations of their countries of asylum;

d. Governments and other relevant actors should create comprehensive conditions that allow for the voluntary repatriation of refugees in safety and dignity, and the voluntary and safe return of internally displaced persons to their homes of origin and their smooth reintegration into society;

e. Governments are urged to abide by international law concerning refugees. States that have not already done so are invited toconsidre acceding to the international instruments concerning refugees, in particular the 1951 Convention relating to the Status of Refugees and the 1967 Protocol to the Convention. Governments are furthermore urged to respect the principle of non-refoulement, that is, the principle of no forcible return of persons to places where their lives or freedom would be threatened because of race, religion, nationality, membership in a particular social group or political opinion. Governments should ensure that asylum-seekers in the Government's territory have access to a fair hearing and should facilitate the expeditious processing of asylum requests, ensuring that guidelines and procedures for the determination of refugee status are sensitive to the particular situation of women;

f. Governments and relevant actors should respect the right of people to seek and enjoy in other countries asylum from persecution.

77. To promote the equitable treatment and integration of documented migrants, particularly documented migrant workes and members of their families;

a. Governments should ensure that documented migrants receive fair and equal treatment, including full respect of their human rights, protection of the laws of the host society, appropriate access to economic opportunities and social services; protection against racism, ethnocentrism and xenophobia; and protection from violence and exploitation. Language training should be provided, in recognition of the centrality of language acquisition to the effective integration of documented migrants, including those not destined for the labour market, in so far as resources permit. Early integration is the key to allowing documented migrants to contribute their skills, knowledge and potential to the development of countries of destination, and involves mutual undestanding by documented migrants and the host society. The former need to know and respect the values, laws, traditions and principles of the host society, which in turn should respect the religions, cultures and traditions of documented migrants;

b. Governments of receiving countries are urged to consider giving to documented migrants having the right to long-term residence, civil and political rights and responsibilities, as appropriate, and facilitating their naturalization. Special efforts should be made to enhance the integration of the children of long-term migrants by providing them with educational and training opportunities equal to those of nationals, allowing them to exercise an economic activity and facilitating the naturaliztion of those who have been raised in the receiving country. Consistent with article 10 of the Convention on the Rights of the Child and all relevant universally recognized human rights instruments, all Governments, particularly those of receiving countries, must recognize the vital importance of family reunification and promote its integration into their national legislation in order to ensure protection of the unity of the families of documented migrants. Governments of receiving countries must ensure the protection of migrants and their families, giving priority to programmes and strategies that combat religious intolerance, racism, ethnocentrism, xenophibia and gender discrimination, and that generate the necessary public sensitivity in that regard;

c. Governments and relevant actors should encourage the intenational exchange of information on educational and training institutions in order to promote the productive employment of documented migrants through greater recognition of foregin education and credentials;

d. Governments should encourage interacial harmony and crosscultural understanding through educational programmes, where appropriate, including alternative dispute resolution and conflict prevention training in schools.

78. In order to address the concerns and basic human needs related to undocumented migrants;

a. Governments are urged to cooperate in reducing the causes of undocumented migrantion, safeguarding the basic human rights of undocumented migrants, preventing their exploitation and offering them appropriate means of appeal according to naional legislation, and punishing criminals who organize trafficking in human beings;

b. Countries of destinaion, countries of transit and countries of origin should cooperate, as appropriate, to manage immigration flows, prevent undocumented migrations, and if, appropriate, facilitate the return of migrants and their reintegration in their home communities;

c. Governments are urged to cooperate to reduce the effects of undocumented migrants on receiving countries, bearing in mind the special circumstances and needs of such countries, in particular developing countries;

d. Governments are urged to promote effective measures to protect all undocumented migrants and members of their families against racism, ethnocentrism and xenophibia.

F. Violence, Crime, the Problem of Illicit Drugs and Substance Abuse

79. Addressing the problems created by violence, crime, substance abuse and the production, use and trafficking of illicit drugs, and the rehabilitation of addicts requires;

a. Introducing and implementing specific policies and public health and social service programmes to prevent and eliminate all forms of violence in society, particularly to prevent and eliminate domestic violence and to protect the victims of violence, with particular attention to violence against women, children older persons and persons with disabilities. In particular, the Declaration on the Elimination of Violence against Women should be implemented and enforced nationally. In addition, the provisions of the Convention on the Rights of the Child should be respected;

b. Taking full measures to eliminate all forms of exploitation, abuse, harassment and violence against women, in particular domestic violence and rape. Special attention should be given to violence resulting from harmful traditional or customary practices and all forms of extremism, which implies both preventive actions and the rehabilitation of victims;

c. Implementing programmes that channel the energy and creativity of children and youth towards improving themselves and their communities in order to prevent their participation in crime, violence, and drug abuse and trafficking;

d. Improving mechanisms for resolving conflicts peacefully and reintegrating society following conflicts, including efforts towards reconciliation and confidence-building between the conflicting groups, training in non-violent conflict resolution at all levels of education, the reconstruction of social institutions that have been destroyed, the reintegration of displaced and disabled persons, and the re-establishment of the rule of law and respect for all human rights;

e. Establishing partnerships with non-governmental organizations and community organiztions to make adequate provision for the rehabilitation and reintegration into society of offenders, especially young offenders; measures will include efforts to maintain links with their families during detention and to reintegrate them into productive employment and social life after their release from detention;

f. Strengthening international cooperation and coodination

in devising strategies, policies, legislation and other measures in combating national and transnational organized crime and the use of violence and terrorism;

g. Adopting effective and environmentally sound national strategies to prevent or substantially reduce the cultivation and processing of crops used for the illegal drug trade, paying particular attention to national and international support for development programmes that create viable economic alternatives to drug production and promote the full integration of the social groups involved in such activities;

h. Combating drug and substance abuse and drug trafficking, corruption and related criminal activities through national and internationally coordinated measures, while strengthening integrated, multisectoral programmes to prevent and reduce the demand for consumption of drugs in order to create a society free of illicit drugs. In cooperation with the institutions of civil society and the private sectors, drug abuse prevention should be promoted, as well as preventive education for children and youth, an rehabilitation and education programmes for former drug and alcohol addicts, especially children and youth, to enable them to obtain productive employment and achieve the independence, dignity and responsibility for drug-free, crime-free, productive life;

i. Working nationally and internationally to identify narcotics trafficking and money laundering networks, prosecuting their leaders and seizing assets derived from such criminal activities;

j. Supporting comprehensive drug interdiction strategies and stregthening efforts to control precursor chemicals and firearms, ammunition and explosives in order to prevent their diversion to drug trafficking and terrorist groups;

k. Combating trafficking in women and children through national and internationally coordinated measures, at the same time establishing or strengthening institutions for the rehabilitation of the victims of the trafficking of women and children.

G. Social Integration and Family Responsibilities

80. The family is the basic unit of society and as such should be strengthened. It is entitled to receive comprehensive protection and support. In different cultural, political and social systems, various forms of the family exist. Marriage must be entered into with the free consent of the intending spouses, and husband and wife should be equal partners.

81. Helping the family in its supporting, educating and nurturing roles in cointributing to social integration should involve:

a. Encouraging social and economic policies that are designed to meet the needs of families and their individual members, especially the most disadvantaged and vulunderable members, with particular attention to the care of children;

b. Ensuring opportunities for family members to understand and met their social responsibilities;

c. Promoting mutual respect, tolerance and cooperation within the family and within society;

d. Promoting equal partnership between women and men in the family.

5. Implementation and Follow-up

82. Nothing short of renewed and massive political will at the national and internatioal levels to invest in people and their well being will achieve the objectives of social development. Social development and the implementation of the Programme of Action of the Summit are primarily the responsibility of Governments, although international cooperation and assistance are essential for their full implementation. At all levels of implementation, the crucial and essential requirements are:

- The promotion and protection of all human rights and fundamental freedoms, the support for democractic institutions and the empwerment of women;
- The integration of goals, programmes and review mech-

anisms that have developed separately in response to specific problems;

- Partnership involving States, local authorities, non-governmental organizations, especially voluntary organizations, other major groups as defined in Agenda 21, the media, families and individuals;
- The recognition of the diversity in the world and the need to take measures geared to achieve the Summit's goals;
- The empowerment of people, who are to be assisted so that they fully participate in setting goals, designing programes, implementing activities and evaluating performance;
- Efforts to mobilize new and additional financial resources that are both adequate and predictable, and are mobilized in a way that maximizes the availability of such resources, and uses all available funding sources and mechanisms, *inter alia*, multilateral, bilateral and private sources, including on concessional and grant terms;
- Solidarity, extending the concept of partnership and a moral imperative of mutual respect and concern among individuals, communities and nations.

Actions

A. National Strategies, Evaluations and Reveiws

83. The promotion of an integrated approach to the implementation of the Programme of Action at the national level, in accordance with national speficities, requires:

a. Analysis and reviewing macroeconomic, micro-economic and sectoral policies and their impact on poverty, employment, social intregration and social development;

b. Enhancing government policies and programmes to promote social development by strengthening the coordination of all efforts by naional and international actors, strengthening the efficiently and operational capacity of public management structures, and facilitating the effective and transparent use of resources;

c. Assessing the extent, distribution and characteristics of poverty, unemployment, social tensions and social exclusions, taking measures aiming at eradicating poverty, increasing productive employment and enhancing social integration;

d. Formulating or strengthening, by 1996, comprehensive cross-sectoral strategies for implementing the Summit outcome and national strategies for social development, including government action, actions by States in cooperation with other Governments, international, regional and subregional organizations, and actions taken in partnership and cooperation with actors of civil society, the private sector and cooperatives, with specific responsibilities to be undertaken by each actor and with agreed priorities and time-frames;

e. Integrating social development goals into national development plans, policies and budgets, cutting across traditional sectoral boundries, with transparency and accountability, and formulated and implemented with the participation of the groups directly affected;

f. Defining time-bound goals and targets for reducing overall poverty and eradicating absolute poverty, expanding employment and reducing unemployment, and enhancing social integration, within each national context;

g. Promoting and strengthening institutional capacity-building for inter-ministerial coordination, intersectoral collaboration, the coordinated allocation of resources and vertical integration from national capitals to local districtcs;

h. Developing quantitative and qualitative indicators of social development, including, where possible, disaggregation by gender, to assess poverty, employment, social integration and other social factors, to monitor the impact of social policies and programmes, and to find ways to improve the effectiveness of policies and programmes and introduce new programmes;

i. Strengthening implementation and monitoring mechanisms, including arrangements for the participation of civil society in policy-making and implementation and collaboration with international organizations;

j. Regularly assessing national progress towards implementing the outcome of Summit, possibly in the form of periodic national reports, outlining successes, problems and obstacles. Such reports could be considered with the framework of an appropriate consolidated reporting system, taking into account the different reporting procedures in the economic, social and environmental fields;

84. Internatioal support for the formulation of national strategies for social development will requires actions by bilateral and multilateral agencies for :

a. Assessing countries to strengthen or rebuild their capacities for formulating, coordinating, implementing and monitoring integrated stragies for social development;

b. Coordinating the assistance provided by different agencies for similar planning processes under other international actions plans;

c. Developing improved concepts and programmes for the collection and dissemination of statstics and indicators for social developent to facilitate review and policy analysis and provide expertise, advice and support to countries at their request.

B. Involvement of Civil Society

85. Effective implementation of the Copenhagen Declaration on Social Development and the Programme of Action of the Summit requires strengthening community organizations and non-profit non-governmental organizations in the spheres of education, health, poverty, social integration, human rights, improvement of the quality of life, and relief and rehabilitation, enabling them to participate constructively in policy-making and implementation. This will require;

a. Encouraging and supporting the creation and development of such organizations, particularly among the disadvantaged and vulnerable people;

b. Establishing legislative and regulatory frameworks, institutional, arrangements and consultative mechanisms for involving such organizations in the design, implementation and evaluation of social development strategies and programmes;

c. Supporting capacity-building programmes for such organizations in critical areas, such as participatory plananing, programme design, implementation and evaluation, economic and financial analysis, credit management, research, information and advocacy;

d. Providing resources through such measures as small grant programmes, and technical and other administrative support for initiatives taken and managed at the community level;

e. Strengthening networking and exchange of expertise and experience among such orgnizations.

86. The contributioin of civil society, including the private sector, to social development can be enhanced by :

a. Developing planning and policy-making procedures that facilitate parntership and cooperation between Governments and civil society in social development;

b. Encouraging business enterprises to pursue investment and other policies, including non-commercial activities, that will contribute to social development, especially in relation to the generation of work opportunities, social support services at the workplace, access to productive resources and construction of infrastructure;

c. Enabling and encouraging trade unions to participate in the planning and implementation of social development programmes, especially in relation to the generation of work opportunities under fair conditions, the provision of training, health care and other basic services, and the development of an economic environment that facilitates sustained economic growth and sustainable development.

d. Enabling and encouraging farmers' representative organizations and cooperatives to participate in the formulation and implementation of sustainable agricultural and rural development policies and programmes;

e. Encouraging and facilitating the development of cooperatives, including among people living in poverty or belong to vulnerable groups;

f. Supporting academic and research institutions, particularly in the developing countries, in their contribution to social development programmes, and facilitating mechanisms for independent, detached, impartial and objective monitoring of social progress, especially through collecting, analysing and disseminating information and ideas about economic and social development;

g. Encouraging educational institutions, the media and other srouces of public information and opinion to give special prominence to the challenges of social development and to facilitate widespread and well-informed debate about social policies throughout the community.

C. Mobilization of Financial Resources

87. The implementation of the Copenhagen Declaration and the Programme of Action of the Summit at the national level may require substantial new and additional resources, in both the public and the private sectors. Augmenting the availability of public resources for social development requires at the national level:

a. Implementing macroeconomic and micro-economic policies in accordance with national priorities and policies, aimed at encouraging greater domestic savings and investment required for public spending, through progressive, fair and economically efficient taxes that are cognizant of sustainable development concerns, and through cutting back on subsidies that do not benefit the poor;

b. Reducing, as appropriate, excessive military expenditures and investments for arms production and acquisition, consistent with national security requirements, in order to increase resources for social and economic development;

c. Giving high priority to social development in the allocation of public spending and ensuring predictable funding for the relevant programmes;

d. Ensuring that the resources for social development are available at the level of administration that is responsible for formulating and implementing the relevant programmes;

e. Increasing the effective and transparent utilization of public resources, reducing waste and combating corruption, and concentrating on the areas of greatest social need;

f. Developing innovative sources of funding, both public and private, for social programmes, and creating a supporting environment for the mobilization of resources by civil society for social development, including beneficiary contributions and individual voluntary contributions.

88. Implementation of the Declaration and the Programme of Action in developing countries, in particular in Africa and the least developed countries, will need additional financial resources and more effective development cooperation and assistance. This will require:

a. Translating the commitments of the Summit into financial implications for social development programmes in developing countries, particularly Africa and the least development countries;

b. Striving for the fulfilment of the agreed target of 0.7 per cent of gross national product for overall official development assistance (ODA) as soon as possible, and increasing the share of funding for social development programmes, commensurate with the scope and the scale of activities required to achieve the objectives and goals of the Declaration and Programme of Action;

c. Agreeing on a mutual commitment between interested developed and developing country parnters to allocate, on average, 20 per cent of ODA and 20 per cent of the national budget, respectively, to basic social programmes;

d. Giving high priority in ODA to the eradication of poverty in developing countries, in particular in Africa, low-income countries in Asia and the Pacific, Latin America and the Caribbean, and the least developed countries;

e. Providing assistance for social-sector activities, such as the rehabilitation and development of social infrastructure, including in the form of grants or soft loans;

f. Implementing the commitments of the international community to the special needs and vulnerabilities of the small island developing States, in particular by providing effective means, including adequate, predictable, new and additional resources for social development programmes, in accordance with the Declaration of Barbados and on the basis of the relevant provisions of the Programme of Action for the Sustainable Devleopment of Small Island Developing States;

g. Providing international support and assistance to the land-locked developing countries in their efforts to implement the outcome of the Summit, taking into account the challenges and problems, characteristic to those countries;

h. Giving preference, wherever possible, to the utilization of competent national experts or, where necessary, of competent experts from within the subregion or region or from other developing countries, in project and programme design, preparation and implementation, and to the building of local expertise where it does not exist;

i. Exploring ways and means to strengthen support and expand South-South cooperation based on partnership between developing and developed countries, as well as enhanced cooperation among developing countries;

j. Maximizing project and programme efficiency by keeping overhead costs to a minimum;

k. Developing economic policies to promote and mobilize domestic savings and attract external resources for productive investment, and seeking innovative sources of funding, both public and private, for social programme, while ensuring their effective utilization;

i. Monitoring the impact of trade liberalization on progress made in developing countries to meet basic human needs, giving particular attention to new initiatives to expand the access of developing countries to international markets;

m. Encouraging direct cooperation to promote joint ventures, including in the sector of social programmes and infrastructure;

n. Encouraging recipient Governments to strengthen their national coordination mechanisms for internatioinal co-operation in social development and to ensure the effective use of international assistance so as to assist donors to secure commitment to further resources for natioinal actions plans;

o. Inviting multilateral and bilateral donors to consult with a view to coordinating their financing policies and planning procedures in order to improve the impact, complementarity and cost-effectiveness of their contributions to the achievements of the objectives of social development programmes of developing countries.

89. Implementation of the Copenhagen Declaration and the Programme of Action of the Summit in countries wtih economies in transition will require continued international cooperation and assistance. To this end, there is a need to:

a. Assess the financial implications of the commitments of the Summit for social development programmes in countries with economies in transition;

b. Enhance technical and financial assistance for the implementation of programmes of macroeconomic stabilization in order to ensur sustained economic growth and sustainable development;

c. Support and encourage transformations in the field of human resources development;

d. Invite multilateral and bilateral donors to consult with a view to coordinating their financing policies and planning procedurs in order to improve the impact of their contribution to the achievement of the objectives of social development programmes of countries with economices in transition.

90. Substantial debt reduction is needed to enable developing countries to implement the Declaration and Programme of Action. Building on, *inter alia*, the momentum from the July 1994 meeting of the seven major industrialized countries in Naples and the October 1994 meeting of the governors of

the World Bank and the International Monetary Fund, further progress can be made by:

a. Inviting the international community, including the international financial institutions, to continue to explore ways of implementing additional and innovative measures to alleviate substaintially the debt burdens of developing countries, in particular of the highly indebted low-income countries, in order to help them to achieve sustained economic growth and sustainable development without falling into a new debt crisis;

b. Adopting measures to substaintially reduce the bilateral debts of the least developed countries, in particular the countries of Africa, as soon as possible, and exploring other innovative approaches to managing and alleviating the onerous debts and debt service burdens of other developing countries as soon as possible;

c. Giving special consideration to those developing countries in which multilateral debt constitutes an important part of their total debt in order to seek durable solution to this increasing problem;

d. Encouraging the possibilities of debt swaps for social development, with the resources released by debt cancellation or reduction to be invested in social development programmes, without prejudice to more durable solutions, such as debt reduction and/or cancellation;

e. Mobilizing the resources of the Debt Reduction Facility of the International Development Associaton in order to help eligible developing countries to reduce their commercial debt; considering alternative mechanisims to complement that Facility;

f. Inviting creditor countries, private banks and multilater financial institutions, within their prerogatives, to consider continuing the initiatives and efforts to address the commercial debt problems of the least developed countries and of low and middle-income developing countries, to consider the extention of appropriate new financial support to the low-income countries with substantial debt burdens that continue, at great cost, to srevice debt and meet their international obligations; to continue to explore ways of implementing additional and innovative measures to substantially alleviate the debt burdens of developing countries, in particular of the highly indebted low-income countries, in order to help them achieve sustained economic growth and sustainable development without falling into a new debt crisis.

91. In order to ensure that structural adjustment programmes include social development goals, in particular the eradication of poverty, the genration of productive employment and the enhancement of social integration, Governments, in cooperation with the international financial institutions and other international organizations, should:

a. Protect basic social programmes and expenditures, in particular those affecting the poor and vulnerable segments of society, from budget reductions;

b. Review the impact of structural adjustment programmes on social development by means by gender-sensitive social -impact assessments and other relevant methods, and develop policies to reduce their negative effects and improve their positive impact;

c. Further promote policies enabling small enterprises, cooperatives and other forms of micro-enterprises to develop their capacities for income generation and employment creation.

92. International financial institutions sould contribute to the mobiliztaion of resources for the implementation of the Declaration and Programme of Action. To this end, the relevant institutions are urged to take the following measures;

a. The World Bank, the International Monetary Fund, the regional and subregional development banks and funds, and all other international finance organizations should further integrate social development goals in their policies, programmes and operations, including by giving higher priority to social-sector lending, where applicable, in their lending programmes;

b. The Bretton Woods institutions and other organizations

and bodies of the United Nations system should work together with concerned countries to improve policy dialogues and develop new initiatives to ensure that structural adjustment programmes promote sustained economic and social development, with particular attention to their impact on people living in poverty and vunerable groups;

c. The United Nations, in cooperation with the World Bank, the International Monetary Fund and other multilateral development institutioins, should study the impact of structural adjustment programmes on economic and social development and assist adjusting countries in creating conditions for economic growth, job creation, poverty eradication and social development.

93. In addition to augmenting the flow of the resources through established channels, relevant United Nations bodies, in particular the Economic and Social Council, should be requested to consider new and innovative ideas for generating funds, and for this purpose, to offer my useful suggestions.

D. The Role of the United Nations System

94. A framework for international cooperation must be developed in the context of the agenda for development in order to ensure the integrated and comprehensive implementation, follow-up and assessment of the outcome of the Summit, together with the results of other recent and plnned United Nations conferences related to social development, in particular the World Summit for Children, the United Nations Conference on Environment and Development, the World Conference on Human Rights, the Global Conference on the Sustainable Development of Small Island Devloping states, the International Conference on Population and Development, the Fourth World Conference on Women, and the United Nations Conference on Human Settlements (Habitate II). At the international level, as at the national, the financial and organiztional implications of the commitments, goals and targets should be assessed, priorities established, and budgets and work programmes planned.

95. With regard to the consideration of social development at the intergovernmental level, special consideration should be

given to the roles of the General Assembly and of the Economic and Social Council. To this end:

a. The Genreal Assembly, as the highest intergovernmental mechanism, is the principal policy-making and appraisal organ on matters relating to the follow-up to the Summit. The Assembly should include the follow-up to the Summit in its agenda as an item entitled "Implementation of the outcome of the World Summit for Social Development". In 1996, it should review the effectiveness of the steps taken to implement the outcome of the Summit with regard to poverty eradication, as part of the activities relating to the International Year for the Eradication of Poverty;

b. The General Assembly should hold a special session in the year 2000 for an overall review and appraisal of the implementation of the outcome of the Summit, and should consider further action and initiatives;

c. The General Assembly, as its fiftieth session, should declare the first United Nations decade for the eradication of poverty, following the International Year for the Eradication of Poverty (1996), with a view to its consideration further initiatives on the eradication of poverty;

d. The General Assembly, as well as the Economic and Social Council, could convene meetings of high-level representatives to promote international dialogue on critical social issues and on policies for adressing them through international cooperation;

e. The General Assembly should draw up the initial work of the agenda for development working group on a common framework for the implementation of the outcome of the conferences;

f. The Economic and Social Council, in the context of its role under the Charter of the United Nations *vis-a-vis* the General Assembly, would oversee system-wide coordination in the implementation of the Summit outcome and make recommendations in this regard. It should look at ways to strengthen, consistent with the mandates of the Charter of the United Nations, the role and authority, structures, resources and processes of the Council, bringing specialized agencies into a closer working relationship with the Council so that it can review progress made towards implementing the outcome of the Summit as well as improving the Council's effectiveness. The Council, as its substantive session of 1995, should be invited to review the mandate, agenda and composition of the Commission for Social Development, including considerations of the strengthening of the Commission, taking into account the need for synergy with other related commissions, and conference follow-up. The Council should also draw upon any initial work completed by that time on a common framework for the implementation of conference outcomes (see paras, 94 and 95 (e) above). The Council should also be invited to review the reporting system in the area of social development with a view to establishing a coherent system that would result in clear policy recommendations for Governments and international actors;

g. Within the framework of the discussions on an agenda for development and the discussion of the Economic and Social Council at its coordination segment of 1995 on a common framework for the implementation of the outcome of United Nations conference in the economic and social fields, consideration should be given to the possibility of the holding joint meetings of the Council and the Development Committee of the World Bank and the International Monetary Fund. The Secretary-General and the heads of IMF, the World Bank, ILO, the United Nations funds and programmes, and other relevant agencies should consider the possiblity of holding joint meetings for the purpose of considering the implementation of the Declaration and the Programme of Action prior to the Development Committee sessions;

h. To promote implementation of the outcomes at the regional and subregional levels, the regional commissions, in cooperation with the regional intergovernmental organizations and banks, could convene, on a biennial basis, a meeting at a high political level to review progress made towards implementing the outcome of the Summit, exchange views on their respective experiences and adopt the appropriate measures. The regional commissions should report to the Council on the outcome of such meetings through the appropriate mechanisms;

i. The important role of the Committee on Economic, Social and Cultural Rights in monitoring those aspect of the Declaration and Programme of Action that relate to compliance, by States Parties, with the International Covenant on Economic, Social and Cultural Rights should be emphasized.

96. The United Nations system should provide technical cooperation and other forms of assistance to the developing countries, in particular in Africa and least developed countries, in implementing the Declaration and Programme of Action. To this end:

a. The United Nations systems, including the technical and sectoral agencies and Bretton Woods institutions, should expand and improve their cooperation in the field of social devlopment to ensure that their efforts are complementary and, where possible, should combine resources in joint initiatives for social development built around common objectives of the Summit;

b. In order to improve the efficiency and effectiveness of United Nations organization in providing supportt for social development efforts at the national level, and to enhance their capacity to serve the objectives of the Summit, there is a need to renew, reform and revitalize the various parts of the United Nations system, in particular its operational activities. All specialized agencies and related organizations of the United Nations system are invited to strenthen and adjust their activities, programmes and medium-term strategies, as appropriate, to take into account the follow-up to the Summit. Relavent governing bodies should review their policies, programmes, budgets and activities in this regard;

c. The Administrative Committee on Coordination should consider how its participating entities might best coordinate their activities to implement the objectives of the

Summit;

d. Regular reports on their plans and programmes related to implementation should be provided to the appropriate forums by United Nationl funds and programmes and the specilalized agencies.

97. The United Nations systems should consider and provide appropriate technical cooperation and other forms of assistance to the countries with economies in transition. To this end:

a. The respective United Nations bodies should assist the efforts of those countries in designing and implementing social development programmes;

b. The United Nations Development Programme should continue to undertake efforts to support the implementation of the social development programmes, taking into the account the specific needs of the countries with economies in transition;

c. The organizations and bodies of the United Nations system, including the technical and sectoral agencies, the International Monetary Fund and the World Bank, should, continue their cooperation in the field of social development of countries with economies in transition.

98. The implementation of the Copenhagen Declaration and the Programme of Action of the Summit will involve many entites of the United Nations systems. In order to ensure coherence in this effort, the General Assembly should give consideration to:

a. Promoting and strengthening the coordination of United Nations system activities, the Bretton Woords institutions and the World Trade Organization at the global, regional and national levels in the area of economic and social development programmes, including, *inter alia*, through reports to and meetings in coordination with the Economic and Social Council;

b. Inviting the World Trade Orgnization to consider how it might contribute to the implementation of the Programme of Action, including activities in cooperation with the

United Nations system;

c. Requesting the International Labour Organization, which because of its mandate, tripartite structures and expertise has a special role a play in the field of employment and social development, to contribute to the implementation of the Programme of Action;

d. Requesting the Secretary-General to ensure effective coordination of the implementation of the Declaration and Programme of Action.

99. United Nations operational activities for development should be strengthened in order to implement the Summit outcome, in accordance with relevant resolutions, particularly General Assembly resolution 47/199, and to this end:

a. The United Nations Development Programme should organize United Nations system efforts towards capacity-building at the local, national and regional levels, and should support the coordinated implementation of social development programmes through its network of field officies;

b. Coordination at the country level should be improved through the resident coordinator system to take full account of the Copenhagen Declaration and the Programme of Action of the Summit and related international agreemetns;

c. The United Nations system should encourage and assist South-South cooperation and technical cooperation among developing countries, at all levels, as an important instrument for social development and the implementation of the Programme of Action;

d. United Nations development efforts should be supported by a substantial increase in resources for operational activites for development on a predictable, continuous and assured basis, commensurate with the increasing needs of developing countries, as stated in resolution 47/199;

e. The United Nations system's capacity for gathering and analysing information and developing indicators of social development should be strengthened, taking into account the work carried out by differnt countries, in particular by developing countries. The capacity of the United Nations system for providing policy and technical support and advice, upon request, to improve national capacities in this regard should also be strengthened.

100. The support and participation of major groups as defined in Agenda 21 as essential to the success of the implementation of the Programme of Action. To ensur the commitment of these groups, they must be involved in planning, elaboration, implementation and evaluaion at both the national and the international levels. To this end, mechanisms, are needed to support, promote and allow their effective participation in all relevant United Nations bodies, including the mechanisms, responsible for reviewing the implementation of the Programme of Action.

APPENDICES

Appendix 1

RESOLUTIONS ADOPTED BY THE SUMMIT

Resolution 1

Copenhagen Declaration on Social Development and Programme of Action of the World Summit for Social Development*

The World Summit for Social Development

Having met in Copenhagen from 6 to 12 March 1995,

1. *Adopts* the Copenhagen Declaration on Social Development and the Programme of Action of the World Summit for Social Development;

2. *Recommends* to the General Assembly of the United Nations at its fiftieth session that it endorses the Copenhagen Declaration and the Programme of Action, as adopted by the Summit.

Resolution 2

Expression of thanks to the people and Government of Denmark**

The World Summit for Social Development

Having met in Copenhagen from 6 to 12 March 1995 at the

* Adopted at the 14th plenary meeting on 12 March, 1995.

** Adopted at the 14th plenary meeting, on 12 March, 1995.

invitation of the Government of Denmark,

1. Expresses its profound gratitude to the Government of Denmark for having made it possible for the World Summit for Social Development to be held in Copenhagen and for the excellent facilities, staff and services so graciously placed at its disposal;

2. Requests the Government of Denmark to convey to the city of Copenhagen and to the people of Denmark the gratutide of the Summit for the hospitability and warm welcome extended to all participants.

Resolution 3

Credentials of representatives to the World Summit for Social Development***

The World Summit for Social Development,

Having considered the report of the Credentials Committee and the recommendation contained therein,

Approves the report of the Credentials Committee.

*** Adopted at the 10th plenary meeting, on 10 March 1995,

Appendix 2

ATTENDANCE AND ORGANIZATION OF WORK

A. Date and place of the Summit

1. The World Summit for Social Development was held at Copenhagen from 6 to 12 March 1995, in conformity with General Assembly resolution 47/92 of 16 December 1992. During that period, the Summit held 14 plenary meetings.

B. Attendance

The following States and regional economic integration organization were represented at the Summit:

Afghanistan
Albania
Algeria
Andorra
Angola
Antigua and Barbuda
Argentina
Armenia
Australia
Austria
Azerbaijan
Bahamas
Bahrain
Bangladesh
Barbados
Belarus
Belgium
Belize
Benin
Bhutan
Bolivia
Bosnia and Herzegovina

Botswana
Brazil
Brunei Darussalam
Bulgaria
Burkina Faso
Burundi
Cambodia
Cameroon
Canada
Cape Verde
Central African Republic
Chad
Chile
China
Colombia
Comoros
Congo
Cook Islands
Costa Rica
Cote d'Ivoire
Croatia
Cuba
Cyprus
Czech Republic
Democratic People's
 Republic of Korea
Denmark
Djibouti
Dominica
Dominican Republic
Ecuador
Egypt
El Salvador
Equatorial Guinea
Eritrea
Estonia
Ethiopia
European Community
Finland
France
Gabon
Gambia
Georgia
Germany
Ghana
Greece
Grenada
Guatemala
Guinea
Guinea-Bissau
Guyana
Haiti
Holy See
Honduras
Hungary
Iceland
India
Indonesia
Iran (Islamic Republic of)
Iraq

Ireland
Israel
Italy
Jamaica
Japan
Jordan
Kazakhstan
Kenya
Kuwait
Kyrgyzstan
Lao People's Democratic Republic
Latvia
Lebanon
Lesotho
Liberia
Libyan Arab Jamahiriya
Liechtenstein
Lithuania
Luxembourg
Madagascar
Malawi
Malaysia
Maldives
Mali
Malta
Marshall Islands
Mauritania
Mauritius
Mexico
Micronesia (Federated States of)
Monaco
Mongolia
Morocco
Mozambique
Myanmar
Namibia
Nepal
Netherlands
New Zealand
Nicaragua
Niger
Nigeria
Niue
Norway
Oman
Pakistan
Panama
Papua New Guinea
Paraguay
Peru
Philippines
Poland
Portugal
Qatar
Republic of Korea
Republic of Moldova
Romania
Russian Federation

Rwanda
Saint Kitts and Nevis
Saint Lucia
Saint Vincent and the Grenadines
San Marino
Sao Tome and Principe
Saudi Arabia
Senegal
Seychelles
Sierra Leone
Singapore
Slovakia
Slovenia
Solomon Islands
South Africa
Spain
Sri Lanka
Sudan
Suriname
Swaziland
Sweden
Switzerland
Syrian Arab Republic
Tajikistan
Thailand
The former Yugoslav Republic of Macedonia
Togo
Tonga
Trinidad and Tobago
Tunisia
Turkey
Turkmenistan
Uganda
Ukraine
United Arab Emirates
United Kingdom of Great Britain and Northern Ireland
United Republic of Tanzania
United States of America
Uruguay
Uzbekistan
Vanuatu
Venezuela
Viet Nam
Yemen
Zaire
Zambia
Zimbabwe

3. The observer for Palestine attended the Summit.
4. The following associate members of the regional commissions were represented by observers: Macau Netherlands Antilles.

5. The secretariats of the following regional commissions were represented:

Economic Commission for Africa

Economic Commission for Europe

Economic Commission for Latin America and the Caribbean

Economic and Social Commission for Asia and the Pacific

Economic and Social Commission for Western Asia

6. The following United Nations bodies and programmes were represented:

United Nations Children's Fund

United Nations Conference on Trade and Development

United Nations Development Fund for Women

United Nations Development Programme

United Nations Environment Programme

United Nations Population Fund

United Nations Relief and Works Agency for Palestine Refugees in the Near East

United Nations University

World Food Programme

United Nations Centre for Human Settlements (Habitat)

United Nations High Commissioner for Human Rights, Office of the United Nations High Commissioner for Refugees, Office of the

United Nations International Drug Control Programme

International Research and Training Institute for the Advancement of Women

United Nations Research Institute for Social Development

7. The following specialized agencies were represented:

International Labour Organization

Food and Agriculture Organization of the United Nations

United Nations Educational, Scientific and Cultural Organization

World Health Organization

World Bank

International Monetary Fund

World Meteorological Organization

World Intellectual Property Organization

International Fund for Agricultural Development

United Nations Industrial Development Organization

8. The following intergovernmental organizations were accredited to participate in the Summit:

African, Caribbean and Pacific Group of States

African Development Bank

African Society for Humanitarian Aid and Development Sudan

Andean Parliament

Arab Fund for Economic and Social Development

Asian-African Legal Consultative Committee

Asian and pacific Development Centre

Asian Development Bank

Asian Forum of Parliamentarians on Population and Development

Association of South-East Asian Nations

Commonwealth of Independent States

Commonwealth Secretariat

Council of Europe

Economic Affairs Secretariat

Gulf Cooperation Council

Inter-American Development Bank

International Committee of the Red Cross

International Federation of Red Cross and Red Crescent Societies

International Food Policy Research Institute

International Organization for Migration

Islamic Educational, Scientific and Cultural Organization

Latin American Economic System

Latin American Parliament

League of Arab States

Nordic Council Secretariat of the Presidium

Organisation for Economic Cooperation and Development

Organization of African Unity

Organization of American States

Organization of Eastern Caribbean States

Organization of the Islamic Conference

South Pacific Commission

9. A large number of non-governmental organizations attended the Summit.

C. Openins of the Summit and election of the President

10. The Summit was declared open by the Secretary-General of the United Nations. The Secretary-General then addressed the Summit.

11. At the Ist plenary meeting, on 6 March, the Summit elected, by acclamation, as president of the Summit, His Excellency Mr. Poul Nyrup Rasmussen, Prime Minister of the Kingdom of Denmark. The President of the Summit made a statement.

D. Messages from heads of State

12. The Summit received a message wishing it success from His Excellency Mr. Jose Eduardo dos Santos, President of the Republic of Angola.

E. Adoption of the rules of procedure

13. At the Ist plenary meeting, on 6 March, the Summit adopted the provisional rules of procedure as recommended by the Preparatory Committee for the Summit and approved by the General Assembly in its decision 49/446 of 23 December 1994.

F. Adoption of the agenda

14. At the Ist plenary meeting, on 6 March, the Summit adopted as its agenda the provisional agenda recommended by the Preparatory Committee in its decision 3/3. The agenda as adopted was as follows:

1. Inaugural ceremony.
2. Election of the President.
3. Adoption of the rules of procedure.
4. Adoption of the agenda and other organizational matters.
5. Election of officers other than the President.
6. Organization of work, including establishment of the Main Committee.
7. Credentials of representatives to the Summit:
   (a) Appointment of the members of the Credentials Committee;
   (b) Report of the Credentials Committee.
8. General exchange of views.
9. Meeting of heads of State or Government.
10. Declaration and Programme of Action of the World Summit for Social Development.
11. Adoption of the report of the Summit.

G. Election of officers other than the President

15. At the Ist and 7th plenary meetings, on 6 and 9 March, the Summit elected Vice-Presidents from the following regional groups:

African States (7 Vice-Presidents): Algeria, Burkina Faso, Cameroon, Ethiopia, Guinea-Bissau, Sudan and Zimbabwe;

Asian States (6 Vice-Presidents): China, India, Indonesia, Philippines, Qatar and Republic of Korea;

Eastern European States (3 Vice-Presidents): Latvia, Slovakia and Ukraine;

Latin American and Caribbean States (5 Vice-Presidents): Belize, Chile, Cuba, Panama and Paraguay;

Western European and other States (6 Vice-Presidents): Andorra, Australia, Canada, Germany, Portugal and Sweden.

16. At the Ist plenary meeting, on 6 March, the Summit elected, by acclamation, an ex offico Vice-President from the host country, His Excellency Mr. Poul Nielson, Minister for Development Cooperation of the Kingdom of Denmark.

17. At the same meeting, the Summit elected Mr. Sadok Rabah (Tunisia), Rapporteur-General of the Summit.

18. Also at the Ist plenary meeting, the Summit elected Mr Juan Somavia (Chile), Chairman of the Main Committee.

H. Organization of work, including establishment of the Main Committee

19. At the Ist plenary meeting, on 6 March, the Summit approved the organization of work and orally amended. It decided to allocate agenda item 10 (Declaration and Programme of Action of the World Summit for Social Development) to the Main Committee.

I. Accreditation of intergovernmental organizations

20. At the Ist plenary meeting, on 6 March, the Summit approved the accreditation of the intergovernment organizations.

J. Accreditation of On-governmental organizations

21. At the Ist plenary meeting, on 6 March, the Summit approved the accreditation of the non-governmental organizations.

K. Appointment of the members of the Credentials Committee

22. At the Ist plenary meeting, on 6 March, in conformity with rule 4 of the rules of procedure Of the Summit, the Summit established a Credentials Committee composed of China, Fiji, Honduras, Namibia, Portugal, the Russian Federation, Suriname, Togo and the United States of America, on the understanding that if one of those States did not participate in the Summit, it would be replaced by another State from the same regional group.

Apendix 3

GENERAL EXCHANGE OF VIEWS

1. The Summit held a general exchange of views at the Ist to 10th meetings, from 6 to 10 March 1995. Representatives of States, specialized agencies, United Nations bodies, programmes and offices, intergovernmental organizations and non-governmental organizations and observers of associate members of the regional commissions addressed the Summit. All speakers expressed their appreciation of the efforts made by the host Government and the secretariat in preparing for the Summit.

2. At the Ist meeting, on 6 March, statements were made by the representatives of the Philippines (on behalf of the States Members of the United Nations that are members of the Group of 77), France (on behalf of the European Union), Chile, Malaysia, Venezuela, Slovakia, Mall and Ukraine.

3. At the 2nd meeting, on 6 March, statements were made by the representatives of Norway, Kuwait, Jamaica, Italy, Germany, the Republic of Korea, Barbados, Seychelles, Azerbaijan, Bolivia and Papua New Guinea.

4. At the same meeting, the Director-General of the World Health Organization a statement. The Administrator of the United Nations Development Programme made a statement. The representative of the Islamic Educational, Scientific and Cultural Organization, an intergovernmental organization, made a statement. Statements were also made by the repre-

sentatives of the following non-governmental organizations: World Council of Churches, Baha'i International Community and South Asia Caucus. Her Royal Highness Princess Basma Hint Talal of Jordan introduced the report of the forty-seventh annual Department of Public Information/ Non-Govemmental Organizations Conference, held on 20-22 September 1994.

5. At the 3rd meeting, on 7 March, statements were made by the representatives of Mexico, Burkina Faso, the Syrian Arab Republic, Algeria, Romania, Guyana, Kenya, Ethiopia, the Democratic People's Republic of Korea, the Marshall Islands, Mongolia, the Lao People's Democratic Republic, the Gambia, Tunisia and China.

6. At the same meeting, statements were made by the Managing Director of the International Monetary Fund and the Director-General of the Food and Agriculture Organization of the United Nations. The representative of the Commission on Global Governance, a non-governmental organization, also made a statement.

7. At the 4th meeting, on 7 March, statements were made by the representatives of Swaziland, the United Arab Emirates, Austria, India, Benin, the Holy See, the United Republic of Tanzania, Zambia, Switzerland, Malawi, Sri Lanka, Guinea, Peru, Bangladesh, Indonesia, Nepal and the former Yugoslav Republic of Macedonia.

8. At the same meeting, the President of the International Fund for Agricultural Development made a statement. Statements were made by the Executive Director of the United Nations International Drug Control Programme, the Executive Director of the World Food Programme, the Deputy Executive Director of the United Nations Children's Fund and the Executive Director of the United Nations Environment Programme. Statements were made by the representatives of the following intergovernmental organizations: International Committee of the Red Cross, International Organization for Migration and Latin American Parliament. Statements were also made by the representatives of the following non-governmental organizations: International Planned parenthood

Federation, Medecins du Monde, International Council on Social Welfare, International Federation of Agricultural Producers, International Union of Local Authorities and world Assembly of Youth.

9. At the 5th meeting, on 8 March, statements were made by the First Lady of Panama and by the representatives of Pakistan, Spain, Ghana, Namibia, Senegal, Haiti, the Bahamas, Slovenia, the Niger, the United States of America, Botswana, Belize and the Russian Federation.

10. At the same *meeting,* the representative of the Women's Environment' and Development Organization, a non-governmental organization, made a statement.

11. At the 6th meeting, on 8 March, statements were made by His Highness Prince Sisowath Sirirath of Cambodia and by the representatives of Liechtenstein, Brazil, Guinea-Bissau, Malta, Antigua and Barbuda, Iceland, Cameroon, Jordan, the Sudan, Ireland, Sierra Leone, Burundi, Ecuador, Nigeria, Rwanda, the Congo and Chad.

12. At the same meeting, statements were made by the Secretary-General of the, Fourth World Conference on Women, the Executive Director of the United Nations population Fund, the Director of the United Nations Development Fund for Women, the President of the Board of Trustees of the International Research and Training Institute for the Advancement of Women, the Executive Coordinator of the United Nations Volunteers and the Director of the United Nations Research Institute for Social Development. Statements were made by the representative of the following intergovernmental organizations: Organization of African Unity, Asian Development Bank and International Food Policy Research Institute. Statements were also made by the representatives of the following governmental organizations: Inter-Parliamentary Union, Women's Caucus, Union Nationale de la Femme Tunisienne, World Movement of Mothers, National Union of Working Women, Soroptimist International, International Council of Women, International Center for Economic Growth, and World Blind Union.

13. At the 7th meeting, on 9 March, statements were made by

the representatives of Colombia, Belarus, Poland, Finland, Turkey, Canada, Andorra, Portugal, Bulgaria, Uganda, Saudi Arabia, Estonia, Cyprus and Gabon.

14. At the same meeting, statements were made by the Directors-General of the United Nations Educational, Scientific and Cultural Organization, the International Labour Organization and the United Nations Industrial Development Organization. The United Nations High Commissioner for Human Rights made a statement. The representative of the European Commission, an intergovernmental organization, also made a statement.

15. At the 8th meeting, on 9 March, statements were made by the representatives of Mauritius, the Netherlands, Suriname, Guatemala, Greece, Djibouti, Afghanistan, Kazakhstan, Mozambique, Lesotho, Brunei Darussalam, Myanmar, Saint Vincent and the Grenadines, Nicaragua, Niue and the Cook Islands.

16. At the same meeting, statements were made by the Secretary-General of the United Nations Conference on Human Settlements (Habitat *II)*, the Rector of the United Nations University and the Officer-in-Charge of the United Nations Conference on Trade and Development. Statements were made by the representatives of the following intergovernmental organizations: Agency for Cultural and Technical Cooperation and Nordic Council. Statements were also made by the representatives of the following non-governmental organizations: International Chamber of Commerce, International Confederation of Free Trade Unions, Rotary International, Small Farmers, Producers and Micro-entrepreneurs Caucus, World Confederation of Labour, Independent Commission for Population and Quality of Life, Values Caucus, African Caucus, International Movement ATD Fourth World and Bonn International Centre for Conversion. The President of the Conference of Non-Governmental Organizations in Consultative Status with the Economic and Social Council and the representative of the NGO Committee on Ageing made statements.

17. At the 9th meeting, on 10 March, statements were made by the representatives of Viet Nam, Sweden, Vanuatu, Denmark, Singapore, the Islamic Republic of Iran, Trinidad and

Tobago, Japan, Israel, Latvia, Croatia, Belgium, Lithuania and Uruguay. The observer for Palestine made a statement.

18. At the same meeting, the Managing Director of the World Bank made a statement. The United Nations High Commissioner for Refugees made a statement. The representative of the Commonwealth Secretariat, an intergovernmental organization, made a statement. The representative of the Disability Caucus, a non-governmental organization, made a statement.

19. At the 10th meeting, on 10 March, statements were made by the representatives of the United Kingdom of Great Britain and Northern Ireland, Fiji, Thailand, Egypt, Angola, Cuba, Hungary, Lebanon, Bosnia and Herzegovina, Qatar, Iraq, Argentina, Mauritania, Saint Lucia, Morocco, Georgia, the Central African Republic and the Libyan Arab Jamahiriya. The observer for Macau made a statement.

20. At the same meeting, the representative of the World Meteorological Organization made a statement. Statements were made by the following intergovernmental organizations: Organisation for Economic Cooperation and Development, Inter-American Development Bank, Council of Europe, League of Arab States and International Federation of Red Cross and Red Crescent Societies. The following non-governmental organizations also made statements: Business Association for the World Social Summit, Copenhagen Alternative Declaration, Cousteau Society, Development Caucus, Latin American Caucus, Rights of the Child Caucus, Third World Network and Eurostep, People's Alliance of Social Development and Center of Concern.

Appendix 4

REPORT OF THE MAIN COMMITTEE

1. The Main Committee considered agenda item 10 (Declaration and Programme of Action of the World Summit for Social Development) at its 1st to 5th meetings, on 6, 7, 9 and 10 March 1995. It also held a number of informal meetings.
2. The Main Commitee had before it a note by the Secretary-General transmitting the draft declaration and draft programme of action of the World Summit for Social Development and a note by the Secretariat transmitting additional proposals for the draft declaration and draft programme of action.
3. The Chairman of the Main Committee was Jaun Somavia (Chile), who was elected by acclamation at the 1st plenary meeting of the Summit.
4. The Main Committee, at the 1st meeting, on 6 March, elected by acclamation the following States as Vice-Chairmen: Autralia, Cameroon, India, Indonesia, Latvia, mexico, Netherlands, Poland, Zimbabwe and Denmark (ex officio).
5. Also at the 1st meeting, the Main Committee established a Working Group, chaired by Mr. Prakash Shah (India). The Working Group held a number of meetings.

Consideration of the Draft Declaration and Draft Programme of Action

6. At the 2nd to 5th meetings, on 6, 7, 9 and 10 March, the main Committee considered the draft declaration and draft programme of action and the amendments thereto.

7. At the 4th meeting, on 9 March, the Main Committee approved a new commitment for the draft declaration, to be included in the declaration as commitment 6, and recommended it to the Summit for adoption. Statements were made by the representatives of Tunisia, Indonesia, the Holy See, Brazil, India, the United States of America, Egypt, Canada, Benin, Switzerland, Uganda, Guatemala, the Islamic Republic of Iran, Algeria, Malta, France (on behalf of the European Union), the Sudan, Fiji, Pakistan and the Philippines (on behalf of the States Members of the United Nations that are members of the Groups of 77 and China). The Vice-Chairman of the Committee, Mr. Shah (India), also made a statement.

8. The Main Committee then considered the draft declaration as a whole. The Vice-Chairman of the Committee, Mr. Richard Butler (Australia), informed the Committee of the progress made during informal consultations. Statements were made by the representatives of the United State of America, Egypt, the Russian Federation, the Philippines (on behalf of the States Members of the United Nations that are members of the Group of 77 and China) and Cuba.

9. At the same meeting, the Main Committee considered Chapter I of the draft programme of action. The Vice-Chairman of the Committee, Mr. Butler (Australia), informed the Committee of the progress made during informal consultations. Statements were made by the representatives of the United States of America,Egypt, Pakistan, the Sudan, benin, China, Bangladesh, Canada, France (on behalf of the European Union), the Holy See, Azerbaijan and Belize.

10. Also at the 4th meeting, the Main Committee approved Chapter II of the draft programme of action and recommended it to the Summit for the adoption . Statements were made by the representatives of Saudi Arabia, Canada, the Unitede

States of America, Pakistan, Guatemala, the United Arab Emirates, the Sudan, Norway, Mongolia, Zambia, Jamaica, Australia, Malta, Bangladesh, the Holy See, the Islamic Republic of Iran and Egypt.

11. At the same meeting, the Main Committee approved Chapter III of the draft programme of action and recommended it to the Summit for adoption. Statements were made by the representatives of the United States of America and Australia.

12. At the same meeting, the Main Committee approved Chapter IV of the draft programme of action and recommended it to the Summit for adoption. Statements were made by the representatives of the Philippines (on behalf of the States Members, of the United Nations that are members of the Group of 77 and China), Canada and the Holy See.

13. Also at the 4th meeting, the Main Committee considered Chapter V of the draft programme of action. The representative of Malaysia informed the Committee of the progress made during informal consultations. Statements were made by the representatives of Ukraine, Egypt, the United States of America, Benin, Algeria and Indonesia.

14. At the 5th meeting, on 10 March, the Main Committee approved the draft declaration and Chapter I and V of the draft programme of action. It deleted former paragraph 88 (c) of the draft programme of action, concerning the establishment of an international fund for social development, on the understanding that the issue would be considered bythe Economic and Social Council at its substantive session of 1995 in the context of the discussion of the World Summit for Social Development.

15. Statements were made by the representatives of the Philippines (on behalf of the States Members of the United Nations that are members of the Group of 77 and China), the United States of America, Azerbaijan, Egypt, India, Iraq, Tunisia, Guatemala, Kuwait, Belize, Saudi Arabia, Costa Rica, Pakistan, Ecuador, Argentina, malta, Peru, the Holy See, the Sudan and Jordan.

16. At the same meeting, the Chariman of the Main Committee

and the Under-Secretary-General for Policy Coordination and Sustainable Development made statements.

17. The following requested that their reservations or comments be placed on record:

(a) The representative of Egypt expressed a reservation on any reference counter to the laws and Constitution of Egypt and wished to see specific commitments from donor countries on assistance to social development and debt alleviation;

(b) The representatives of Iraq and Kuwait stated that the thrust of commitment 9 of the Copenhagen Declaration should be on social development;

(c) The representative of Peru stated that nothing in the Copenhagen Declaration or the Programme of Action should be contrary to the right to life;

(d) The representative of the Philippines, on behalf of the States Members, of the United Nations that are members of the Group of 77, stated that, owing to inequalities between the developing countries and countries with economies in transition, the two should not be treated on an equal basis. He expressed a reservation on paragraph 6 of the Copenhagen Declaration;

(e) The representative of the Sudan expressed a reservation on any paragraphs that contradict Islamic law (Sharia);

(f) The representative of Ukraine expressed a preference for alternative wording at the end of paragraph 89 (b).

Appendix 5

ADOPTION OF THE COPENHAGEN DECLARATION ON SOCIAL DEVELOPMENT AND THE PROGRAMME OF ACTION OF THE WORLD SUMMIT FOR SOCIAL DEVELOPMENT

1. At the 14th plenary meeting, on 12 March, the representative of the Phillipines, on behalf of the States Members of the United Nations that are members of the Group of 77 and China, introduced and orally revised a draft resolution entitled "Declaration and Programme of Action of the World Summit for Social Development".
2. At the same meeting, the Summit adopt the draft resolution as revised (Resolution 1).
3. Before the adoption of the draft resolution, statements were made by the representatives of Azerbaijan, Saudi Arbia, Iraq, the Islamic Republic of Iran, Qatar, the Libyan Arab Jamahiriya, the United Arab Emirates and the Holy See.

Reservations on the Copenhagen Declaration and the Programme of Action

4. The representatives of a number of countries made statements which they requested the secretariat of the Summit to place on record. Those statement are set out below.
5. The representative of Argentina submitted the follwing written

statement:

The Argentine Republic wishes to place on record the following reservations with regard to the terms "reproductive health" and "forms of family" contained in the text of the Declaration and Programme of Action of the World Summit for Social Development held in Copenhagen, adopted at a plenary meeting of the Summit:

Reproductive Health

The Argentine Republic cannot accept the idea that reproductive health should include abortion, either as a service or as a method of birth control. This reservation, which is based on the universal nature of the right to life, extends to all references of this kind.

Forms of family

The Argentine Republic declares that it accepts those paragraphs that refer to forms of family on the understanding that the references in question do not imply any change in the meaning of the origin and foundation of the family, which is the union of a man and woman from which children are derived.

6. The representative of Azerbaijan submitted the following written statement:

The delegation of Azerbaijan welcomes the adoption of the Declaration and Programme of Action.

Paragraph 26 (k) of the Declaration is based on article 2 of the Vienna Declaration and Programme of Action, adopted at the World Conference on Human Rights. However, this paragraph does not completely reflect the wording of the Vienna Declaration.

In fact, section I, paragraph 2, of the Vienna Declaration stats: "Taking into account the particular situation of peoples under colonial or other forms of alien domination or foreign occupation...".

The wording of paragraph 26 (k) of the Declartion is different from that of the Vienna Declaration. Instead of Stating: "Taking into account the particular situaion of peoples.....", it staes: "... in particular of peoples ...". We would prefer that paragraph 26 (k) reflect the exact wording of the Vienna Declaration.

As far as paragraph 15 (e) of the Programme of Action of the Sumit is concerned, ther is no reference at all to the Vienna Declaration.

For this reason, my delegation would like to reserve its position on paragraph 15 (e) and ask the secretariat to duly reflect this reservation in the records of the Summit.

7. The representative of Costa Rica submitted the following written statement:

Costa Rica respectfully requests the President of the World Summit for Social Development, held in Copenhagen, to include in the reprt Costa Rica's reservation concerning paragraph 21 of the Declaration and the twelfth point in paragraph 70 in chapter IV, on social integration. Even though Costa Rica recognizes the existence of conflicts the differences between nations and peoples and between social groups, it considers that such conflicts should be resolved through negotion, dialogue and efforts to acheive a consensus, and that the resources spent on arms would be better invested in the social develoment of peoples.

8. The representative of Guatemala submitted the following written statement:

My delegation requests that the following statement be included in the final report of the World Summit for the Social Development. For reasons that concern my country, Guatemala wishes to make an express reservation with regard to all uses of the term "territorial integrity" or of any other term which might have implications with respect to the territorial dispute in which Guatemala is involved and which my Government is seeking to resolve in accordance with the principle of the peaceful settlement of disputes between States.

The delegation of Guatemala also has reservations with respect to all such topics as "reproductive health", "family planning" and "health education" which, in one way or another, might be contrary to the Constitution of our country, our laws or the religious, ethical and cultural values upheld by Guatemala.

My delegation also wishes to express the reservations of Guatemala with respect to anything that might in any way be prejudicial to the commitment and positions of Guatemala set forth in the following documents:

The Alliance for the Sustainable Development of Central America, adopted at the Central American environment summit meeting for sustainable development held in Managua, Nicaragua, on 12 October 1994, and circulated as an official document of the General Assembly and the Security Council, dated 27 October 1994.

The Teguciagalpa International Declaration on Peace and Development in Central America Adopted by the Central American Presidents at the International Conference on Peace and Development in Central America, held in Tegucigalpa, Honduras, on 24 and 25 October 1994, and circulated as an official document of the General Assembly and the Security Council, dated 4 November 1994.

The reservations submitted by Guatemala to the Programme of Action of the Conference on Population and Development, held in Cairo on 13 September 1994, and the documents referred to in the aforementioned reservations, in particular:

The Universal Declaration of Human Rights, and the constitutional principles and provisions embodied in the domestic law of the Republic of Guatemala.

9. The representative of the Holy See submitted the following writtten statement:

The Holy See, in conformity with its nature and particular mission, in joining the consensus at the World Summit for Social Development, held in Copenhagen from 6 to 12 March, 1995, wishes to express its understanding of some concepts used in the documents of the Summit.

1. The Holy See reaffirms the reservation it expressed at the conclusion of the International Conference on Population and Development, held in Cairo from 5 to 13 September, 1994, which is included in the report of that Conference,

concerning the interpretation given to the term "reproductive health". In particular, the Holy See reiterates that it does no consider abortion or access to abortion as a dimension of reproductive health or reproductive health services.

2. The Holy See's joining the consensus on the term "family planning" should in no way be interpreted as constituting a change in its well-known position conerning those family planing methods that the Catholic Church considers morally unacceptable or concerning family planning services that do not respect the liberty of spouses, human dignity and the human rights of those concerned.
3. The Holy See, in line with the Universal Declaration of Human Rights, stresses that the family is the basic unit of society and is based on marriage as an equal partnership between husband and wife.
4. With reference to all international agreements and instruments mentioned in the documents of the Summit, the Holy See reserves its position in a manner consistent with its acceptance or non-acceptance of them or of any expression found in them.
5. Nothing that the Holy see has done in this consensus process should be understood or interpreted as an endorsement of concepts that it cannot support for moral reasons. Especially, nothing is to be understood to imply that the Holy See endorses abortion or has in any way changed its moral position concerning abortion or on contraceptivs, sterlization or the use of condoms in HIV/AIDs prevention programmes.

The Holy See ask that these reservations be included in the report of the Summit.

10. The representative of Iraq submitted the following written statement:

Although the delegation of Iraq joined the other delegations in agreeing on the Declaration and the Programme of Action, it is important to point out that this document neglected to deal with a very important question that has negative effects on the process of social development, that is, the "brain drain". It is well known that some of the industrialized countries are enacting legislation and inciting qualified third world persons to emigrate from their home countries. This process has had very advese effects on the development of the affected third world countries.

It is unfortunate that the Sumit did not pay any attention to this question. The delegation of Iraq would, therefore, like to put his question on record.

The pressures that were applied by some Western countries have also resulted in the Summit not dealing with the serious effects of economic sanctions on the Social development of targeted countries that belong to the third world, which are already suffering from social backwardness. Here, also, the delegation of Iraq would like to put on record this defect in the final document of the Summit.

11. The representative of the Libyan Arab Jamahiriya submitted the following written statement:

The delegation of the Libyan Arab Jamahiriya has expressed certain observations during previous meetings namely:

> "What has been ordined to us by God cannot be changed by man. What has been particularly textually defined by the Holy Koran cannot be counters."

The delegation of the Libyan Arab Jamahiriya expresses reservations about what has been stated in the Declaration and the Programme of Action that countries Islamic Sharia.

12. The representative of Malta submitted the following written statement:

The delegation of Malta reserves its position on the use of the term "reproductive health" in the Declaration and the Programme of Action.

The interpretation given by Malta to this term is consistent with its national legislation which considers the termination of pregnancy through procedures of induced abortion as illegal.

The delegation of Malta requests that this reservation be included in the final document of the World Summit for Social Development.

13. The representative of Oman submitted the following written statement:

    The Sultanate of Oman adopts the Declaration and Programme of Action of the World Summit for Social Development, provided they are not in conflict with the requirements, of the Islamic religion and our national laws.

14. The representative of Qatar submitted the following written statement:

    The delegation of the State of Qatar would like to make reservations on any part or paragraph of the Declaration and Programme of Action adopted by the Summit, in case of any contradictions with Islamic principles (Sharia), our moral values or our national traditions.

    The delegation of Qatar requests that its reservations be included in the final report of the Summit.

15. The representative of Saudi Arabia submitted the following written statement:

    The delegation of Saudi Arabia would like to express its reservations on any part of the Declaration or Programme of Action of the Summit that does not conform to, is not in line with or contradicts Islamic Law (Sharia) or our values and tradition.

    We would not be obliged to implement and will not commit ourselves to implementing any such part.

    The delegation of Saudi Arabia requests that its reservations be included in the final report of the Summit.

16. The representative of the United Arab Emirates submitted the following written statement:

    The delegation of the United Arab Emirates would like to express its reservations on any part or paragraph in the Declaration or Programme of Action of the Summit that contradicts in any way Islamic law (Sharia) or does not conform to our ethical values and traditions. It should be noted that we have expressed our reservations during the discussion in the Main Committee.

    The delegation of the United Arab Emirates requests that

its reservations be included in the final report of the Summit.

17. The representative of the United States of America submitted the following written statement:

Declaration, paragraph 16 (d), and Programme of Action, paragraph 10 (c)

As recognized in paragraph 10 of the Declaration, Governments reaffirm and are guided by the principles of the Charter of the United Nations and by the decisions of, inter alia, the United Nations Conference on Environment and Development, held at Rio de Janerio in 1992. We understand and accept the references to consumption in both paragraph 16 (d) of the Declaration and paragraph 10 (c) of the Programme of Action in the context of the full reference from paragraph 4.3 of Agenda 21, as follows:

> Poverty and environmental degradation are closely interrelated. While poverty results in certain kinds of environmental stress, the major causes of the continued deterioration of the global environment is the unsustainable pattern of consumption and production, particularly in industrialized countries, which is a matter of grave convern, aggravating poverty and imbalances.

Declaration, Paragraph 27

We understand and accept that the goals referred to in paragraph 27 refer to achieving social development in general and to creating a suitable framework of action in particular.

Commitment 9 (1) and Programme of Action, Paragraphs 11 (h) and 88 (b)

The United States reiterates that, with respect to commitment 9(1) and paragraphs 11 (h) and 88 (b) of the Programme of Action, it is not one of the countries that have accepted an "agreed target" for official development assistance or have made a commitment to fulfil such a target. We believe that national Governments, not international donnors, must have primary responsibility for thier country's development. Targets detract from the more important issues of the effective and quality of aid and the policies of the recipient country. The

United States has traditionally been one of the largest aid donors in volume terms and will continue to work with developing countries to provide aid in support of their efforts.

In addition, the United States understands and accepts the reference in commitment 9 (l) to increasing the share of official development assistance for social development programmes to apply to only those countries that have accepted the target.

Commitment 9 (m)

The United States understands the word "resources" in commitment 9 (m) to include technical and other non-financial forms of assistance, and accepts the commitment on that basis. The United States will strive to increase resources for the United States Food for Peace Program and will continue to provide resources for major refugee relief and logistic activities. The United States does not accept in interpretation of commitment 9 (m) that would commit States to provide only financial assistance.

Commitment 9 (s)

The United States understands commitment 9 (s) to reiterate, as stated in General Assembly resolution 47/199, that there is a need for a substantial increase in resources for operational activities from all available sources for development and accepts the commitment on that basis. The United States understands the word "resources" to include technical and other non-financial forms of assistance and, in the spirit of commitment 9 (s) and General Assembly resolution 47/199, will seek to increase such resources from governmental and other sources in support of United Nations development efforts.

Programme of Action, Paragraph 54(b)

The United States understands the intention of the inclusion of "equal remuneration for men and women for work of equal value" to be to promote pay equity between men and women and accepts the recommendation on that basis. The United States implements it by observing the principle of "equal pay for equal work".

Programme of Action, Paragraphs 83(b)

The United States understands and accepts the reference in paragraph 83 (b) of the Programme of Action to social development as primarily the responsibility of Governments to refer to Governments' responsibility to create an environment that incudes the promotion and protection of all human rights and fundamental freedoms, thereby allowing each person to reach his or her full human potential.

Terminology

The United States understands and accepts that paragraph 28 of the Declaration and paragraphs 2 and 3 of the Programme of Action confirm that the Programme of Action, like the Declaration, is not legally binding and that it consists of recommendations concerning how States can and should promote social development. Accordingly, the United States understands and accepts that words "requires" and "required" as used in the Declaration and in the Programme of Action suggest practical measures to help achieve social development and do not alter the status of the documents or the recommendations contained therein.

Reservation

Commitment 7 (e) and Programme of Action, Paragraph 11 (h)

As the United States stated several times during the World Summit for Social Development and the preparations for it, owing to domestic funding constraints it cannot agree to increase official development assistance, as called for by commitment 7(e) and as recommended in paragraph 11(h) of the Programme of Action. Accordingly, the United States wishes to express its reservations on commitment 7(e) and on paragraph 11(h) of the Programme of Action. The United States remains none the less committed to working to accelerate the development of Africa and the least development countries.

Appendix 6

REPORT OF THE CREDENTIALS COMMITTEE

1. At the 1st plenary meeting, on 6 March 1995, the World Summit for Social Devlopment, in accordance with rule 4 of its rules of procedure, appointed a Credentials Committee, based on that of the Credentials Committee of the General Assembly of the United Nations at its forty-ninth session, consisting of the following nine members: China, Fiji, Honduras, Namibia, Portugal, Russian Federation, Suriname, Togo and United States of America.
2. The Credentials Committee held on meeting, on 9 March 1995.
3. Mr. Pedro Catarino (Portugal) was unamiously elected Chariman of the Committee.
4. The Committee had before it a memorandum by the Secretary-General dated 8 March 1995 on the status of credentials of representatives participating in the Summit. Additional information on credentials received by the Secretary-General after the issuance of the memorandum was provided to the Committee by its Secretary.
5. The Chairman proposed that the Committee accept the credentials of all the representatives mentioned in the mem-

orandum by the Secretary-General, on the understanding that formal credentials for representatives referred to in paragraph 2 of the Secretary-General as soon as possible. The following draft resolution was proposed by the chairman for adoption by the Committee:

> <u>The Credentials Committee:</u>
>
> Having examined the credentials of the representatives to the World Summit for Social Development referred to in the memorandum by the Secretary-General dated 8 March 1995,
>
> *Accepts* the credentials of the representatives concerned.

6. The draft resolution was adopted by the Committee without a vote.
7. Subsequently, on the proposal of the Chairman, the Comittee agreed to recommend to the Summit the adoption of a draft resolution approving the report of the Credentials Committee.

Action Taken by the Summit

8. At the 10th plenary meeting, on 10 March 1995, the Sumit considered the report of the Credentials Committee.
9. The Summit adopted the draft resolution recommended by the Committee in its report. The States and regional economic integration organization that participated in the Summit are listed.

Appendix 7

MEETING OF HEADS OF STATE OR GOVERNMENT

The meeting of the heads of State or Government took place on 11 and 12 March 1995. The following 134 heads of State or Government or their personal representatives made statements:

H.E. Mr. Poul Nyrup Rasmussen
Prime Minister of the Kingdom of Denmark and
President of the Sumit

H.E. Sr. Eduardo Frei Ruiz Tagle
President of the Republic of Chile

H.E. President Soeharto
Republic of Indonesia

H.E. Sardar Farooq Ahmad Khan Leghari
President of the Islamic Republic of Pakistan

H.E. Mr. Li Peng
Premier of the State Council of the People's Republic of China

H.E. Mr. P.V. Narasimha Rao
Prime Minister of the Republic of India

H.E. Mr. Franz Vranitzky
Federal Chancellor of the Republic of Austria

H.E. Mr. Tomiichi Murayama
Prime Ministr of Japan

H.E. Mr. Ingvar Carlsson
Prime Minister of the Kingdom of Sweden

H.E. Mr. Leonid D. Kuchma
President of Ukraine

H.E. Sr. Felipe Gonzalez
Prime Minister of the Kingdom of Spain

H.E.M. Francois Mitterrand
President of the French Republic

H.E. Mr. Willem Kok
Prime Minister of the Kingdom of the Netherlands

H.E. Mr. Robert G. Mugabe
President of the Republic of Zimbabwe

H.E. Mr. Kim Young Sam
President of the Republic of Korea

H.E. Mr. Suleyman Demirel
President of the Republic of Turkey

H.E. Mr. Sam Nujoma
President of the Republic of Namibia

H.E. Me Blaise Compaore
President of Burkina Faso

H.E. Sr. Marc Forne Molne
Head of Government of the Principality of Andorra

H.E. Flt. Lt. (Rtd.) Jerry Jogn Rawlings
President of the Republic of Ghana

H.E. Mr. Lamberto Dini
President of the Council of Ministers of the Italian Republic

H.E. Dr. Cheddi. B. Jagan
President of the Republic of Guyana

H.E. Mr. Martti Ahtisaarri
President of the Republic of Finland

H.E. Mr. Helmut Kohl
Chancellor of the Federal Republic of Germany

H.E. Mrs. Gro Harlem Brundtland
Prime Minister of the Kingdom of Norway

H.E. Mr. Lech Walesa
President of the Republic of Poland

H.E. Mr. Jean-Luc Dehaene
Prime Minister of the Kingdom of Belgium

H.E. Mr. Liamine Zeroual
President of the People's Democractic Republic of Algeria

H.E. Mr. Ion Iliescu
President of Romania

H.E. Sheikh Jaber Al-Ahmad Al-Jaber Al-Sabah
Amir of the State of Kuwait

H.E. Dato' Seri Dr. Mahathir Mohamad
Prime Minister of Malasia

H.E. Dr. Janez Drnovsek
Prime Minister of the Republic of Slovenia

H.E. El Hadj Omar Bonjo
President of the Gabonese Republic

H.E. Mr. Levon Ter-Petrossian
President of the Republic of Armenia

H.E. Mr. Paul Biya
President of the Republic of Cameroon

H.E. Mr. Habib Thiam
Prime Minister of the Republic of Sengeal

H.E. Mr. Vaclav Klaus
Prime Minister of the Czech Republic

H.E. Mr. Alberto Fujimori Fujimori
President of the Republic of Peru

H.E. Mr. Chuan Leekpai
Prime Minister of the Kingdom of Thailand

H.E. The Hon. Ali Hassan Mwinyi
President of the United Republic of the Tanzania

His Majesty King Mswati III
Kingdom of Swaziland

H.E. Mr. Joaquim Alberto Chassano
President of the Republic of Mozambique

H.E. Mr. Kim Pyong Sik
Vice-President of the Democratic People's Republic of Korea

H.E. Mr. Victor S. Chernomyrdin
Prime Minister of the Russian Federation

H.E. Dr. Ernesto Samper Pizano
President of the Republic of Colombia

H.E. Ing, Juan Carlos Wasmosy
President of the Republic of Paraguay

H.E. The Rt. Hon. Percival James Patterson
Prime Minister of Jamaica

H.E. Mr. Fidel V. Ramos
President of the Republic of the Philippines

H.E. Ms. Begum Khaleda Zia
Prime Minister of the People's Republic of Bangladesh

H.E. Mr. Albert Gore
Vice-President of the United States of Amercia

H.E. Mr. Lennart Meri
President of the Republic of Estonia

H.E. Mr. Heydar Alirza Ogly Aliyev
President of the Azerbaijani Republic

H.E. Dr. Ramiro de Leon Carpio
President of the Republic of Guatemala

H.E. Mr. Marechal Mobuto Sese Seko
President of the Republic of Zaire

H.E. Dr. Fidel Castro Ruz
President of the Council of State and Council of Ministers of the Republic of Cuba

H.E. The Rt. Hon. Dr. Ntsu Mokhele
Prime Minister of the Kingdom of Lesotho

H.E. Sir Ketumile Masire
President of the Republic of Botswana

H.E. Mr. Puntsagiin Jasrai
Prime Minister of Mongolia

H.E. The Hon. Paul Keating
Prime Minister of Australia

H.E. The Hon. Daniel Torotich arap Moi
President and Commander-in-Chief of the Armed Forces of the Republic of Kenya

H.E. Dr. Franjo Tudjman
President of the Republic of Croatia

H.E. Madame Ruth Dreifuss
Federal Counsellor, Head of the Federal Department of the In-

terior of the Swiss Confederation

H.E. Dr. Haris Silajdzic
Prime Minister of the Republic of Bosnia and Herzegovina

H.E. The Hon. Dr. Edward Fenech Adami
Prime Minister of the Republic of Malta

H.E. Lic. Gonzalo Sanchez de Lozada
President of the Repblic of Bolivia

H.E. Mrs. Violeta barrios de Chamorro
President of Nicaragua

H.E. Mr. Jacques Santer
President of the European Community

H.E. Mr. Nelson Rorihlahla Mandela
President of the Repblic of South Africa

H.E. Mr. Alberto Dahik
Vice-President of the Republic of Ecuador

H.E. The Hon. Chandrika Bandaranaike Kumaratunga
President of the Democractic Socialist Republic of Sri Lanka

H.E. Mr. Danial Kablan Duncan
Prime Minister of the Republic of Cote d'Ivoire

H.E. Mr. Eduard A. Shevardnadze
President of the Republic of Georgia

H.E. Ing. Jose Maria Figueres Oslen
President of the Republic of Costa Rica

H.E. Mr. Yoweri Kaguta Museveni
President of the Republic of Uganda

H.E. Mr. Alpha Oumar Konare
President of the Republic of Mali

H.E. Mr. Abdellatif Fialli
Prime Minister of the Kingdom of Morocco

His Eminence Angelo Cardinal Sadono
Secretary of State of the Holy See

H.E. Mr. Alyaksandr Lukashenka
President of the Republic of Belarus

H.E. Mr. Jogn Bruton
Prime Minister of the Ireland

H.E. Mr. Guntis Ulmanis
President of the Republic of Latvia

H.E. Mr. Islam A. Karimov

President of the Republic of Uzbekistan

H.E. General Lansana Conte
President of the Republic of Guinea

H.E. Dr. Mario Frick
Prime Minster of the Principality of Liechtenstein

H.E. Dr. Sali Berisha
President of the Republic of Albania

H.E. Captain Yahya A.J.J. Jammeh
President of the Republic of the Gambia

H.E. Dr. Arpad Goncz
President of the Republic of Hungary

H.E. Mr. Algirdas Mykolas Brazauskas
President of the Republic of Lithuania

H.E. Mr. David Oddsson
Prime Minister of the Republic of Iceland

H.E. Dr. Carlos Roberto Reina Idiaquez
President of the Republic of Honduras

H.E. The Rt. Hon. Man Mohan Adhikari
Prime Minister of the Kingdom of Nepal

H.E. Mr. Hassan Gouled Aptidon
President of the Republic of Djibouti

H.E. Mr. Zhelyu Zhelev
President of the Republic of Bulgaria

H.E. General Joao Bernardo Vieira
President of the Republic of Guinea-Bissau

H.E. Mr. Jean-Claude Juncker
Prime Minister of the Grand Duchy of Luxembourg

H.E. Mr. Glafcos Clerides
President of the Republic of Cyprus

H.E. Mr. Ange-Felix Patasse
President of the Cental African Republic

H.E. Mr. Sidi Mohamed Ould Boubacar
Prime Minister of the Islamic Republic of Mauritania

H.E. Mr. Kiro Gligorov
President of the former Yoguslav Republic of Macedonia

H.E. Dr. Carlos Alberto Wahnon de Carvalho Veiga
Prime Miniser of the Republic of Cape Verde

H.E. Lt. Gen. Omer Hassan Ahmed Al Bashir

President of the Republic of the Sudan

H.E. Dr. Armando Calderon Sol
President of the Republic of El Slavador

H.E. Mr. Andrei Nicolae Sangheli
Prime Minister of the Republic of Moldova

H.E. Mr. Renso Ghiotti
Captain Regent of the Republic of San Marino

H.E. Mr. Emomaili Rakhmonov
President of the Republic of Tajikistan

H.E. Mr. Runaldo Ronald Venetiaan
President of the Republic of Suriname

H.E. Mr. Michal Kovac
President of the Slovak Republic

H.E. Mr. Edem Kadjo
President Minister of the Togolese Republic

H.E. The Hon. Dr. Kennedy A. Simmonds
Prime Minister of the Saind Kitts and Nevis

H.E. Mr. Jacinto Peynado
Vice-President of the Dominican Republic

H.E. Mr. Halifa Houmadi
Prime Minister of the Islamic Federal Republic of the Comoros

H.E. Mr. Sylvestre Ntibantunganya
President of the Republic of Burundi

H.E. Mr. Abdorabo Mansoor Hadi
Vice-President of the Republic of Yemen

H.E. Mr. Miguel dos Angos das Canha Lisboa Trovoada
Head of State of the Democractic Republic of Sao Tome and Principe

H.E. Mr. Francisque Ravony
Prime Minister of the Republic of Madagascar

His Highness Sheikh Sultan Bin Zayed Al-Nahayan
Deputy Prime Minister of the United Arab Emirates

H.E. The Hon. Philip Muller
Minister of the Foreign Affairs of the Republic of the Marshall Islands

H.E. Dr. Paulo Renato de Souza
Minister for Education and Sports of the Federative Republic of Brazil

H.E. Mr. Jose Angel Gurria Trevina
Minister for Foreign Affairs of the United Maxican States

H.E. Mr. Abdallah Kalle
Minister of the State, Adviser to the President of the Republic of Tunisia

H.E. Mr. Desire Vieyra
Minister of the d'Etate, Charge de la Coordination de l'Action Gourvenementale of the Republic of Benin

H.E. The Hon. Peter Gresham
Minister for Social Welfare of New Zealand

H.E. Shaikh Isa Bin Ali Al-Khalifa
Minister for Labour and Social Affairs of the State of Bahrain

H.E. Mr. Sadoom Hamadi
Adviser to the Officer of the President of the Republic of Iraq

H.E. The Hon. Ratu Jo Nacola
Minister for Regional Development and Multi-Ethnic Affairs of the Republic of Fiji

H.E. The Hon. Dharmanand Goopt Fokeer
Minister for Social Security and National Solidarity of the Republic of Martitius

H.E. The Hon. Ismail Shafeeu
Minister for Planning, Human Resources and Environment of the Republic of Maldives

H.E. Mr. Ali Khalil
Minister of Social Afairs and Labour of the Syrian Arab Republic

H.E. Mr. Fares Bouez
Minister for Foreign Affairs of the Lebanese Republic

H.E. Mrs. Salwa Damen Al-Masri
Minister for Social Development of the Hashemite Kingdom of Jordan

H.E. Mr. Omar Mustafa Muntasser
Minister for Foreign Affairs of the Libyan Arab Jamahiriya

H.E. Chief Anthony A. Ani
Minister for Foreign Affairs and Finance of the Federal Republic of Nigeria

H.E. Mr. Arsene Tsaty-Boungou
Minster for Foreign Affairs of the Republic of the Congo

H.R. Mr. Usmonakum Ibraimov

Vice-Prime Minister of the Republic of Kyrgyzstan

H.E. Dr. Ali Akbar Velayati
Minister for Foreign Affairs of the Islamic Republic of Iran.

The largest gathering yet of world leaders —117 heads of state or Government—pledged to bring social development. over 14,000 participants attended the Summit, among them delegates from 186 countries. Included were some 2,300 representatives from 811 NGOs, and over 2,800 journalists. Additionally, some 12,000 NGO representatives and others gathered daily from 3 to 12 March on the ground of a former naval base, called Holmen, for a parallel event called NGO Forum 95.

Appendix 8

ADOPTION OF THE REPORT OF THE SUMMIT

1. The Rapporteur-General introduced and orally revised the draft report of the Summit at the 14th plenary meeting, on 12 March, 1995.
2. At the same meeting, the Summit adopted the draft report, as revised, and authorized the Rapporteur-General to complete the report, in conformity with practice of the United Nations, with a view to submitting it to the Geneal Assembly at its fiftieth session.

Appendix 9

CLOSURE OF THE SUMMIT

1. At the 14 plenary meeting, on 12 March, 1995, the representative of the Philippines on behalf of the States of the United Nations that are members of the Group of 77 and china, introduced a draft resolution expressding the Summit's gratitidue to the host counry.
2. At the same meeting, the Summit adopted the draft resolution (for the text, see chap, I resolution 2).
3. Also at the same meeting, statements were made by the representatives of the Philippines (on behalf of the States Members of the United Nations that are members of the Group of 77 and China), France (on behalf of the European Union) and the United States of America.
4. After a statement had been made by the Secretary-General, the President of the Summit made a concluding statement and declared the Summit closed.

Appendix 10

OPENING STATEMENTS

Statement by Poul Nyrup Rasmussen, Prime Minister of Denmark and President of the World Summit for Social Development

The American astronaut, James Lovell, had no doubts about the qualities of the planet Earth, when in 1968 on board Apolo 8 he described the Earth as a grand oasis to the vastness of space.

But we have not treated our planet in a way that warrants this description. Man has often treated nature unwisely and short-sightedly. We are gruaually beginning to do things better. But man has treaded man even worse. In this centruy alone we have lived in the shadow of two world wars and of totalitarian regimes, not to mention the nuclear bomb.

Security of the State has been more important than security of people. We have now learned real lasting security is based upon the security of people.

We have come to a turning-point for making. At last we recognize that the security of people is the main topic of the international agenda.

Let this Summit focus on the security of people.

The Summit is the first of kind: a World Summit for Social Development. We will provide leadership and direction.

I wish to thank the General Assembly of the United Nations for having chosen Copenhagen as the venue for the World Summit for Social Development. Thc Government and people of Denmark are proud to be hosting this Summit.

I welcome you to Copenhagen and Denmark. I hope that you will find time to get to know this country, its people, its culture and its social development.

I wish to express my deep appreciation to the Summit for having elected me President.

My task is made easier through the tremendous work done by the Secrtary-General of the United Nations, his collaborators in the Secretariat, and the Preparatory Committee.

In particular, I wish to pay tribute the the Chairman of the Preparatory Committee, Ambassador Juan Somavia of Chile. For years he has worked hard and with dedication to make this Summit come true.

Let us use the Summit to turn the analysis of problems and possibilities into concrete commitments and actions as we did in Rio.

If we are to shape the future, we must have goals, ambition and decisions. These we have. We are gatherred here to promote social development and social justice, placing the needs, rights and aspirations of people at the centre of our decisions and joint actions.We want to open a new era of international cooperation between Governments and people based on a spirit of partnership.

The core issues to be discussed at the Summit - poverty, employment and social integration - are well chosen. At this Summit we are discussing the real problems, which concern all people. Therefore the Summit is at the very heart of all political work and governance.

We need to focus on human security. Human security and social progress must be maintained by ensuring proper living conditions.

Each person's security has to do with adequate income and employment, education and training, health and housing, equality and legal protection and the exercise of human rights.

The key word is solidarity. The means are political power

and economic and sustainable growth used for the right purposes. It is not a question of whether we can afford it. It is a question of priorities and determination.

We must find new answers to these well-known, fundamental questions.

Poverty is linked to lack of access to resources, including knowledge. Poor people are easily neglected by policy makers. Anti-poverty programmes alone are not sufficient. Democratic participation is necessary to ensur equal access to opportunties, public services and political life.

All governments should undertake policies geared to a better distribution of wealth and income. We must offer social protection and opportunities for those who cannot support themselves. We must assist people in social distress. In short, we must empower people to become genuine partners in developing our societies.

For the poorest countries, we must extend the natonal effort to include international actions of solidarity.

For many years the international community was divided into ideological blocs. This Summit is historic as it gives us the chance-for the first time after the cold war-to share a common vision on how to solve the social problems of the world.

Let this Summit of hope result in better opportunities for an exchagne of experiences. No country can claim to have solved its social problems. Some countries are rich. Some are poor. The acuteness of the problems varies. But they have one thing is common: they are an offence to human dignity and a threat to manking if not attended to in time.

Social problems are of a size and complexity that call for new solutions, new alliances and new values. Many nations have welfare systems that could be an inspiration to others. It is our task to encourage peoplle to take an active part in creating new soceities.

We have learned that social progress will not be realized simply through the free market forces. Nothing short of the political will to invest-nationally and internationally - in poeple's well-being will accomplish the objective of social security.

The private sector, including businesses and enterprises,

must assume a co-responsibility for the solution of social problems.

This new partntership for social development must include actions that enable poor and disadvantaged people to participate fully and productively in the economy and in society.

This Summit is a historic and unique platform for global social development. But we must not give the impression that the Summi alone will dramatically change daily life. We still have to put actions behind the words.

The true significance of the Summit therefore have to be mesured by what happens after the Summit. This is only the beginning of a new, global process. But the difference between last week and next week should be increased awareness and the mobilization of resources for social development.

We gather here in Copenhagen for a Summit for hope, commitment and action.

Let us transform hope into action. That is what people expect from us.

I am confident that we can forge a new partnership for social development. The Copenhagen Summit willl a difference. Because we have decided so.

<u>Statement by Boutros Boutros-Ghali, Secretary-General of the United Nations</u>

The message of this World Summit for Social Development should be clear. The international community is today taking a clear stand against social injustice, exclusion and poverty in the world.

So, as we celebrate the fiftieth anniversary of the Organization, we should ask ourselves some searching questions about our own record.

We should ask how seriously we have taken our Charter commitments. Can we say that we have fulfilled our solemn undertaking, entered into 50 years ago at San Francisco, to promote "the economic and social advancement of all people"?

Today's global economy affects everyone. We also know that it effects are not all positive. It erodes traditional ties of solidarity among individuals. It has marginalized entire countries and regions. The gap between rich and poor is getting wider.

So the task before us today is nothing more nor less than to rethink the notion of collective social responsibility.

A new social contract, at the global level, is required, to bring hope to States and nations, and to men and women around the world. That should be the focus of this World Summit. That is how I believe its work should be seen.

When, in 1992, the General Assembly took the initiative of calling this World Sumit, its aim was to make social development a major priority for the international community. The agenda for this summit meeting faithfully reflects that intentions. We will be discussing how to carry forward the fight against poverty; how to combat social exclusion and disintegration, how to create productive employment; and how to awaken a new awareness of social responsibility at the international level.

It is clear from these concerns that this Copenhagen World Summit is part of a process. It is part of the process of profound reflection and debate on which the international community has embarked - about itself and its future, and about the role of the individual human being.

As part of this collective rethinking, the international community has given a good deal of the thought to the position of the individual human being. At Rio we debated the relationship between the human being and the environment. At Vienna we looked at the human being as the bearer of rights. The human person as collective being was the theme of the Cairo Population Conference. And once more, the human person—this time through the rights and status of women-will bring as together next September, at Beijing.

The concept of social development gives coherence and perspective to the entire process of reflection in which the international community has been engaged.

Social development says that only within a social order based on justice can the individual human being reach his or her full potential. Social development says, too, that real economic progress is impossible without progress in the social sphere. Social development is also the internaional community's political response -

political in the fullest sense of the term - to the global socicty in which we live. That is why I see it as part of the task of the United Nations to attempt to provide such a response - starting now.

Clearly, no one has a ready-made model or answer. But it is possible for us to define what I would call "priority objectives", which are basically three in number:

Providing social protection for the individual;

Assisting social integration;

Maintaining social peace.

These are the three priority goals which I would like to consider with you for a few moments.

Providing social protection for the individual is the ultimate goal of this Conference and, as we are about to begin or work, I think it is important not to lose slight of the indissoluble link between the promotion of social development and the protction of human rights.

In 1948, the Universal Declaration made explicit the social dimension of human rights.That dimension was to be still more strongly reaffirmed in the Covenants of 1966, particularly the Internaioinal Covenant on Economic, Social and Cultural Rights, to whose importance I would call attention. It was in that context that basic concept of the Right to development came into being a few years later.

In the name of that concept and its underlying values, we are now under a compelling obligation to tackle the problem of poverty in the world.

It has to be remembered that 1.3 billion people are currenly living in a state of absolute poverty, and that 1.5 billion have a access to the most elementary health care. We also know that the principal victims of poverty are women, since they represent more than 70 per cent of the disinherited of the Earth.

It should be emphasized that, although a struggle against social inequalities must be waged all over the planet, the scale of the problem, as well as its severity, differ from one region to another.

Only through constant awarness of the realities of the world can we, here in Copenhagen, truely be the spokesmen of all those who desire improved social justice, and play a part in creating a new social policy on a global scale.

The second priority goal I wish to propose is that of assisting social integration. This is all the more necessary as disturbing situations of exclusion and marginalization are developing all over the world.

To struggle for social integration, therefore, means condemning selfishness and indifference first of all. It also means combating all forms of discrimination throughout the world, whatever their cause. It also means calling upon all humanity to show tolerance, solidarity, and involvement. Lastly, it means giving all men, women, and children the education they need in order to take their place in society.

The World Summit for Social Development has quite rightly emphasized the connection between the struggle against poverty, the compaign for social integration and the creation of productive jobs. In fact in the world of today, employment is an essential factor in integration. On the other hand, unemployment is a form of exclusion leading to a combination of social handicaps.

It is primarily the duty of States to implement dynamic social policies. Social development calls for wide-ranging political action, particularly in the areas of laws and regulations.

But social development is a mater, not only for States, but also for the entire United Nations system. The latter has long been active in the service of social progress. Many of its organs, such as the United Nations Development Programme, and numerous specialized agencies, including the Internatioinal Labour Organization and the United Nations Educational, Scientific and Cultural Organization, have done pioneering work in this area.

However, in this social project of ours, we must also take account of the extraordinary capacity for mobilization of the non-governmental organizations, and the force for integration represented by private enterprise and investors.

Maintaining social peace is the third priority goal which I invite you to pursue. In fact, there is a clear interaction between political issues and social issues.

On the one hand, it is obvious that a stable political environment is essential to harmonious social development. One of the purposes of political activity is to give tangible reality to social aspirations.

On the other hand, it is equally clear that a dynamic social environment is one of the requirements for political stability itself. For a State in which inequality and privilege prevail is potentially in danger of suffering the gravest social upheavals. A State which, by not permitting satisfactory social integration, generates large numbers of marginalised people has to fear the most unpredictable social explosions. It has to be clearly stated: political serenity goes hand in hand with social contentment.

Furthermore, it is now well know that most of the armed conflicts facing the United Nations are internal conflicts taking place within nations.

We also know that most of those conflicts have clear economic and social causes. Consequently, we can reaffirm once more the indissoluble link between the promotion of development and the preservation of peace.

I have sought to place the World Summit for Social Development in the perspective of the major goals of United Nations because, as Secretary-General of the Organizations, I am conscious of our collective responsibility towards futher generations. I therefore hope that the United Nations may acquire the necessary means to follow up this Conference, so that the important recommendations adopted here may have a genuine impact on the lives of peoples and nations. I sincerely trust that the Bretton Woods insitutions will play a full role in the social action which we are now redefining and reinventing.

For the social development project is an opportunity for the international community as a whole to say:

No to the inevitability of crisis!

No to the persistence of inequalities!

No to the division of the world!

Giving social issues the status of universal priorities shows our determinaion to accept responsibility for the collective destiny of international society and to establish a new planet—wide pact of solidarity.

Appendix 11

CLOSING STATEMENT

Statement by Poul Nyrup Rasmussen, Prime Minister of Denmark and President of the World Summit for Social Development

It falls upon me now to bring to a close the World Summit for Social Development.

What lies ahead of us is a task even more important than the one we have just successfully completed. For documents, well crafted as they may be, and commitments, forceful as they may be, must stand the test of time. It is our duty to ensur that this is done.

I would not want to close this meeting without expressing my profound appreciation for all those whose personal contribution has made this Summit possible.

> To Ambassador Somavia, whose country proposed the Summit, and on whose broad shoulders so much of its preparations fell. May I comment his untiring work on behalf of the Summit; he guided the negotiating process with tenacity, skill and commitment; his intellect, spirit, constancy of purpose and optimism were instrumental to our success. Our gratitude also goes to the talented diplomats who so ably assisted Ambassador Somavia in his work, both here and in

New York: Ambassadors Richard Butler of Asutralia, Koos Richelle of the Netherlands, Ismail Razali of Malaysia and Prakesh Shah of India;

To, you Secretary-General, for your personal and untiring efforts on behalf of the Summit which demostrate your commitment to the role of the United Nations in development. Many of the heads of State and Government who have been with us over the past two days know first hand the strength of our conviction. If this Summit was attended by so many eminent statesmen and women, it is in no small measure due to you pesonally, but also to the entire United Nations Secretariat staff, led by Under-Secretaries-General Ismat Kittani and Nitin Desai and Conference Coordinator Jacques Baudot, who were the true backbone of the Summit;

And, finally, to all the other participants of civil society, who have brought their expertise, their talent and, above all, their imagination and enthusiasm to this Summit and its preparations. Their spirit and impatience for change brought much passion and energy to our task.

The Declaration we have just adopted states that the General Assembly should hold a special session in the year 2000 to appraise how far we will have gone by then in implementing the results of this meeting. I would like, when we meet five years hence, to look back to this Summit of hope, as many have called it, as a Summt of fulfilled expectations.

Appendix 12

HEADS OF STATE OF GOVERNMENT

The World Summit for Social Development was attended by the following heads of State or Government, representing 117 States and the European Community:

Albania
H.E. Dr. Sali Berisha,
President

Algeria
H.E. M. Liamine Zeroual,
President

Andorra
H.E. Sr. Marc Forné Molné,
Head of Government

Armenia
H.E. Mr. Levon Ter-Petrossian
President

Australia
H.E. The Hon. Paul Keating,
Prime Minister

Austria
H.E. Mr. Franz Vranitzky,
Federal Chancellor

Azerbaijan
H.E. Mr. Heydar Alirza ogly Aliyev,
President

Bangladesh
H.E. Begum Khaleda Zia,
Prime Minister

Belarus
H.E. Mr. Alyaksandr Lukashenka,
President

Belgium
H.E. M. Jean-Luc Dehaene,
Prime Minister

Bolivia
H.E. Lic. Gonzalo Sanchez de Lozada,
President

Bosnia and Herzegovina
H.E. Dr. Haris Silajdzic,
Prime Minister

Botswana
H.E. Sir Ketumile Masire,
President

Bulgari
H.E. Mr. Zhelyu Zhelev,
President

Burkina Faso
H.E. M. Blaise Compare,
President

Burundi
H.E. Mr. Sylvestre Ntibantunganya,
President

Cambodia
H.R.H. Sdech Krom Luong Norodom Ranariddh,
First Prime Minister

Cameroon
H.E. M. Paul Biya,
President

Cape Verde
H.E. Dr. Carlos Alberto Wahnon de Carvalho Veiga,
Prime Minister

Central African Republic
H.E. Mr. Ange-Félix Patasse,
Presdient

Chile
H.E. Sr. Eduardo Frei Ruiz Tagle,
President

China
H.E. Mr. Li Peng,
Premier of the State Council

Colombia
H.E. Dr. Ernesto Samper Pizano,
President

Comoros
H.E. Mr. Halifa Houmadi,
Prime Minister

Costa Rica
H.E. Ing. José María Figueres Olsen,
President

Côte d'Ivoire
H.E. Mr. Daniel Kablan Duncan,
Prime Minister

Croatia
H.E. Dr. Fanjo Tudjman,
President

Cuba
H.E. Dr. Fidel Castro Ruz,
President of the Coucil of State

Cyprus
H.E. Mr. Glafcos Clerides,
President

Czech Republic
H.E. Mr. Václav Klaus,
Prime Minister

Democratic People's Republic of Korea
H.E. Mr. Kim Pyong Sik,
Vice-President

Denmark
H.E. Mr. Poul Nyrup Rasmussen,
Prime Minister

Djibouti
H.E. Mr. Hassan Gouled Aptidon,
President

Dominican Republic
H.E. Mr. Jacinto Peynado,
Vice-President

Ecuador
H.E. Mr. Alberto Dahik,
Vice-President

El Salvador
H.E. Dr. Armando Calderon Sol,
President

Eritrea
H.E. Mr. Isaias Afwerki,
President

Estonia
H.E. Mr. Lennart Meri,
President

Ethiopia
H.E. Mr. Meles Zenawi,
President

European Community
H.E. Mr. Jacques Santer,
President

Finland
H.E. Mr. Martti Ahtisaari,
President

France
H.E. M. François Mitterrand,
President

Gabon
H.E. El Hadj Omar Bongo,
President

Gambia
H.E. Captain Yahya A. J. J. Jammeh,
President

Georgia
H.E. Mr. Eduard A. Shevardnadze,
President

Germany
H.E. Mr. Helmut Kohl,
Chancellor

Ghana
H.E. Flt. Lt. (Rtd.) Jerry John Rawlings,
President

Guatemala
H.E. Dr. Ramiro de Leon Carpio,
President

Guinea
H.E. General Lansana Conte,
President

Guinea-Bissau
H.E. General Joao Bernardo Vieira,
President

Guyana
H.E. Dr. Cheddi B. Jagan,
President

Holy See
His Eminence Angelo Cardinal Sodano,
Secretary of State

Honduras
H.E. Dr. Carlos Roberto Reina Idiaquez,
President

Hungary
H.E. Dr. Arpád Göncz,
President

Iceland
H.E. Mr. David Oddsson,
Prime Minister

India
H.E. Mr. P.V. Narasimha Rao,
Prime Minister

Indonesia
H.E. President Soeharto

Ireland
H.E. Mr. John Bruton,
Prime Minister

Italy
H.E. Mr. Lamberto Dini,
President

Jamaica
H.E. The Rt. Hon. Percival James Patterson,
Prime Minister

Kenya
H.E. The Hon. Daniel Toroitich arap Moi,
President

Kuwait
H.E. Sheikh Jaber Al-Ahmad Al-Jaber Al-Sabah,
Amir

Latvia
H.E. Mr. Guntis Ulmanis,
President

Lesotho
H.E. The Rt. Hon. Dr. Ntsu Mokhehle,
Prime Minister

Liechtenstein
H.E. Dr. Mario Frick,
Prime Minister

Lithuania
H.E. Mr. Algirdas Mykolas Brazauskas,
President

Luxembourg
H.E. Mr. Jean-Claude Juncker,
Prime Minister

Madagascar
H.E. Mr. Francisquc Ravony,
Prime Minister

Malaysia
H.E. Dato' Seri Dr. Mahathir Mohamad,
Prime Minster

Mali
H.E. Mr. Alpha Oumar Konare,
President

Malta
H.E. The Hon. Dr. Edward Fenech Adami,
Prime Minister

Mauritania
H.E. Mr. Sidi Mohamed Ould Boubacar,
Prime Minister

Monaco
H.E. M. Paul Dijoud,
Prime Minister

Mongolia
H.E. Mr. Puntsagiin Jasrai,
Prime Minister

Morocco
H.E. Mr. Abdellatif Filali,
Prime Minister

Mozambique
H.E. Mr. Joaquim Alberto Chissano,
President

Namibia
H.E. Mr. Sam Nujoma,
President

Nepal
H.E. The Rt. Hon. Man Mohan Adhikari,
Prime Minister

Netherlands
H.E. Mr. Willem Kok,
Prime Minister

Nicargua
H.E. Mrs. Violeta Barrios de Chamorro,
President

Norway
H.E. Mrs. Gro Harlem Brundtland,
Prime Minister

Pakistan
H.E. Sardar Farooq Ahmad Khan Leghari,
President

Paraguay
H.E. Ing. Juan Carlos Wasmosy,
President

Peru
H.E. Mr. Alberto Fujimori Fujimori,
President

Philippines
H.E. Mr. Fidel V. Ramos,
President

Poland
H.E. Mr. Lech Walesa,
President

Republic of Korea
H.E. Mr. Kim Young Sam,
President

Republic of Moldova
H.E. Mr. Andrei Nicolae Sangheli,
Prime Minister

Romania
H.E. Mr. Ion Iliescu,
President

Russian Federation
H.E. Mr. Victor S. Chernomyrdin,
Prime Minister

Saint Kitts and Nevis
H.E. The Hon. Dr. Kennedy A. Simmonds,
Prime Minister

San Marino
H.E. Mr. Renzo Ghiotti,
Captain Regent

H.E. Mr. Luciano Ciavatta,
Captain Reagent

Sao Tome and Principe
H.E. Mr. Miguel dos Angos da Canha Lisboa Trovoada,
Head of State

Senegal
H.E. Mr. Habib Thiam,
Prime Minister

Slovakia
H.E. Mr. Michal Kovac,
President

Slovenia
H.E. Dr. Janez Drnovsek,
Prime Minister

South Africa
H.E. Mr. Nelson Rorihlahla Mandela,
President

Spain
H.E. Sr. Felipe Gonzalez,
Prime Minister

Sri Lanka
H.E. The Hon. Chandrika Bandaranaike Kumaratunga,
President

Sudan
H.E. Lt. Gen. Omer Hassan Ahmed Al Bashir,
President

Suriname
H.E. Mr. Runaldo Ronald Venetiaan,
President

Swaziland
His Majesty King Mswati III

Sweden
H.E. Mr. Ingvar Carlsson,
Prime Minister

Switzerland
H.E. Madame Ruth Dreifuss,
Federal Counsellor

Tajikistan
H.E. Mr. Emomaili Rakhmonov,
President

Thailand
H.E. Mr. Chuan Leekpai,
Prime Minister

The Former Yugoslav Republic of Macedonia
H.E. Mr. Kiro Gligorov,
President

Togo
H.E. Mr. Edem Kodjo,
Prime Minister

Turkey
H.E. Mr. Süleyman Demierel,
President

Uganda
H.E. Mr. Yoweri Kaguta Museveni,
President

Ukraine
H.E. Mr. Leonid D. Kuchma,
President

United Republic of Tanzania
H.E. The Hon. Ali Hassan Mwinyi,
President

United States of America
H.E. Mr. Albert Gore,
Vice-President

Uzbekistan
H.E. Mr. Islam A. Karimov,
President

Yemen
H.E. Mr. Abdorabo Mansoor Hadi,
Vice-President

Zaire
H.E. Mr. Maréchal Mobuto Sese Seko,
President

Zimbabwe
H.E. Mr. Robert G. Mugabe,
President

Appendix 13

BACKGROUND PAPERS

Attacking Poverty

The reduction and elimination of poverty—a goal implicit in the 1945 Charter of the United Nations—is one of three core issues to be addressed by heads of State or Government when they gather at the World Summit for Social Development, 6-12 March 1995 in Copenhagen, Denmark. This backgrounder offers an overview of the problem, and examines the range of approaches being considered in advance of the Social Summit. It draws on a varity of sources, especially a report of the United Nations secretary-General to the first meeting of the Summit Preparatory Committee held 31 Janruary—11 February 1994 in New York.

A Challenge for Development

The half-century since the founding of the United Nations has been a time of exhilaration in the world—and deepening despair for hundreds of millions.

Amid unprecedented material progress, human miery has reached almost unimaginable proportions.

Poverty, in tandem with prosperity, has become globalized.

"Absolute poverty, hunger, disease and illiteracy are the lot of one fifth of the world's populaion", the United Nations Secretary-General, Boutros Boutros-Ghali, has said. "There can be no more urgent task for development than to attack both the causes and the symptoms of these ills."

The Basic Symptoms

The key facts about poverty are these:

Poverty affects individuals and families in every part of the world, although most of the very poorest people-a total of 1.1 billion—live in the developing world, where they represent one third of the population.

* Poverty has increased in recent years, in both relative and absolute terms, in Africa, Latin America and the Industrialized countries, while decreasing in Asia.
* Its impact is heaviest on women, followed by the elderly and children.

The World Social Summit

"The struggle against poverty has been part and parcel of the intellectual and political evolution of the notion of social progress in world culture since the end of the eigtheenth century", the Secretary-General has noted.

That long and honourable tradition will be advanced at the 1995 World Summit for Social Development, which was authorised in December 1992 by the United Nations General Assembly.

The Copenhagen Summit, one in a constellation of United Nations-sponsored conferences on devlopment, will seek internationl and country-specific commitments to alleviate and ultimately eradicate global poverty.

Governments will examine the issue in the context of two other interrelated core issues: unemployment and social disintegration. Solutions to all three are vital prerequisites to social development.

"The expansion of productive employment is central to the alleviation and reduction of poverty and enhancement of social integration", the Secretary-General said in his report.

The Nature of the Problem

The 1.1 billion absolute poor live in conditions that Robert, S. McNamara, president of the World Bank from 1968 to 1981, described in 1978 as " so limited by malnutrition, illiteracy, disese, squalid surroundings, high infant mortality, and low life expectancy as to be beneath any reasonable definitioin of human decency".

Among all poor people, 1.5 billion have no sources of clean drinking water or access to sanitation. Most go to bed hungry.

They are particularly vulnerabloe to natural disasters such as drought, floods and storms, having little or no margin for survival when their housing, possessions and means of production are destroyed.,

Out of the world labour force of 2.8 billion, there are 120 million people who are actively looking for work, but without result.

The vast majority of the absolute poor—700 million people — are classified as under employed, working long hours, often at back-breaking jobs that don't come close to covering their most basic needs. A startlingly disproportionate number of these people are women.

The largest number of poor people — about half of the total—eke out existence in the countries of South Asia.

One quarter live in East Asia.

Eighty per cent of the World's poor in rural areas, with the great majority in Asia and Africa. But the rural poor are mostly landless, or have farms that are too small to yield an adequate income.

Extreme poverty is most concentrated in Africa, particularly in the band of countries south of the Sahara Desert. Africa has about 16 per cent of the World's total—but fully half of all Africans are impoverished.

Poverty Amid Plenty

Poverty is also making significant in roads inthe recesion-battered rich countries.

In both the United States and the 12 countries of the 11European Union, nearly 15 percent of the populaion live below the poverty line.

Over the last decade, the number of jobs in the industrialized countries has decreased at a rate only half that of GDP growth.

This phenomenon—dubbed "jobless growth"-combined with budged-dictated cuts in welfare and unemployment benefits, has swelled the unemployed and weakened social safety nets, especially for the most vounerable people: women, the young, the old, the disabled.

The effects are dramatized in the numbers and faces of the urban homeless.

"Nearly a quarter of a million New Yorkers — more than 3 per cent of the city's population and more than 8 per cent of its black children — have statyed in shelters over the past five years", according to Human Development Report 1994, an annual study commissioned by the United Nations Development Programme. "London has about 400,000 registered homeless people. France has more than 500,000—nealy 10,000 in Paris."

But the situation is worse still in the developing countries, the Report says. "In Calcutta, Dhaka and Mexico City, more than 25 per cent of the people constitute, what is sometimes called a floating population".

Poverty and Gender

Impoverished women suffer disproportionately from social and cultural problems and from underdevelopment. An increasing number, in both developed and developing countries, are falling into crushing cycles of poverty.

More than 70 per cent of the world's poor are women, followed closely by the elderly.

"They are also the ones, who, in the midst of destitution, poverty and disintegrating social structures, sacrifice their comfort and sometimes their lives to hold their families together", the Sectary-General has said.

The so-called feminization of poverty grows out of a stark

demographic reality: since women control fewer resources, enjoy a considerably smaller share of the world's wealth and earn lower incomes, they are poorer than men.

In fact, men generally fare better than women on almost every socio-economic indicator except life expectancy.

Human Development Report 1994 found that, in industrial countries, gender discrimination is generally reflected in employment and wages, with women often getting less than two thirds of the employment opportunities and about half the earnings of men.

"In developing countries", the Report notes, "the discrimination is more broadely based. It occurs not only in empowerment but also in education, nutritional support and health care."

Children also suffer more. They are exploited for their labour at a young age, and hurt nutritionally, educationally and in susceptibility to disease.

"Child labour and the impoverishment of children are not unieuqly urban phenomena", the Secretary-General has said. " Some of the worst manifestations are to be found in rural areas, but with increased crowding into shanty towns and urban slums as well as the growing plight of street children in many large cities, the effects of poverty on children are becoming more well known."

"Children in slum neighbourhoods are often the exposed to hazards of

The widening gap between the rich and the poor

Ratio of income shares—richest 20% : poorest 20% of world population

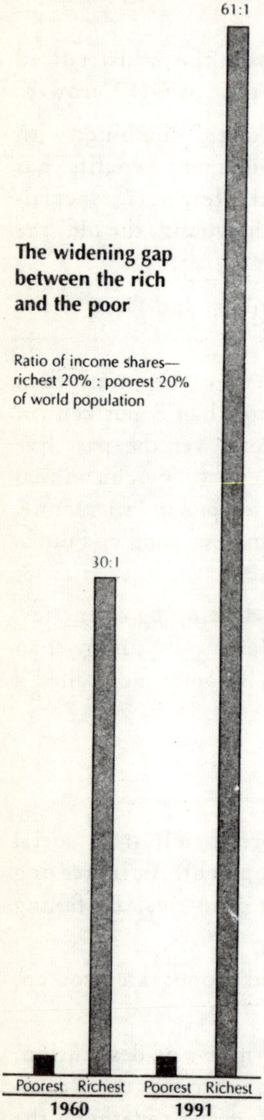

61:1

30:1

Poorest Richest Poorest Richest

1960 **1991**

Source: Human Development Report, 1994, UNDP, p. 35.

urban poverty", he added, "and the morbidity and mortality rates are three to four times higher than the average for their age group".

Good News and bad

The indicators used to assess the severity of poverty vary, and there is disagreement about whether poverty is increasing or decreasing on a global scale, as opposed to just regionally.

But there is consensus among experts that there has ben a significant reduction in the proportion of poor people in the world in recent decades.

"The last two and a half decades have been remarkable progress in the developing world", said Lewis T. Preston, President of the World Bank. "The per capita incomes of the poorest countries have doubled. Life expectancy has risen by 10 years. And with increased immunization rates, child death rates have decreased."

While nearly 70 per cent of humanity were living in abysmal conditions in 1960, only 32 per cent were in that state in 1992, according to Human Development Report 1994.

"The share of the world population enjoying fairly satisfactory human development levels {above an HDI of 0.6) increased from 25 per cent in 1960 to 60 per cent in 1992", the Report said.

Moreover, both the numbers and the proportion of poor people have decreased in many countries in East and South-East Asia.

The downside of these statistics is that the improvement has slowed, and the absolute number of poor people has actually increased, particularly in Africa, where economic growth since 1980 has fallen considerably behind popolation growth.

The World Bank has estimated that, if economic growth remains low and recent trends in poverty continue, there could be 200 million more poor people in the developing world by the yeare 2000.

There has also been a substantial increase in poverty levels in Eastern Europe. But experts say it is not yet clear whether this is a temporary phase en route to renewed economic and social development or a longer-term trend.

"Taken as a whole, the available data suggest that the gap between the 20 per cent of the world population at the bottom of the income ladder and the 20 per cent at the top of that ladder is widening", Secretary-Geneal Boutros-Ghali has noted.

"It increased from 1 to 20 in 1960 to 1 to 60 in 1990. In other words, the top 20 per cent received 83 per cent of the world's income, while the bottom 20 per cent received only 1.5 per cent".

Poverty and Population

There are many reasons for the international community's failure to stem the tide of world poverty.

Rapid population growth is one.

Worldwide, the human population — 5.6 billion by the end of 1994 - is growing by 90 million a year. Although the rate of growth has slowed, plausible estimates are that there will be 6.2 billion people by the year 2000 and between 7.8 and 12.5 billion by the year 2050.

In the developing countries, the annual rate of population growth—currently 1.94 per cent—is "making it extremely difficult to raise living standard and reduce poverty", Secretary-General Boutros-Ghali has noted.

Thers is growing fear that the combined effects of poverty, population growth, social and economic inequality and wasteful consumption patterns pose a serious threat to the basic resources that future generations will need for their survival and well-being.

The intensity and rapidity of population growth in the cities-where the poor, many fleeing rural privation, congregate in sprawling, disease-ridden slums—has thrown old assumptions about consumption and development into doubt.

Already, an average of 51 per cent of the world's people live in cities —77 per cent in the industrialized North, and 72 per cent in Latin America.

"Towns and large cities—the sources of economic activity, innovation, freedom and culture—are suffering today from prob-

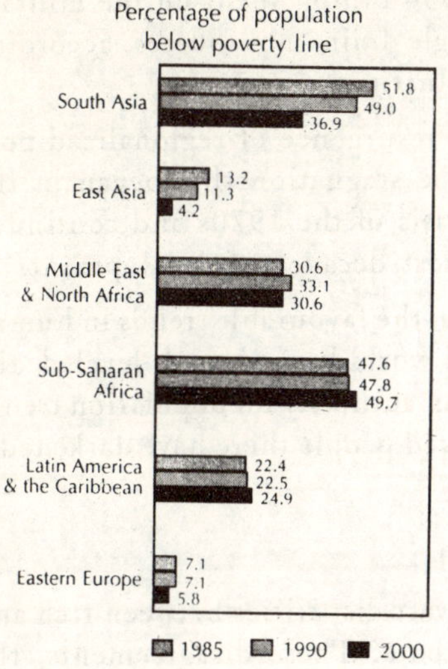

Source: The UNESCO Courier No. 143, p. 79.

lems of overcrowding, inadequate public services and insecurity", the Secretary-Geneal has observed.

On its face, the situation seems grim, especially looked at in terms of simple logic.

"Of the 90 million new people on earth this year", the philosopher Holmes Rolston 3rd said, "85 million will appear in the countries least able to support them".

"Even if there were an equitable distribution of wealth", Professor Rolston argues, "it would be illogical to assume the human population could continue escalating without people becoming poorer as a result. The pie would continually need to be divided into smaller pieces as the population grew".

Other experts agrue that it is too early to make assumptions.

"We do not know that the next generation's consumption preferences will be", caution the authors of *Human Development Report* 1994. "Nor can we anticipate future increases in population that may require more Capital to sustain the same opportunities per head. It is also difficult to predict the technological breakthroughs that may reduce the capital that would be required to achieve the same level of well-being."

The Lost Decade

Besides population, another factor in the persistence of extreme poverty has been the failure of many Governments to reform their economic and political systems.

Also, foreign aid donations have stagnated since the mid-80s. And $1.2 trillion worth of foreign debt has accumulated, sapping financial earnings and undermining the credit-worthiness of low-income countries. The $950 billion spent on the military in 1990 alone was the biggest single drain on resources, according to a report by the Worldwatch Institute.

Many authorities trace the resurgence of regionalized poverty, particularly in Africa, to the stagnation that began in the world economy during the oil crisis of the 1970s. and continued into the 1980s—the so-called "lost decade" of development.

"In the course of that decade, the favourable trends in human devleopment in the preindustrial world have slowed, leveled, the even reversed", and Gerard Piel, an authority on population trend. "The prospects of the most deprived people there have darkened".

Political and Social Perils

The presice reasons for the vast disparities between rich and poor are the source of much debate. These disagreements, the Secretary-General suggests, miss the point.

"While issues relating to the distribution of income and of basic services elicit reactions, views and theories which vary gratly according to time and place", Mr. Boutros-Ghali notes, poverty is nonetheless "universally recognized as morally repugnant, economically destructive and politically dangerous."

The danger is inherent in the perception that to be impoverished is not simply to be without the basic necessaties of life. It implies exclusion from the goods, services, rights and activities that constitute the basis of citizenship.

"If poverty persists or increases and there is neglect of the human condition, political and social strains will endanger stability over time", the Secretary-General has warned. "The reduction of poverty requires development in which access to the benefits of economic progress is as widely available as possible, and not concentrated excessively in certain localities, sectors or groups of the population."

Histroians reexamining certain periods have found striking parallels in the past. The situation in eighteenth-century France is a classic example of the explosive power of extreme poverty and population pressure, according to the historian Paul Kennedy:

"Although the French Revolution had specific causes—for example, worsening state finances during the 1780's—many felt that there were deeper reasons for these social upheavals", he notes in his study *Preparing for the Twenty-First Century.*

"One such was obvious to anyone who visited Europe's crowded cities or noted the growing incidence of rural unemployment: it was the sheer press of human beings, all needing food, clothing, shelter, and work in societies not well equipped to meet those demands, at least on such as scale".

Poverty and the Environment

There is wide agreement that the industrialized nations are responsible for most of the world's pollution.

But the poor, struggling for survival cn a day-to-day basis, often lack the resources to avoid degarding the environment.

"Most of the rural poor in the world. live in areas of low agricultural productivity and have little alternative to unsustainable practices that will make it even more difficult for their children to escape from poverty", Mr. Boutros-Ghali notes.

At the same time, most of the world's poorest countries depend for increasing export earning on tropical agricultural products that are vulnerable to fluctuating or declining terms of trade. Expansion can occur only at the rice of environmental damage.

The connection between poverty and destruction of the natual environment was officially acknowledged, more than two decades ago, at the 1972 United Nations Conference on the Human Environment in Stockholm, Sweden, a watershed moment in world-wide awareness of environment and development issues.

Twenty years later, the link between poverty and sustainable development became the basis for a sweeping series of affirmations.

The 178 Member states represented at history's largest diplomatic gathering, the 1992 United Nations Conference on Environment and Development, in Rio de Janerio, Brazil, called for an end to poverty, and recommended that all nations move to attack the problem in country-specific ways.

"All States and all peple", says the Rio Declaration on Environment and Development, "shall cooperate in the essential task or eradicating poverty as an indispensable requirement for sustaiable development, in order to decrease the disaparities in standards of living and better meet the needs of the majority of the people of world."

In "Combating Poverty", one of the 40 chapters in Agenda 21, the UNCED blueprint for devlopment into the twenty-first century, the Governments set out a series of recommendations to "enable the poor to achieve sustainable livelihoods".

The document notes that because poverty is "a complex multidimensional problem with origin in both the national and international domains", "no unifrom solution can be found for global application".

Instead, it says, what is needed for "country-specific programme to tackle poverty and international efforts supporting national efforts, as well as the parallel process of creating a suportive international environment".

The Role of the UN

The 1995 World Social Sumit is part of multifaceted drirve against poverty by the United Nations and its agencies. These include the World Bank, United Nations Children's Fund, the United Nations Development Programme, the United Nations Environment Programme, the United Nations Conference on Trade and Development, the International Fund for Agricultural Development and the Food and Agriculture Organization of the United Nations, among many other organizations.

The World Bank, which has made the reduction of poverty and the improvement of living standards its overall objective, has charted a two-pronged strategy against poverty. The strategy was first detailed in the Bank's 1990 *World Development Report*.

One element involves expanding employment and income-earning opportunities among the poor, and is thus necessarily concerned with the nature and rate of economic growth.

The second aspect of the Bank's strategy is to enhance the ability of poor people to respond to the opportunities presented. It is thus involved with improving access to such aspects of social infrastructure as health services and education.

The General Assembly has called the eradication of poverty-particularly in the least developed countries, sub-Saharan Africa and other countries that have areas of concentrated poverty— "one of the priority development objectives for the 1990s".

In its· call—a resolution of 31 March 1994—it invited all countries to begin implementing domestic policies to help create jobs and assure food security, health, eduction, housing and population programmes for all citizens, especially the most vulnerable and disadvantaged.

The chairman of the Preparatory Conference of the World Summit for Social Development, Ambassador Juan Somavia of Chile, has said that he hopes the meeting will result in a commitment from every nation to eliminate poverty.

"A political decision to eliminate—and yes, I mean eliminate—extreme poverty within a time frame distinctly specificed by each nation would be a true achievement in which we could take legitimate pride", he said.

Source: United Nations

Towards a Society for All

How to strengthen social integration-ensuring that a society reflects and is responsible to the needs of all its citizens— is one of three core issues to be addressed by national leaders at the World summit for Social Development, 6-12 March 1995 in Copenhagen, Denmark.

This backgrounder offers an overview of the issue. It draws on the Januray 1994 Report of the United Nations Secretary-General, the recommendations of an Expert Group Meeting held 27 September-1 October 1993, and other relevant studies.

The sense of deepening social inequalities worldwide, fragmenting societies, and polarizing population and income groups is more than just, "perception", according to United Nations

Secretary-General Boutros Boutros-Ghali. He reports that "the previously attained level of social security, an thus inclusion in society, is increasingly under threat".

The *Human Development Report* 1994, an annual study commissioned by the United Natons Development Programme, cites ten indicators which reflect a "weakening social facibric": homocides, rapes, divorces, births outside marriage, single parent homes, drug crimes, suicides, requests for asylum, numbers of prisoners and the percentage of juveniles in the prison populations. These figures are increasing, especially in economically developed countries and countries in transition.

The irony is that evidence of the social development and the social deterioration often appear juxtaposed within the same socities. For example, for United States, ranking eighth highest on the Human Development Index, is simultaneously the aggregate leader in indicators of a weakenig social fabric.

What is Social Integration?

What is a socially integrated society? The Secretary-General defines it as one that is "able to accommodate different and divergent individual and group aspirations within a flexible framework of shared basic values and common interests."

Seen in the context of sustainable human development, social integration is a synonym for greater justice, equality, material well-being and democratic freedom that implies equal opportunities and rights for all.

Within society, it manifests itself as solidarity, interdependence, respect for cultural divesity, tolerance for non-mainstream life styles and the courage to replace dysfunctional systems (eg, slavery, apartheid) with more equaitable ones.

In the words of the Secretary-General, the goal of constructive social integration is a "society for all" in which citizens feel that the state is responsive to their needs; one that promotes "development consistent with justice for the individual, harmony among groups and social cohesion."

It is clear that this goal cannot be achieved without successfully addressing the Summit's other two core issues of poverty and productive employment. In fact, the common thread that links all three issues is their "crucial importance for the development of individuals and societies," according to the Secretary-General.

Because most of the world's abjectly poor people live in the developing world, where they account for a third of the population, poverty is a major threat to social integration in these regions.

At the same time, poverty is increasing in industrialized countries-for example, nearly 15 per cent of the population of the twelve European Union countries live below national poverty lines.

Social integration is also threatened by the rising tide of unemployment and "jobless growth" which, if it persists, inevitably produces poverty. This downward spiral of social disintegration is characterized by marginalization of large portions of a society's population through exclusion and neglect, homelessness, and high crime and mortality rates.

Symptoms of Disintegration

Rapid, far-reaching change is a hallmark of contemporary society. In the realms of economics, technology, culture and social values, change is ironically one of the few "permanent" features of the world. Yet, although change has brought a multitude of improvements, one of its most adverse repercussions has been its tendency to marginalize, discriminate and exclude groups and even entire nations.

Who ar the marginalized and excluded? They include:

- illiterate migrants moving from rural poverty to urban slums, their search for a better life often unattainable;
- unemployed teenagers hanging out on street corners, "looking for trouble" because they can't find worthwhile work;
- orphaned children, victims of ethnic conflict, subsisting in the nether world of refugee camps;
- elederly widows, strugling with too little money to make ends meet.

Profile of human distress in industrial Countries

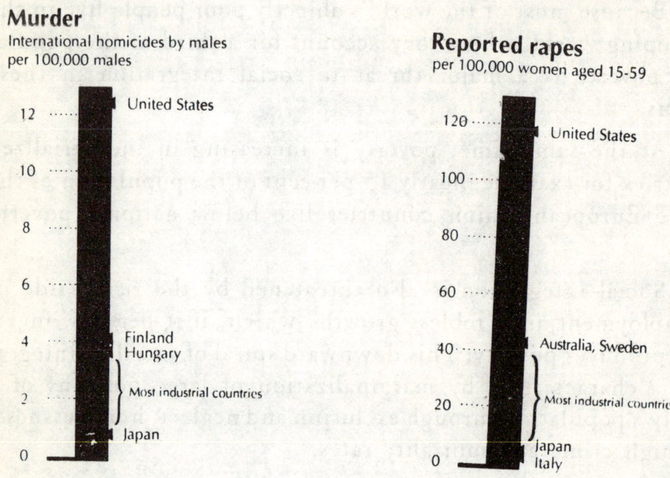

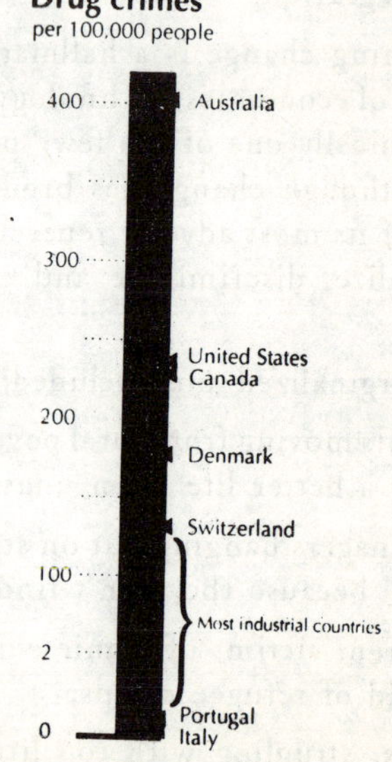

Source : Human Development Report, 1994, UNDP, p. 30.

Exclusion

As with poverty, exclusion anywhere poses a threat everywhere, particularly when sheer numbers of there marginalized minorities attain critical mass. And their numbers are increasing.

Consider the elderly, one of the most volunerable population groups: by the year 2025, the world's elderly population (people aged 60 or more) will number 1.2 billion, 14 per cent of the projected total global population. That means that this portion of the world population will have grown approximately by a factor of six, double the growth rate of the overall population.

Exclusion and discrimination are not only economics-driven. They are often based on racial, ethnic or tribal differences and may also be gender-based. Harvard economist Amartya Sen estimated that some 100,000,000 women are missing from the global population figures, most of them from South and East Asia, where female foetuses ar routinely aborted after amniocentesis or ultrasound scanning.

Statistics from 43 developing countries reveal that mortality rates for female children between a few months and four years old exceed those of boys in the same age groups. Even if they survive early childhood, discrimination against girls continues, fueling further societal marginalization.

Take education: of the 100 million children worldwide between the ages of 6-11 who do not attend school, 70 per cent are girls. Some 660 million people—two thirds of the world's illiterates-are women. And, althogh they are making progress, women as a group as still subject to varying degrees of discrimination of virtually every country of the world.,

Ethnic Conflict

All too often, institutionalized discrimination results in ethnic or racial violence and armed conflict, as societies disintegrate under the weight of their own prejudice. As the *Human Development Report* 1994 revealed, of the 82 conflicts since 1990, 79 were within national borders.

Played out in both political and military arenas, these conflicts characteristically take a high toll of civilian casualities. Fully

90 per cent of war casualities since 1990 have been civilian as opposed to only 10 per cent at the beginning of the twentieth century. Those who survive often become refugees.

As case in point, the prolonged warfar in the former Yugoslavia has generated the largest refugee exodus in Europe since the Second World, War. Another example is Tajikistan (in the former Soviet Union) where war has taken the lives of more than 20,000 citizens and made refugees of over half a million people, the equaivalent of 10 per cent of the country's total population.

Yet another example is Africa, which accounts for one third of the world's refugee population. Since April 1994, an estimated 3.5 million, or almost half the entire pre-war population of Rwanda, were either killed or forced to flee their homes due to ethnic conflict. Many who survived the slaughter fell victim to cholera and other diseases sweeping the refugee camps.

Migration

Whether because they are seeking a better life or because they are forced to flee from hostile political conditions or natural disasters, more poeple today are living outside their home villages, countries or regions than ever before. Although many migrants and refugees expect to remain only temporarily in thier host communities, increasingly, they are they to stay.

In search to work or higher wages, economic migrants often move to urban areas, leaving their families behind. Although the majority are men, in recent years economic migration rates for women have almost caught up, especially in southern and south-east Asia where more than 70 per cent of women migrants are under 25 years old.

Economic migration may bring privation, even physical danger, as well as a cultural backflash when groups who often share neither a comon language nor a common religion or culture are thrown together, straining existing social services as well as human tolerance.

Most problematic is migration that involves political refugees. The current human tidal wave of some 20 million refugees who have fled across borders, along with another 26 million

The top ten performers in human development, 1960-92

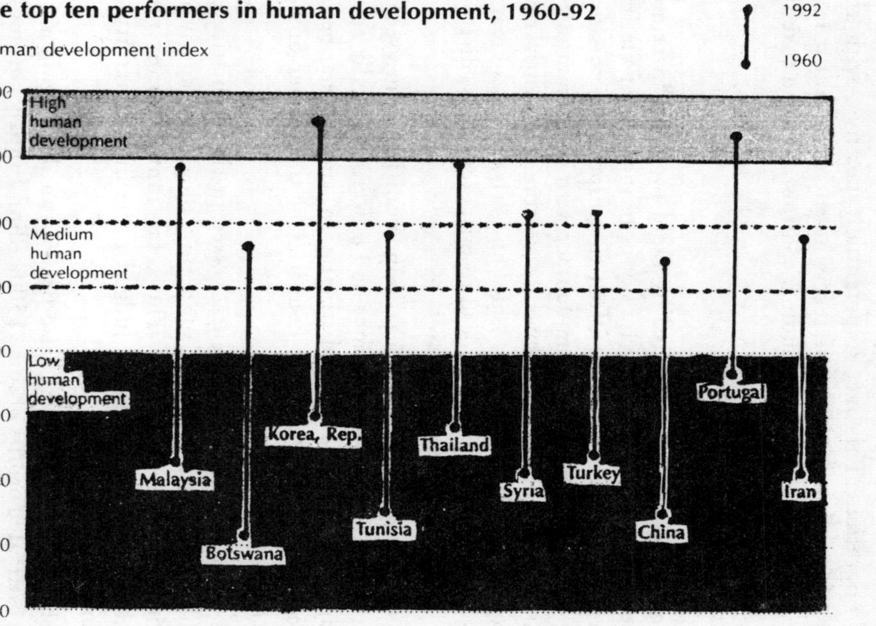

These ten countries have made the most progress in human development over the last three decades.

Source: Human Development Report 1994, UNDP. p.96

internally displaced persons, is swelled by armed conflicts, political instability, violations of human rights and persecution.

Many socities are becoming increasintly multi-cultural as a result of migration. This fact is potentially positive, with the posibility of greatly enriching the receiving societies, but it may equally lead to greater misunderstanding, confrontation and anxeity.

Crime

Many societies are threatened by rapid increases in crime, which seem to be outpaced only by skyrocketing fear of victimization felt by ordinary citizens. Often the response to this fear has been to seek to withdraw from contact with the community, behind high walls or barred windows. Increasing fragmentization of the physical environment into "safe" and "risky" areas creates distances among residents which lead to misperceptions, distrust and eventually, social disintegration.

Frustrated at diminishing legal opportunities, crime seems to offer a tempting path to affluance and power. Especially amid the nearanarchy of severe social distingration, such as that being experienced in Russia and other countries of the former Soviet Union, crime proliferates.

For a handful of entrepreneurs, versed in the sophisticated niceties of marketing and money laundering, illegality may pay off big—at least in the short run. The total annual turnover of organized transnational crime is judged to be in the vicinity of $1,000 billion.

Global trade in drugs has also become an illegal goldmine, raking in estimated profits of some $500 billion annualy, an amout which exceeds the GDP of many of countries. it is estimated that, in the United States alone, $85 billion a year from the sale of cocaine, heroin and cannabis is available for money laundering and black market investment. This illegally acquired wealth only serves to exacerbate the already yawning chasm between the very rich and very poor in the world.

The Vision

How do we transform the vision of a "society for all" into

reality? This is the challenge of the Social Summit. Even at this early stage, the Secretary-General's report has identified certain criteria, including:

* an "enabling environment";
* fulfilment of basic human needs (eg, health, shelter);
* literacy and primary education for all;
* economic growth with social justice;
* respect for, and protection of, diversity
* equal opportunities for all;
* accurate, timely information for all so that citizens can fully participate in their soceities;
* means to measure social development over time.

Setting New Priorities

The real goal is not merely to integrate a social dimension into the development process, but to redefine the very concept of development so that it truly becomes socially relevant. That means setting new priorities.

First of all, it will be vital to bring governments closer to the people, humanizing their bureaucracies and making them more responsible and responsive to their citizens.

Within countries, governments have prime responsibility for assuring overall social security by ensuring an environment which encourages sustainable economic growth, increase the number of productive jobs, guarantees social safety nets, and empowers the disadvantaged.

Governments have a very powerful means at their disposal: the power to redistribute economic and taxation burdens which can discourage exorbitant income differentiation and target needy portions of the population through well-difined social programmes. For example, progressive taxation, if not excessive, can be effective in creating socially supportive incentives.

Governments also must take "preventive action" against social exclusion. They must pass, and enforce, legislaion to ensur equal rights for all and to respect diversity. Where discrimination has previously set the tone, equal opportunities must be created through affirmative action and similar policies.

Government is not the sole actor when it comes to promoting social integration. It must work with the private sector and civil society.

Socially Responsible Businesses

The role of the private sector in promoting social integration is clearly evolving and it is likely to take an added importance in the years to come. Gone are the days when clear distinctions could be made between the role of government and the role of private companies in promoting social and economic well-being. Increasingly, there is a need for partnership between private the public institutions to ensure quality and choice in the goods and services people require.

This is where is growing sense of corporate social responsibility comes in. As experts at a 1993 meeting in The Hague put it, " in order to survive, private enterprises will have to change from a model based on maximizing profit to a model which emphasizes social responsibility and accountability to the community. Through the vehicle of private sector initiatives, the focus of productive employment must shift from profit towards people".

An Engaged Civil Society

Equally important for promoting social integration is the community of non-governmental organizations, religious institutions, professional associations, labour unions, cooperatives, community groups and other social networks which make up civil society. Such organizations often provide the means and the structures for people to express their aspirations, meet their needs, represents their interests and participate in local and national decision-making. They can also provide the forum for various interest groups to reconcile their differences democractically and peacefully, thus avoiding conflict and potential social disintegration.

To be able to function effectively, the orgaizations of civil society may need the active support of government. By decentralizing responsibilities and authority, by guaranteeing freedom of association and organization, and by ensuring active, two-way communications, governments can promote a lively, active and functioning civil society. This "enabling" action by government will promote social integration.

Vision to Reality

"No one goes through life alone. All of us are created within, and influenced by, networks of social relations which provide us with our identity and establish a framework for our actions," said the United Nations Research Institute for Social Development report on social integration. It stressed that people live and pursue their goals within a structure of institutions, ranging from families and households to schools, street gangs, sweatshops, stroes and offices in which they work.

On a more general level, their opportunities in life are affected by the larger economic and political context, ranging from bartering for food to betting on the stock market, from decisions of tribal councils to those of international tribunals.

As of August 1994, the United Nations numbered 184 Member States, actually made up of several thousand "nations" or "peoples". In this multi-ethnic, multi-cultural patchwork world, a flexible, socially responsive framework which supports civilized cultural change while, at the same time, fostering respect for tradition is crucial to sustainable human development.

Social integration, states the Secretary General's Report, should be very clearly and firmly based on "a platform of principles built on respect for human dignity, individual freedom and equality of rights and duties."

Empowering of UN

There is a pressing need for the world community to recognize its common heritage. Dur to the increasing interdependence between nations, many proposals for social integraton and socially just global system of governance can be implemented only at the international level. Here the United Nations has a unique and vital role to play.

Convened by the United Nations, the Social Summit will produce a political Declaration as well as a Programme of Action aimed at alleviating and finally eliminating extreme poverty, at creating adequate productive employment for an increasing population and at enhancing social integration. The Social Summit will endorse an agenda for social development—but that is the beginning.

Empowering the United Nations to meet this challenge effectively means paving the way for "social progress and better standards of life in larger freedom" as envisaged almost fifty years ago in the United Nations Charter.

Source: United Nations

Appendix 14
Fact Sheets

HELPING THE POOR TO HELP THEMSELVES

World Bank

The task of reducing poverty is daunting, but by no means hopeless. We know that rapid and sustained development is not a dream but an achievable reality. The Social Summit offers an opportunity to focus the world's attention on global poverty and to agree on strategies for faster progress to reduce it.

A person born in the developing world today can expect to live 63 years-longer than at any time in human history. Many countries have achieved striking gains in health and education. In the past 25 years alone, average per caita incomes inthe developing world have doubled.

Yet, despite these achievements, the stark reality is that between 1.1 billion and 1.3 billion people in developing countries are still desperately poor, living on an income of less than $1 per day. Hundreds of millions more have incomes so narrowly above this threshold they live at constant risk of sinking below it. Their poverty is not just a lack of income. It is a deprivation of welfare and, very profoundly, a lack of capability, social power and opportunities.

Investing in Poor People

What must developing countries do to increase the well-being of their people? Sustained economic growth is essential, but it is not enough. Efforts to reduce poverty are unlikely to suceed in the long run unless there is greater investment in (the human resources of) the poor themselves. Improvements in education, health and nutrition directly address the worst consequences of being poor. And investing in people, especially in their education, also attacks some of the most important causes of poverty. Improving social services is an integral of any long-term strategy for reducing poverty.

To be cost-effective, interventions must be well-targeted and carefully designed to meet the specific needs of poor people. This means developing technologies suited to the risky environment that confronts small farmers, devising credit schemes to serve small borrowers, combining feeding programs for especially vulnerable groups with education on health and nutrition. The success of these programmes usually means involving the poor both at the design and implementation stages.

Shifting the allocation of funds from higher-level services to basic health and primary education will help to offer more efficient and equiptable servics to the poor.

In Brazil, for example, 23 per cent of the public education budget goes to higher education, even though only 2 per cent of the student population attends university. In Morocco, only 5 per cent of young people eventually obtain university degrees, but those inthis fortunate minority receive 35 per cent of total government expenditures on education.

Recommending a shift to funding more basic services does not mean denying the importance of higher-level services; it does mean shifting the emphasis and targeting first things first. In particular, any country that wants to compete in the world economy needs a comprehensive education policy that includes spending on higher education, science and technology, and professional training.

In health-care systems, hospitals are the educational and research institutions that train new staff and generage new knowledge. However, maintaing a modern urban hospital could take half

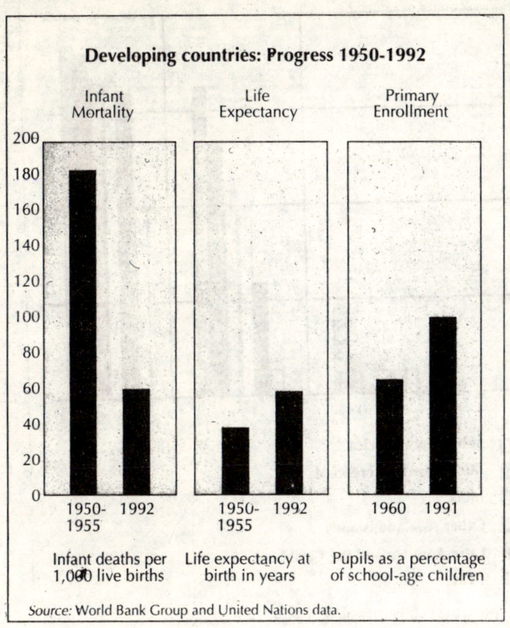

Source: World Bank Group and United Nations data.

a country's annual health budget: funds which could otherwise benefit vast numbers of poor people through the provision of primary health care at the community level. Therefore, what is needed is financial reform, including greater reliance on alternative financing mechanisms such as student loans and health insurance plans, to free up resources that could be used to expand and improve basic services and provide better access to the poor.

Investing in Health

The world is facing serious new health challenges. By 2000 the growing toll from acquired immune deficiency syndrome (AIDS) in developing countries could easily rise to more than 1.8 million deaths annually, erasing decades of hard-won reductions in mortality. The malaria parasite's increased resistance to avail-

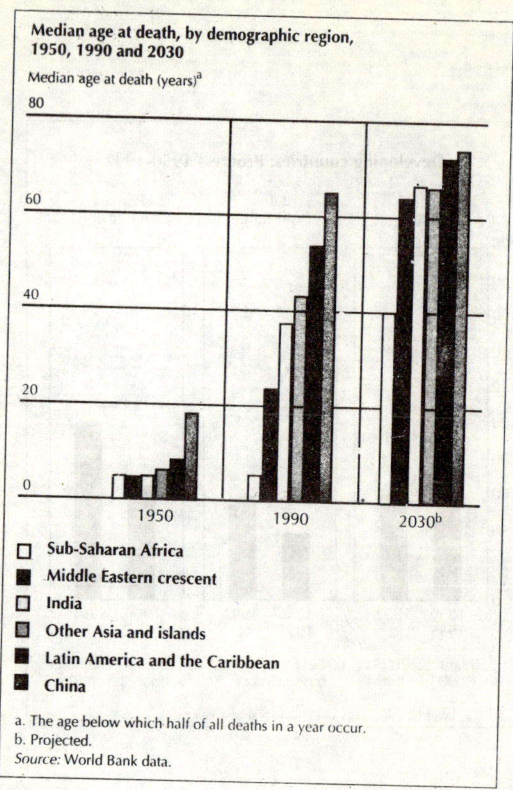

a. The age below which half of all deaths in a year occur.
b. Projected.
Source: World Bank data.

able drugs, could lead to a doubling of malaria deaths, to nearly 2 million a year within a decade.

Rapid progress in reducing child mortality and fertility rates will create new demands on health-care systems to provide for ageing populations. Yet, despite increasing demands for health care, millions of lives and billions of dollars could be saved if governments pursued sound macroeconomic policies that focus on the poor.

Governments need to adopt a three-part approach to improving health, re-directing funds towards:

- Fostering an enabling economic environment for households to improve their own health. This includes policies that ensure rising incomes for the poor and increased investment in school's basic health education, particularly for girls;

- Providing more support public health programmes, essential clinical services and more cost-effective programmes that do more to help the poor. Currently, government spending accounts for half of the $168 billion annual expenditure on health in devleoping countries. Too much of this goes to specialized care in hospitals while too little gocs to low-cost, highly effective programmes, such as control and treatment of infectious diseases and of malnutrition. Developing countries as a group could reduce their burden of disease by 25 per cent - the equivalent of averting more than 9 million infant deaths- by redirecting about half, on average, of government spending;
- Encouraging more private sector initiatives. Governments needs to promote greater diversity and competition in the financing and deliverty of health services. Government financing of public health and basic clinical services would leave the coverage of remaining clinical services to private finance, usually mediated through insurance. Government regulation can stregthen private insurance markets by improving social insurance incentive for wider coverage and cost control. Even for publicly financed clinical sevices, governments can encourage competition and private-sector involvement in sevice supply and help the private sector more by generating and disseminating key information. A combination of these measures would improve the health of the entire population, especially the poor, and help save millions of lives and billions of dollars while providing better servics for everyone.

Investing in Education

Most developing countries are officially committed to providing universal primary schooling for children but few of them have achieved that goal. Although middle-income countries provide primary education to virtually all schools-age children, in low-income countries (other than China and India), primary school places are limited.

Boys in developing countries are much more likely than girls to be enrolled in primary or secondary school. And in all countries, children from poor families are less apt to enroll in school and

World Bank lending for human resource development has risen dramatically

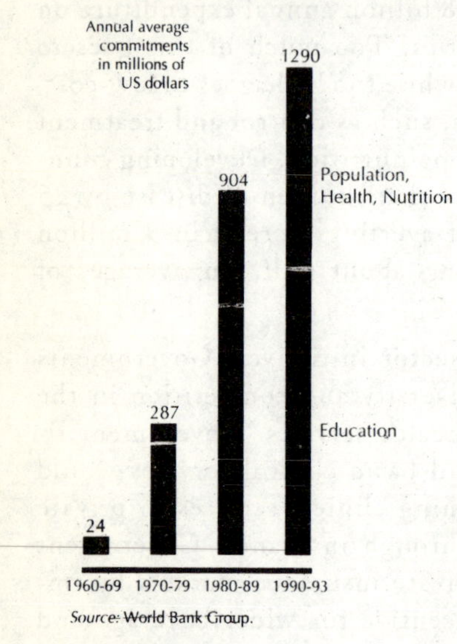

Source: World Bank Group.

more apt to drop out than children from more affluent families. It is disconcerting that even children who complete primary school often have not learned the core skills in their national curriculum. Students in low income countries tend to peform poorly on national and international measures in mathematics, science and reading comprehension.

Education must reach beyond the fortunate few. Those living in rural areas, women, the poor and minorities suffer most from limited access to education. In all region of the world, except Latin America and the Caribbean, women and girls, in particular, face economic and cultural bariers to attending school at each level of education.

Many schools in developing countries fail to reach or teach children because of inadequate resources of because available resources are not used efficiently. In primary schools, drop-out and repetition rates are high, so that countries have to pay for as many as nine years of education simply to produce one pupil who has completed the fifth grade—something few nations can afford. In many countries, a disproportionate amount may go for salaries instead of books, educational supplies and teachers training. The same constraint hampers secondary schools and universities.

Weaknesses in school management systems have been identified in almost of developing countries as rapid expansion of education systems has increased the need for managers and administrators. The absence of effective managers is evident at the intermediate and higher levels of education. Strengthening managerial capability at all levels of the education system will require substantial resources and a long-term perspective. To maintain managerial competence, countries eventually must develop specialized institutes for training educational managers.

Resource constraints are a principal barriers to bridging the widening education gap between developing and industrialized countries. Industrialized countries typically invest almost 6 per cent of their gross national product (GDP) on education and training while low income countries invest scarcely more than half (i.e., 3 per cent) on average, although their school-age population is 75 per cent larger.

For low-income countries to be able to provide a place in primary school for 95 per cent of their school-age children, they would probably have to spend as much as 3.5 per cent of gross national product on this goal over the next ten years. Their actual resource commitments fall far short of such a goal.

Targetting Social Expenditures and Social Safety Nets

Individuals, families and communities frequently join forces as a means of coping with poverty. Thus, in many parts of Sub-Saharan Africa the term for being poor is synonymous with lacking kin or friends.

At the community level these "social security" arrangements are sometimes quite sophisticated. For example, fishing villages in South Asia, Sub-Saharan Africa and Latin America often provide for subsistence needs of old fishermen or of poor fishing families whose male income earnes have died. Old fishermen are commonly assigned comparatively easy tasks on shore, and children from needy families are allowed to take some fish from each boat. In some Senegalese villages, retired fishermen are granted a fixed share of the catch. This "tax" is paid not only by local fishermen but also by fishermen from other areas.

But there are limits to what those unable to work can do to protect themselves, and limits to what the households looking after them can do to raise household income to workable levels. The state, therefore, has a role in aiding households or communities, especially during periods of transition while economic reforms are under way.

Increasing social expenditures is essential for poverty reduc-

Poverty in the developing world 1985 and 2000

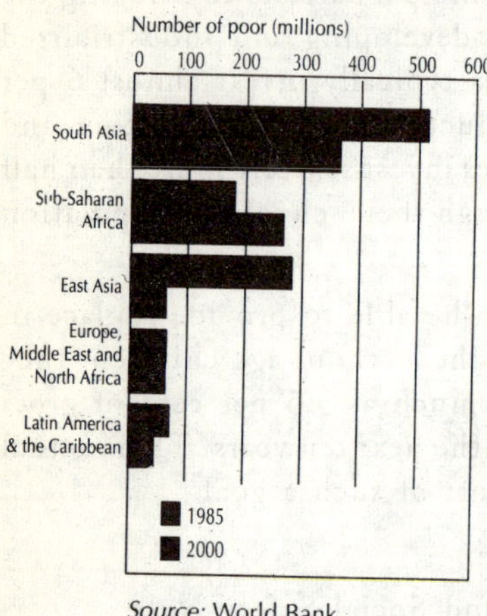

Source: World Bank.

tion, but it is not enough. Careful monitoring of scarce resources to ensure that they reach those most in need is imperative. Studies of poverty alleviation programmes inMalasia and Indonesia, for example, show that the poor benefit most from broad targeting of basic services, such as primary schools and health centres, while more narrowly targeted programmes can be designed to reach particularly vulnerable groups. Among these are health and nutrition schemes for mothers and infants; feeding programmes for the victims of drought or famine,safety nets for the sick, the old and the newly unemployed.

During the "first generation" of structural adjustment programmes, issues and such as primary health care and education were not given sufficient attention but the lessons are being learned.

Since the late 1980s World Bank-supported structural adjustment operations have included the provision of safety nets and social funds for vulnerable groups in many countries (e.g., in Bolivia, Honduras and Zambia). In addition, 21 per cent of total World Bank lending in fiscal year 1994 supported specific, targeted programmes aimed at poverty reduction — for instance, water and sanitation for low-income communities in Brazil; AIDS prevention in Uganda; and primary health care, education and water supply in Pakistan. These are and importance complement to other World Bank operations and enhance the effectiveness of the overall effort to reduce poverty.

The Road Ahead

It is sometimes suggested that there is an inherent tension between social development and economic development; yet the evidence unequivocally shows that they are mutually reinforcing.

Social development requires economic growth. But it also requires much more - the expansion of people's human potential through better health and education, the guarantee of political rights, equality of opportunity, and better-functioning institutions.

The Social Summit offers and unique opporunity to reaffirm our commitment to the goals of reducing poverty, creating stable employment, and improving social integration and to collaborate on strategies for faster progress in achieving them. Most important, the Summit will focus the attention on global poverty, the greatest threat to social development. Projections for this decade are that continued progress will be made, but the global tragedy of more than 1 billion people living on the margin of existence presses us all to do more, and faster.

Source: World Bank

HEALTH: CORNERSTONE OF SOCIAL DEVELOPMENT

World Health Organisation

The Health Gap

When looking at overall global health trends, the good news is that health status has improved during the second half of this century. Life expectancy at birth increased by more than 20 years (i.e. from 41 to 62 years) in the less developed regions between 1950 and the early 1990s, and by 8 years, (i.e. from 66 to 74 years) in the more developed regions over the same period. A major reason for this progress was the falling infant mortality rates during this period: from 179 to 70 per 1,000 children in less developed regions, and from 59 to 10 per 1,000 children in more developed regions.

Nevertheless, the gap between rich and poor remaines an all but unbridgeable chasm. For example, average life expectacy is 12 years greater (74 years as compared to 62 years) in more developed areas, while seven times as many infants die in least developed areas. Moreover, estimates indicate that 40 times as many women die as a consequence of complications of pregnancy and childbirth in the less developed regions.

Furthermore, despite improved survival in all developing regions, the least developed countries' progress was sluggish. Whereas they were only 5 years behind less developed regions as a whole in life expectancy in 1950- (36 vs. 41 years), by the early 1990s the difference had doubled to over 10 years (51 vs. 62 years.)

The infant mortality profile in the least developed regions actually worsened. From a level from 8 per cent higher than developing regions as a whole in 1950 (194 vs. 179 per 1,000), it rose to almost 60 per cent higher by 1990 (110 vs. 70 per 1,000).

In sub-Saharan Africa, home to the majority of least developed countries, it is estimated that, at the end of the 1980s, women died of maternal complications three times more often than in less developed regions as a whole, and nearly 150 times more often than in more developed regions.

These differences in mortality risk are highly dependent on the causes of death. At present, of the 50 million people who die each year worldwide, some 38 million live in less developed regions. In addition, in the less developed regions, ten times as many death-44 per cent of the total—are due to communicable diseases, as opposed to only 4.3 per cent in developed areas.

Recent years have seen a shift in disease trends towards noncommunicable diseases such as cencer, cardiovascular diseases and diabetes, resulting largely from changes in lifestyles, environmental changes and the ageing of populations, in both developed and developing countries. Yet, even for diseases that are greater killers in the more developed regions, their burden of death can be greater in the less developed regions. Although nearly half (48 per cent) of deaths in more developed regions are due to diseases of the circulatory system, in absolute numbers more people die from these diseases in the less developed regions.

In addition to the relatively recent emergence of HIV/AIDS, there has been a resurgence of old scourges such as tuberculosis, malaria and cholera.

The health dimensions of today's complex social problems call for multifaceted response that is not restricted to medical solutions. Strategies that address health problems will also need to relate them to the other major social problems of the 1990s.

Health status gaps between regions mirror the unequal development of health infrastructures that varies both by population groups and by community within a given country. Affluent populations enjoy

Estimated annual number of deaths, by cause, in developing and developed countries, 1990

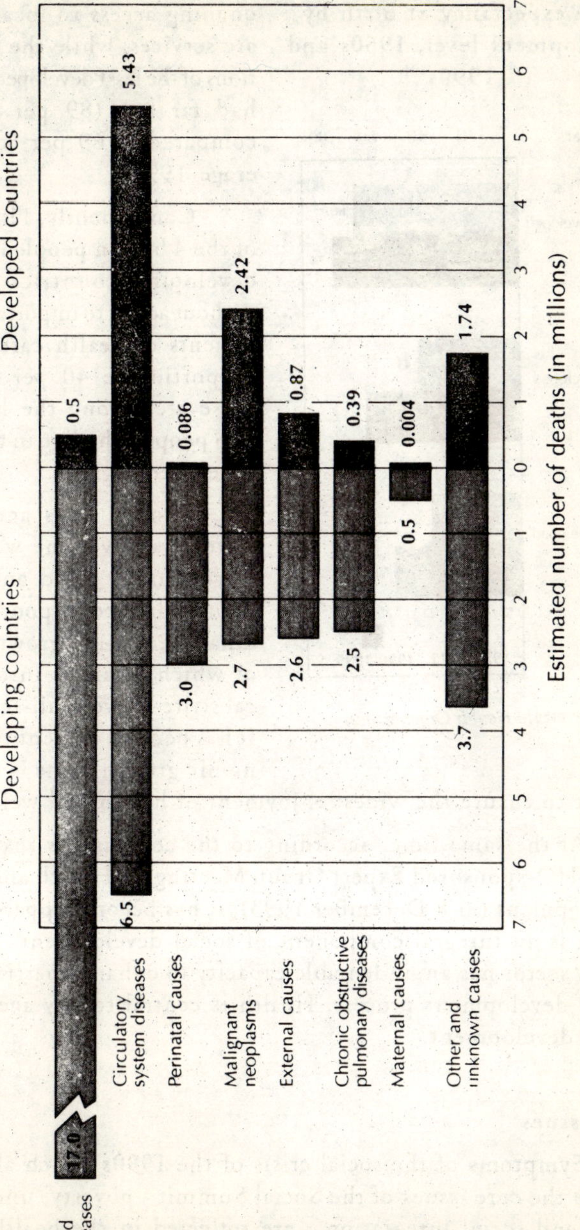

Source: World Health Organization

Life expectancy at birth by development level, 1950s and 1990s

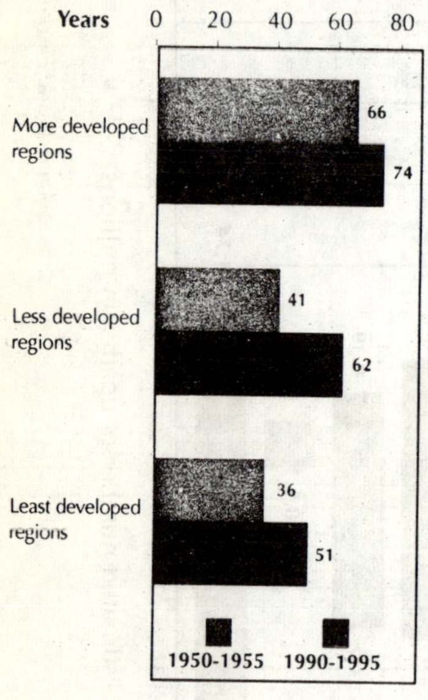

Source: World Health Organization

ongoing access to local health are services, while the populations of the least developed regions had far less (89 per cent as compared to 69 per cent coverage 1991).

Consequently, 11 per cent of the 4 billion people living in developing countries remain without access to important components of health care; a disproportionate 40 per cent of these are among the half billion people who live in the least developed regions.

Communities and social systems all over the world are disrupted by rapid and often poorly planned or poorly coordinated economic growth, some of which escalates into political strife or even full-scale war. It has become evident that economic growth alone is not sufficient to ensure the widest enjoyment of health and well-being.

At the same time, according to the conclusions reached by the WHO-sponsored Expert Group Meeting on Health and Social Development (6-8 December 1993), it has become apparent that health is an integral component of social development, and the health sector has an undeniable capacity to enhance participation in the development process. Health is central to any agenda for social development.

The Issues

Symptoms of the social crisis of the 1990s which also constitute the core issues of the Social Summit - poverty, unemployment and social integration - are reflected in the health status profiles presented above.

The World Health Organization (WHO) considers that health is both a goal and a means of achieving social development. Health is inseparable from economic and social productivity and family cohesiveness. Equity in access to health services, therefore, is an essential component of strategies for social development. This outlook is fundamental in addressing each of the three core themes of the World Summit for Social Development - the reduction and elimination of poverty, productive employment and the reduction of unemployment, and social integration.

WHO is working with a growing number of countries of define health reform policies that take into consideration the complex interaction of factors at play in an evolving political and economic environment. This work is being conducted by WHO is close collaboration with the United Nations system, financial institutions and other development partners. The health and well-being of people, particularly the poor and the marginalized, is the main target of such policies, aiming, in the long term, at self-reliance and sustainable development. This collaboration, implemented within the ftamework of the WHO policy for intensified cooperation with countries and peoples in greatest need, deals with many of the issues involved in the three core themes of the Summit.

WHO's Constitution defines health as"a complete state of physical, mental, and social well-being, and not merely the absence of disease or infirmity". The attainment by all peoples of the world by the year 2000 of a level of health that will permit them to lead socially and economically productive lives was defined as a main social target by the World Health Assembly in 1977. This goal is to be attained through the implementation of a primary health-care policy based on equity and social justice and the firm belief that health is a fundamental human right and world-wide social goal.

Future Priorities

WHO has established for interrelated policy orientations as the foci for action by the international health community. These orientations provide the framework for WHO's work during the period 1996-2001.

1. **Integrating health and human development in public policies:** WHO's primary responsibility is to examine how the existing development strategies and policies of countries can be strengthened to protect and improve the health status of their people bring health objectives into the centre of current development strategies.` Health must become an integral part of the political, social and economic issues which are emerging as the current major priorities of development policy makers.

2. **Ensuring equitable access to health services:** Equity of access to care, with special reference to the poor and marginalized, is basic to development strategies aiming at social justice. WHO strives to bring Governments to reconfirm their commitment to equity through appropriate health financing policies, including health insurance, and the control of overall levels of health expenduture. This commitment is directed especially towards those populations who have least access to health care—such as the rural and urban poor, the unemployed, women, children, youth, the elderly, migrants and refugees.

3. **Promoting and protecting health:** According to WHO, individuals, families and communicaties should actively participate in their own health development. This means adopting healthy lifestyles and improving nutritional status, living conditioins and environment.

   Protecting the health of minorities, the underprivileged and high-risk population groups, including nomads and indigenous peoples, is an important challenge, to be met through the application of integrated approaches that increase both the capacity of individuals to be self-sufficient and the capacity of services to respond to their changing needs.

4. **Preventing and controlling specific health problems:** Primary health care and programmes for the control and elimination of diseases are essential components in the fight against poverty and social exclusion. The health and well-being of people, particularly the poor and marginalized, should be the main target of policies aiming at self-reliance and sustainable development. WHO's role in this connection is to stimulate authorities to develop national policies

addressing specific health problems and to implement integrated measures for disease prevention and control.

Source: World Health Organization

AGRICULTURE AND SOCIAL DEVELOPMENT

Food and Agriculture organisation

The Situation

On a global scale...

Poverty is a rural problem

Poor countries are agrarian countries

In the world's poorest countries:

* More than three quarters of the people live in rural areas and depend on agriculture for work and income;
* Agriculture accounts for nealy 40 per cent of the gross domestic product and more than half of export earnings.

Poor people are rural people.

* More than 800 million of the world's 1.1 billion poor people live in rural areas, with the majority in Asia and Africa.
* 60 per cent of the rural population sub-Saharan Africa live in poverty, as do 31 per cent of rural Asians.

Underemployment is a rural problem

Around 30 per cent of the world's total labour force is not productively employed. Most of the 800 million jobless and underemployed live in rural areas.

* In sub-Saharan Africa, over 50 per cent of the rural workforce is seasonally underemployed.
* Nearly 40 per cent of rural households in South Asia are landless, or else their farm plots are too small to provide year-round work. Among Bangladesh's 80 million landless and small landholders, nearly one third are underemployed or jobless.

Marginalization is a rural problem

The rural poor suffer not only from low incomes but from marginalization in every sense of the world—geographic, economic, social, cultural and political.

Vulnerable rural groups include those most easily and frequently disinfranchised: small farmers, the landless,women, nomadic pastoralists, artisanal fishermen and dispalced persons. Generally, they lack both entitlement to food and productive resources and access to essential services, such as water, sanitaion, medical care and education.

* In the least developed countries, less than a third of the rural poor have access to clean, safe drinking water. Barely a quarter have adequate sanitation.
* 80 per cent of the doctors in East Africa are based in cities, while more than 80 per cent of the people live in the countryside. In rural East Africa, there is one doctor for every 60,000 people (as opposed to one for every 500 people in developed countries).
* Adults in cities in the developing world are twice as likely to have had some schooling as those in rural areas.

Food insecurity is a rural problme

Worldwide, 800 million people suffer from chronic undernutrition. The vast majority live in rural areas of the developing world.

* The greatest concentration of the chronically undernourished, some 271 million people, live in South Asia. More than 80 per cent of them reside in rural areas.

Rural problems fuel urban problems

Every year, more than 80 million people from rural areas flood into cities in the developing world, driven mainly by poverty and the prospect of food, jobs, services and other opportunities.

* The urban population of the developing countries will grow from less than 1 billion in 1980 to 2.7 billion in 2010.

* Two thirds of the homeless people living on the streets of Bombay came to the city because they had no land; half arrived with little more than the clothes on their backs.

Rural problems threaten the global environment

The poverty of the rural poor in developing countries is a major cause of environmental degradation. In their struggle for survival, the poor are driven to practices that damage the environment, jeopardizing both their own food security and that of future generations.

* Shortening of fallow periods and continuous cultivation without replacing the soil nutrients damages soils and reduces crop yields. All countries in sub-Saharan Africa are estimated to suffer from nutrient mining.
* Every year about 15.4 million hectares of tropical forests are lost. A large part of the cutting and burning results from extention of grazing and cultivation, particularly shifting cultivation practiced by the poor.
* Overgrazing and overcultivation of fragile soils have been identifed as major factors in dryland degradation and desertificaion. Croplands and rangelands covering an estimated 30 per cent of the world's land surface are threatened.

Seeking Solutions

Rural problems need rural solutions

Since over 80 per cent of the world's poor live in rural areas, large-scale reduction in poverty, will depend on gains in agricultural and rural development.

Attacking rural poverty

Most of the 800 million rural poor live in low-income food-deficit countries, where food ensecurity, poverty, malnutrition and environmental degradation go hand in hand. In these countries, improvements in food production and productity must be the engine of equitable and sustainable development. Keys to achieving such improvements include:

* **Developing areas with adequate to high agricultural poten-**

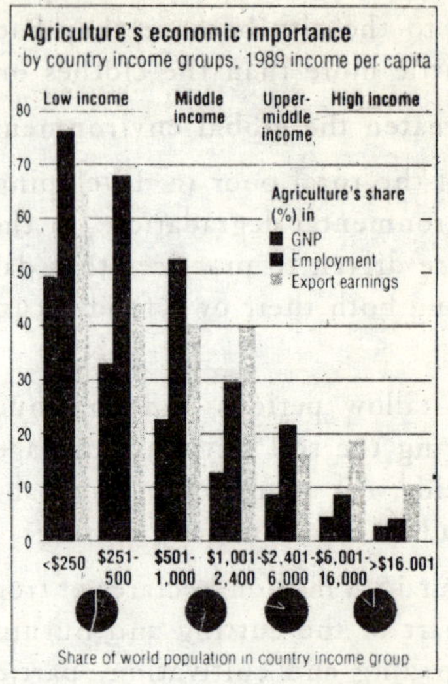
Agriculture's economic importance
by country income groups, 1989 income per capita
Low income
Middle income
Upper-middle income
High income
Agriculture's share (%) in
GNP
Employment
Export earnings
<$250
$251-500
$501-1,000
$1,001-2,400
$2,401-6,000
$6,001-16,000
>$16,001
Share of world population in country income group

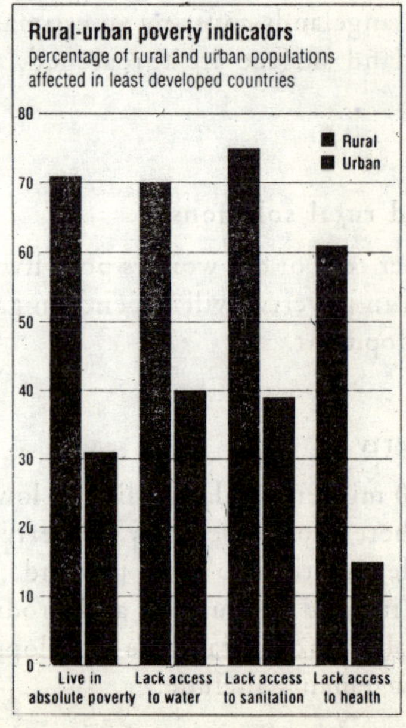
Rural-urban poverty indicators
percentage of rural and urban populations affected in least developed countries
Rural
Urban
Live in absolute poverty
Lack access to water
Lack access to sanitation
Lack access to health

tial: An FAO study of 91 developing countries found that seven countries (i.e. Afghanistan, Burundi, Central African Republic, Chad, Ethiopia—including Eritrea—Mozambique and Somalia) with very low household food security index ratings had the potential to produce more than enough essential food crops to meet their needs. Nearly half the countries studied could potentially meet mroe than twice their total requirements. Most of these gains would result from higher yields achieved through diffusion of improved technology— a green revolution";

* **Emphasizing food crops for local consumption:** Worsening terms of trade have steadily erodded the value of many cash crops. The fall in prices of Africa's export commodities between 1986 and 1990 is estimated to have cost the continent $ 50 billion in lost revenues. Low-income food-deficit countries, in particular, would benefit from reallocating resources to production of food crops for local consumption, including those traditional crops and varities that so often are neglected in favour of high-yielding hybrids;
* **Establishing forestry or agro-forestry systems in areas with poor soils or steep slopes:** Millions of households in the developing world depend on trees and on forests for shelter, fuel, food and fodder. In marginal areas, community-based forestry and agro-frsstery can increase production and food security without endangering fragile ecosystems.

Other proven weapons in the battle against rural poverty include:

• **Labour-intensive public works:** Irrigation and road-building projects provide jobs and income, while reducing the isolation of the rural poor and increasing the assets of the community;

* **Improving access to land and credit:** Where small farmers, particularly women, have benefited from land reform and specialized credit institutions, harvests and incomes have increased and hunger has fallen. Effective reforms favouring small farmers have been shown to be among the most important factors in raising agricultural income.

Building solidarity with the rural poor

Rural development—and particularly eradication of rural poverty-can be achieved only with the voluntary and active participation of the rural people themselves. Therefore, policies and priorities must be directed towards promoting.

* **People's participation:** Of particular importance in rural areas is the strengthening of agricultural cooperatives, water users' associations, agricultural workers' unions and self-help community organisations:
* **Investment in rural infrastructure:** Studies show that investments in rural infrastructure—irrigation, roads, electricity, markets and communications—increase agricultural production and rural industry while reducing rural poverty;
* **Investment in rural people:** Providing basic education to the rural poor, particularly women, yields dramatic improvements in food production and household food security. According to one study, providing 10 years of education for every women would have a more direct impact on child mortality than doubling income, providing sanitation and piped water, and turning every agricultural worker into a white—collar worker.

Creating rural jobs

Major increases in rural non-farm employment will be required to absorb the rapid growth in the rural labour force and stem the tide of migration to the cities. Steps to generate employment include:

- **Development of rural industries:** Food processing and other industries related to agriculture create jobs and retain value added in the rural areas. Making local produce available year-round improves food security and reduces micro-nutrient deficiences;
- **Improving market infrastructure:** Efficient and equitable agricultural marketing systems contribute both to rural development and to increasing the supply of low-cost food to the urban poor.

Source: Food and Agriculture Organisation of United Nations

RURAL POVERTY: THE STRUGGLE TO SURVIVE

International Fund for Agricultural Development

Situation

Although some parts of the world have made great strides in development during the second half of the twentieth century, according to a report by the Secretary-General (A/CONF. 166/PC/6), "poverty and inequality remain and appear to the worsening". Moreover, the draft Declaration and Programme of Action (A/CONF.166/L.22) for the upcoming World Summit for Social Development reveals that:

* More than 1 billion people live in abject poverty; more than half of those go hungry every day. A large proportion of men and women, particularly in Africa and the least developed countries, have very limited or no access to income and resources.
* Over 120 million people worldwide are without employment; many more are underemployed or have no viable sustainable livelihoods.
* Far too many people, particularly women, increasingly face vulnerability, isolation, marginalization, violence and insecurity about the future—their own and their children's—as poverty, joblessness and social disintegration become ever more ubiquitous features of today's world.

Especially since the "lost decade" of the 1980s, the numbers of rural poor have been increasing steadily, and they now encompass about one fifth of the entire global population. The figures portray a bleak picture:

* In 1988, it was estimated that the percentage of the rural population living below the poverty line was 61 per cent in Latin America and the Caribbean, 60 per cent in sub-Saharan Africa, 31 per cent in Asia and 26 per cent in North Africa and the Near East.
* Some 55 per cent of those living below the poverty line are women; over the past two decades, their numbers have grown by 50 per cent, compared to 30 per cent for men.
* With mounting populations, landholdings inall regions of the developing world except Latin America and Caribbean

are becoming smaller and more fragemented; rural landlessness or near landlessness is on the rise, affecting at least 40 per cent of households in South Asia.

Poverty and the struggle to survive have undermined the vital natural resource base of the rural population. For example, just within the brief timespan of the past thirty years:

* Nearly 20 per cent of the topsoil from croplands has been lost, largely due to lack of capital and technology to undertake appropriate soil conservation measures;
* Millions of hectares have become wasteland due to poorly constructed and illmaintained irrigiation systems;
* Deforestation of tropical forests and woodlands has occured at the rate of 11 million hectares a year, in a desperate attempt to clear land or to obtain fuelwood.

As rural conditions deteriorate, more and more rural people flock to urban centres. Most of these are men, leaving women behind tol manage the homestead and the family.

Issues

Considering the abundance and affluence in some parts of the world, the central question is: how can the rural poor obtain the resources they need to become more productive? Their requirements are relatively modest; the rural poor need:

* Land or off-farm opportunities for employment;
* Technical support (extension services and adaptive research);
* Agricultural inputs: seeds, fertilizers, etc;
* Credit for investment;
* Access to markets; and
* Community services: schooling, health care, sanitaion and transport.

Women are a crucial factor in alleviating rural poverty. In order to successfully harness rural women's productive potential, specific attention must be paid to their particular interests and needs. Women must be full and active partners in the development process.

IFAD lending by region under the Regular and Special Programmes for Africa, 1978-1994

Total lending $4.2 billion

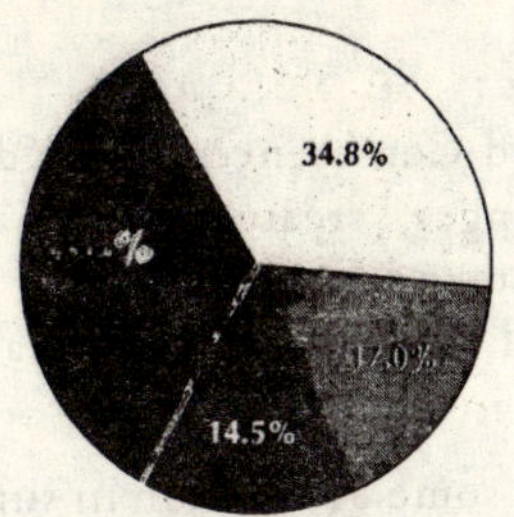

- Africa
- Asia
- Latin America and Caribbean
- Near East and North Africa

IFAD projects by type under the Regular and Special Programmes for Africa, 1978-1994

Total number of projects: 380

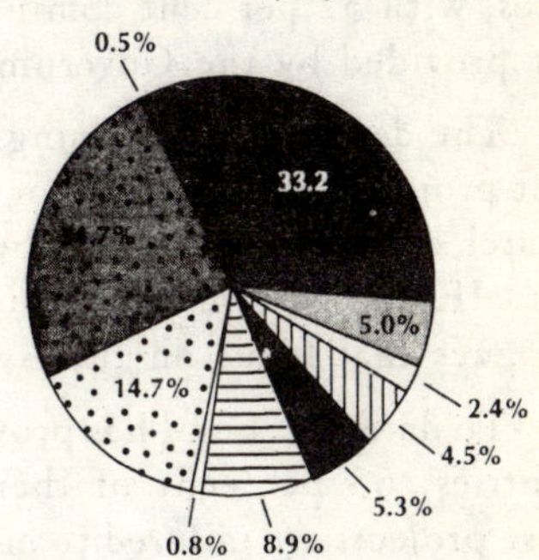

- Agricultural/Development
- Marketing/Storage/Processing
- Rural Development
- Credit
- Settlement
- Irrigation
- Livestock
- Research/Extension/Training
- Programme Loan
- Fisheries

Source: IFAD

When necessary, indigenous peoples must also be helped to adopt more appropriate technologies without undermining social cohesion and values.

Responses

In 1974, the Fourth World Food Conference, alarmed by a rising tide of rural poverty and hunger, created a specialized United Nations agency whose sole mandate was that of rural poverty alleviation. The International Fund for Agricultural Development (IFAD) began operations in 1978.

Since 1978, IFAD has mobilized some $14 billion in support of initiatives to assist the poorest of the rural poor to produce more food, earn more income and improve the quality of their lives. About 29 per cent of the total comes from the Fund's own resources, replenished by voluntary contributions of its 157 member States, with 32 per cent coming from outside donors and 39 per cent provided by the Governments of recipient countries.

The design and financing of agricultural and rural development projects is IFAD's major activity. It also finances adaptive research and local institution-building directly related to the rural poor. IFAD also initiates country, regional and international dialogues that focus on the issues of rural poverty.

To date, the Fund has provided loans for 386 projects in 102 countries, 65 per cent of them on highly concessional terms. These projects are tailored to meet the needs of a particular target group. Some focus on agricultural development through such components as the provision of the inputs, improved irrigation schemes and strengthened extension services. Others focus on livestock or fisheries development, or on providing credit to the poor.

A number of projects invovle soil and water conservation, a high-priority obejctive of the Special Programe for sub-Saharan Countries Affected by Drought and Desertification (SPA), launched in1986 and designed specifically to assit smallholders.

Direct Benefits to the Rural Poor

Small-scale: With the objective of directly benefiting intended target groups, priority has shifted gradually from larger, less targeted projects to the development of smallar, but more cost-effective, irrigation shemes.

Women: With an intentional focus on the gender of recipients, at least 30 per cent of IFAD's funding will be directed towards providing women the resources and support they need to realize their productive potential.

Credit: Innovative approaches to credit delivery have also been tested and proved successful through the formation of small groups acting as guarantors for their members' loans. Often terms are formed to bring credit services directly to the villages, instead of the villagers having to travel to the bank. There are also arrangements for in-kind credit and repayment, and increasingly, credit is provided for off-farm enterprises.

Grants: By the end of 1993, IFAD had provided a total of $191.7 million to cover 481 grants for adaptive research and institution building. The former have focused on improved varieties of staple food crops, small farming systems and low-cost soil and water conservation measures, while the latter have concentrated on strengthening extension services, input delivery, credit facilities and NGO support in rural areas.

Future Priorities:

Dialogue and Collaboration

Repeated intiatives have been taken to bring the issues of rural poverty to the attention of the international community. To this end, a series of national and regional seminars and workshops have brought together experts to share views and formulate action plans.

IFAD's collaboration with NGOs inthe field has received added impetus by the creation in 1987 of the IFAD/NGO Extended Coorperation Programme. By the end of 1992, some 74 NGOs had participated in 59 IFAD projects, 64 per cent of them from sub-Saharan Africa, 16 per cent from Asia, 15 per cent from Latin America and the Caribbean and 5 per cent from the near East and North Africa.

IFAD is explicitly manded to assist the rural poor. Thus,

three creteria have been constant in all IFAD projects and programmes to date:

* Identification of the concrete obstacles faced by the poor producer;
* Targeted delivery of relevant assistance; and
* Assistance in the development of an appropriate organizational framework.

These components have worked well on the micro level. The challenge now is for all donor institutions working in a coordinated way to build them into the overall structure of the national policy and international development assistance.

This approach involves more active dialogue with Governments about the consequences of their policies. It also means a more searching scrutiny among donors themselves on the concrete relations between their macroeconomic growth prescriptions and the simultaneous reduction of poverty.

In addition, there must be greater coordination and co-financing of projects and programmes, broad sectoral frameworks specifically designed for complementary projects and programmes targeted specifically towards the poor.

The Social Summit: The opporunity provided by the convening of the World Summit for Social Development, from 6 to 12 March 1995 in Copenhagen, Denmark, should be seen as unique in the evolution of social development thinking.

The second commitment in the Summit's draft Declaration states: "We commit ourselves to the goal of eradicating poverty in the world, through decisive national actions and international cooperation, as a moral, political and economic imperative of humankind."

Endorsement of this commitment, along with the other measures contained in the final Declaration and Programme of Action, will go a long way in bringing IFAD's work to fruition.

Source: International Fund for Agricultural Development

SHELTER, EMPLOYMENT AND THE URBAN POOR

UN Centre for Human Settlements (Habitat)

An every-increasing share of the world's population lives in urban areas. According to the United Nations Secretariat, the urban population has gorwn from less than 30 per cent of the humanity in 1950 to about 45 per cent in 1995. By the year 2005, every second human being will live in cities and towns. This global picture, however, shows considerable regional differences. While already today three quarters of all inhabitants in the developed countries and in Latin America live in urban areas, less than a third of the population in Africa and Asia (excluding the Arab countries) is urban. Yet it is in those countries that the rate of urbanization is highest. The population of urban areas in developing countries grows currently at a rate of at least 3.6 per cent annualy, about four times faster than in rural areas. This means that the urban population of developing countries increases by some 170,000 persons every day, compared to "only" 60,000 per day in rural areas. United Nations Secretariat projections show that 40 per cent of the population in developing countries will live in urban areas by the turn of this century and that the urban population will overtake the rural population in about 20 years. By the year 2030, two thirds of the population in developing countries will live in urban areas.

The urbanizations of humanity

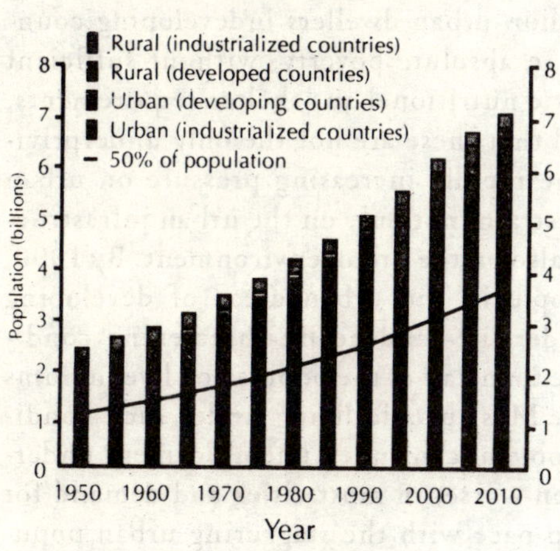

The Urbanization of poverty

Today, one fifth of all human beings (about 1.4 billion people) live in absolute poverty, without adequate food, clothing and shelter. Some 1.3 billion live in developing countries, most of these (about one billion) in rural areas. This situations, however, is changing swiftly. Although there are stilll uncertainties on the exact year when the urban poor will outnumber the rural poor, the trend is clear: not only are we living in an increasingly urbanized world,we are also experiencing an urbanization of poverty. One of the most visible characteristics of poverty is the shelter conditions under which poeple live.

The vast majority of those with incomes below the poverty line are also living under inadequate shelter conditions. Adequate shelter implies more than a roof a one's head: it means adequate privacy, adequate space, adequate security, adequate lighting and ventilation, adequate basic infrastructure and adequate location with regard to work and basic facilities—all at a reasonable cost. Although "only" 300 million urban dwellers indeveloping countries are currently living in absolute poverty, without sufficient incomes to fulfil even basic nutritional ans shelter requirements, it should be kept in mind that these are not the only underprivileged urban dwellers. The rapidly increasing pressure on urban areas casues considerable strain, not only on the urban infrastructure and on housing, but also on the urban environment. By 1990, at least 600 million people in the urban areas of developing countries were living under life- and health-threatening conditions. In some cities, more than half of the population live in slums and squatter settlements. Most people living under such conditions also face another problem: continued unemployment underemployment. What is even worse, in most cities and demand for labour are unable to keep pace with the staggering urban population growth. It is thus not surprising that a large proportion of the 700 million people added to the urban population of developing countries during this decade alone may end up unemployed or with very low incomes, living in slums or squatter settlements.

The Global Strategy for Shelter

The main objective of the Global Strategy for Shelter to the Year 2000—as adopted by the General Assembly of the United Nations in December 1988—is to facilitate adequate shelter for all. The Strategy recognizes that despite decades of direct government intervention in housing supply, the present housing situation in developing countries is worse than ever. It thus calls for Governments to leave the actual production of housing units to the private sector and to community efforts, and to provide legal, financial and institutional support to this process instead. This principle of enabling shelter strategies has since been adopted by many Governments. The sheer magnitude of the shelter problem, however, remains the main obstacle to the success of the Strategy. Although exact global figures are not available, the experiences from individual coutnries suggest that inadequate shelter is still increasing. Althoug the introduction of enabling strategies has improved the shelter conditions of large population groups, the needs and potential of the poorest groups may not have been properly addressed. Experience suggests that direct interventions-targeted subsidies-may be required to improve the shelter conditions of the poorest groups, i.e. those that are unable to take advantage of fre-market condtions. More and more cities are faced with growing unemployment, homelessness, crime, disease and pollution. It was this dilemma that, in 1992, prompted Governments to call upon the United Nations to convene the second United Nations Conference on Human Settlements (Habitat II) —the "City Summit" — 1996.

Investing in Shelter

Habitat's strategy for povery reduction emphasizes that investments in shelter are productive investments, rather than consumption expenditure. Investments in housing generate income and increase the labour productivity of the occupants. This has one major implication for development policies: it implies that housing is not only a goal, but more importantly it is a tool of development policy. Any investment in housing or infrastructure has effects on the national income that go far beyond the direct investment itself. Increased housing activities trigger additional investments in building-materials production, transport and marketing. They also lead to higher demand for a variety of local goods from the additional employees in these sectors — who are mainly semi-skilled and unskilled labourers with little propensity for buying imported goods — and thus increased investments in the production of such goods as well. Experiences from a number of countries indicate that, for every unit of currency spent directly on house construction, an additional unit of currency is added to the national income through such multiplier effects.

...and Small-scale Enterprises

In addition, low-cost housing construction generates more jobs per unit of investment than high-cost housing, and informal-sector construction methods are more labour-intensive than formal ones. Experiences from several countries indicate that informal-sector housing creates about 20 per cent more jobs per unit of expenditure than formal-sector housing and, at the same time, six times as many (although lower standard) dwellings can be built for the same investment. Similar lessons apply to the provision, operation and maintenance of various types of infrastructure and services: the construction of roads, the laying of water pipes, drains and sewers, and solid-waste management. The involvement of small-scale informal construction enterprises in the execution of housing and infrastructure projects should therefore be supported, as they use more unskilled labour, fewer imports and less hard currency than their large-scale, formal-sector counterparts. Experience also demonstrates that formal-sector housing is unaffordable for the poor. In most cases such housing, although officially intended for the poor, is inhabited by middle- and high-income households.

The informal housing sector, despite advantages and considerable output, is often neglected in favour of a relatively inefficient formal sector. One should, however, be careful not to embrace the activities of the informal sector without reservation. Its non-compliance with health, safety and internationally accepted labour standards is very serious indeed. Yet the reality is that the vast majority of housing units in most developing countries continue to be constructed through informal-sector activities. The formal sector is unable to address increasing housing needs. There is thus an urgent need to facilitate the activities of the informal part of the economy, while at the same time actively encouraging adherence to acceptable health, safety and labour standards.

A Common Strategy

The fact is that even an increasing number of middle-income salary earners also have to live under inadequate shelter conditions. Higher income alone does not solve the problem. What is required is a strategy that increases incomes and housing supply at the same time. The future priorities of local and national Governments — and of international develop- ment programmes — must therefore be to ac- tively support and advocate poverty-reduction strategies based on labour-intensive shelter delivery using local resources and linking the goals of shelter and employment for all as a common strategy for poverty reduction.

Source: United Nations Centre for Human Settlements (Habitat)

REFUGEES:

Victims of Social Disintegration

UN High Commissioner for Refugees

For years to come, a single word will sum up both social disintegration and the plight of refugees in their most extreme forms: Rwanda.

In less than four months, from 6 April to the end of July 1994, this tiny overcrowded country of some 8 million people suffered one of the most sudden and devastating collapses in history. Within the first lew weeks, an apparently orchestrated campaign of genocide led to an estimated 1 million deaths. By late April, 50,000 refugres had fletd to Burundi (which had itself produced 700,000 refugees only six months earlier), Uganda and Zaire. Then, in the space of 24 hours starting on 28 April, some 250,000 Rwandese refugees poured into Tanzania. At the time, the Office of the United Nations High Commissioner for Refugees (UNHCR) described it as the "largest and fastest exodus" it had ever witnessed. That label remained valid until mid-July, when a million Rwandese refugees crossed into Zaire near the town of Goma, totally overwhelming the relief agencies. Another 400,000 had entered Zaire further south, and 200,000 had gone to Burundi. By August, between half and two-thirds of the country's population were refugees, displaced or dead. Hundreds of villages were empty; ripened crops were rotting in the fields; and the refugees in Goma were dying in the thousands from cholera, dysentery and other diseases.

Complex Causes of Refugee Flows

Refugees are the ultimate symptom of social disintegration They are the last, most obvious, link in a chain of causes and effects that define the extent of a country's social and political breakdown. Looked at globally, they are a barometer of the current state of human civilization.

* By the end of 1993, before the latest Rwanda disaster, UNHCR was responsible for the protection and assistance of 23 million refugees and others in a similar predicament, including 4.1 million people in the former Yugoslavia alone.
* Taking an additional 26 million inter nally displaced people into account, one in every 115 people on Earth had been forced from their homes.
* There were still 3.3 million Afghan reiugecs in the Islamic Republic of Iran and Pakistan, and 1.3 million Mozambican refugees remained in six neighbouring countries. A fur- ther 19 countries or regions had between 100,000 and 1 million of their citizens living as refugees in other countries.
* Iran was hosting more refugees than any other country, namely 1.85 million Afghans and 645,000 Iraqis, making a total of 2.5 mil- lion. Pakistan had 1.5 million refugees. A fur ther 32 countries were hosting between 100,000 and 1 million refugees each. Of these countries, 18 were in Africa, five in Asia, four in Europe, and *tcvo* each in North America and the former Soviet Union.
* A total of 47 states and regions—one quarter of all the countries in the world—were either the recipient or the place of origin of more than 100,000 refugees.
* Eight countries were simultaneously the recipient and the place of origin of over 100,000 refugees: namely, Azerbaijan,. Croatia, Iraq, Burundi, Ethiopia Liberia, Rwanda and the Sudan.

The immediate causes of refugee flows of this magnitude are

Global Refugee Statistics*

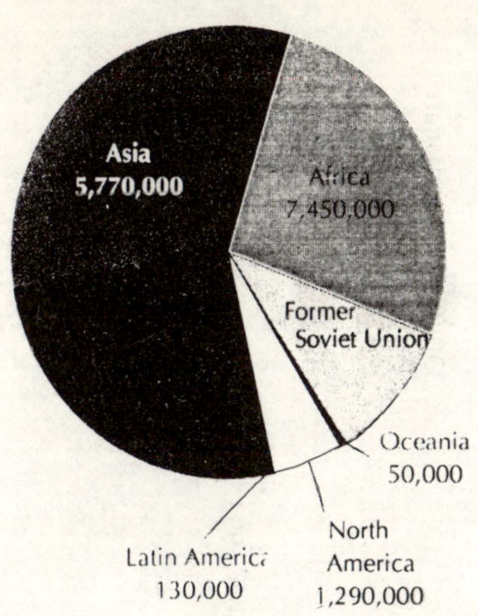

*Includes some persons in refugee-like situations who are of concern to UNHCR; excludes ca. 3 million Palestinian refugees under the direct mandate of UNRWA.

Source: UNHCR

invariably conflict or massive human rights violations. Since the end of the cold war, virtually all conflicts have been either predominantly or wholly internal in nature.

The long-simmering root causes that lead to the final explosion of violence and displacement, however, are often a complex and inter related mixture of social, political, economic and environmental forces. Poverty and population pressures leading to competition over scarce resources, serious social inequalities, divisive or exclusionary politics, arms proliferation and inadequate or decayed central and local government structures may all play a role. The ingredients will differ from situation to situationl but the results — dfestruction, death and displacement— are depressingly similar.

Rising Numbers of Refugees

UNHCR was set up in 1951 with a mandate to protect and assist refugees — mainly those left over from World War II — and to find lasting solutions to their problems. The organization was seen as temporary, with an initial life-span of only three years, as a result of misplaced optimism that once the massive displacement created by the second "war to end all wars" had been cleared up, refugees would by and large become a phenomenon of the past. Instead, since the mid-1970s, the number of refugees around the world has soared:

* In 1976, UNHCR was looking after 2.8 million refugees.
* By 1980, that number had tripled, to 8.2 million.

Top Ten Countries of Asylum

Country	Refugees
Islamic Republic of Iran*	2,400,000
Zaire*	1,580,000
Pakistan	1,480,000
USA	950,000
Sudan	750,000
Guinea	580,000
Tanzania*	540,000
Fed. Rep. of Yugoslavia*	450,000
Canada	340,000
Armenia	340,000

Top Ten Countries of Origin

Country	Refugees
Afghanistan*	3,270,000
Rwanda*	2,200,000
Iraq	720,000
Liberia	700,000
Somalia	520,000
Eritrea	430,000
Sudan	370,000
Azerbaijan	330,000
Angola	330,000
Sierra Leone	310,000

All figures as of 31.12.1993, except those marked (*), which are as of September 1994.
Source: UNHCR

* Since 1986, when there were 12.4 million people of concern to UNHCR, the global total has risen at an average rate of 1.5 million people per year.

Since the end of the cold war, the nature of most refugee-producing situations has changed, but the general trend of inexorably rising numbers has, if anything, grown more intense as States splinter bloodily along historical or ethnic lines. In addition, displacement has spread to new areas, such as the Caucasus and Central Asia.

Already several of the States that have gainetd independence over the past few years have experienced tremendous damage: Armenia, Azerbaijan, Bosnia and Herzegovina, Croatia, Georgia and Tajikistan, for example, have all suffered from major conflicts that have led to refugee exoduses or massive internal displacement. In all these cases, the ethnic or nationalist nature of the conflict was underpinned, to varying degrees, by the political, social and economic upheaval that accompanied independence. Other newly independent States, however, including many in Eastern Europe, as well as Namibia and Eritrea, have been making the transition from one political system to another without succumbing to the fatal cockta it of causes that lead to conflict and forced displacement.

Social Development: A Key to Prevention

Many young States lack the basic social and legal apparatus necessary to protect human rights. Nationalism thrives in such conditions, compounded by poor education, distorted or unforgiving history and unscrupulous politicians prepared to exploit ethnic tensions to further their own political ends.

Without extensive social, economic and political development to shore up fragile coun-tries that have either already produced refugees or are in danger of doing so, it seems likely that more countries will join those — such as Angola, Rwanda and Afghanistan—which have been locked in a vicious cycle of war and dis placement for years, or even decades.

Improvement of the social fabric and the establishment of responsible political leadership, particularly with regard to the

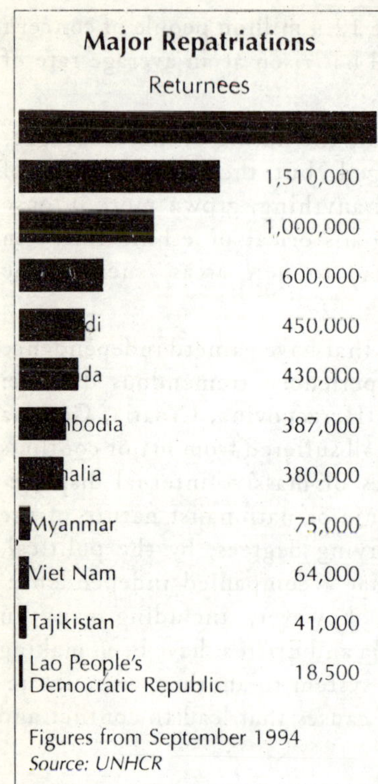

Figures from September 1994
Source: UNHCR

accommodation of minorities, are key factors in solving existing refugee problems. They are also essen- tial if embryonic crises are to be prevented from creating large numbers of new refugees.

Declining economies have another, indirect, detrimental effect on refugees. Fearing large numbers of immigrants — both refugees and economic migrants — many Governments have reacted by placing stricter limits on immigration. Under the 1951 Convention relating to the Status of Refugees, a refugee is someone who can prove "a well-founded fear of persecution for reasons of race, religion, nationality, member of a particular social group or political opinion" in his or her country of origin. A perceived or real rise in the number of economic migrants posing as asylum-seekers has in turn led to a tightening of asylum procedures, with the inevitable result that genuine asylum-seekers are faced with a wall of suspicion that lowers their chances to obtain refugee status.

Development: Crucial for Durable Solutions

The refugee story is not, however, one of unmitigated gloom. In some corners of the world — especially Central America, South-East Asia and southern Africa—the advent of peace has led to large numbers of refugees returning home in recent years. Between the beginning of 1990 and the end of 1993, around 7 million refugees went back to their countries of origin. The vol-untary repatriation of 370,000 Cambodian refugees, many of whom had been outside their home country for more than a decade, was completed in time for the May 1993 elections.

Voluntary repatriation is generally considered the "preferred solution" by UNHCR, the international community in general and the great majority of refugees themselves. For repat- riation to be a truly durable solution, the country of origin needs to have solved the political problems—usually by means of a peace agreement or significant changes in the political and human rights arenas — that led to the original outflow. However, peace and the opportunity to return home are not enough.

The countries to which refugees return are often devastated: villages rared to the ground; bridges blown up; roads and fields mined; irrigation systems collapsed; schools, clinics and other basic infrastructure in ruins. The people themselves — both those who left and those who stayed behind — are often daunted by the task of rebuilding their lives virtually from scratch.

By August 1994, some 900,000 out of the original total of more than 1.5 million Mozambican refugees had returned home to a country shattered by 16 years of civil war. As in Cambodia, the successful social and economic reintegration of the Mozambican returnees—as well as an estimated 4 million internally displaced people — will depend on the maintenance of the political reconciliation process, as well as the design and implementation of social and economic development programmes.

UNHCR can, at most, help returning refugees take their initial steps along the path to development and sell-sufficiency. While they are still in camps in their countries of asylum, UNHCR and other agencies try to make the most of the refugees' existing skills and capabilities. Increasingly, attempts are being made to improve educational facilities for refugee children and to teach adults, particularly women, income-generating skills that will benefit them not only during their time in the camps but also after their return home.

In recent years, in an attempt to boost returnees' chances of reintegrating successfully, UNHCR has broadened its humanitarian assistance inside countries of origin to include small-scale projects designed to fulfill some of the most immediate social development needs of the communities receiving large numbers of returnees. By benefitting the entire community, such projects aim to calm, rather than exacerbate, frictions between returnees and those who remained in their country. They are also intended to capitalize on communities' own expertise and commitment to rebuilding their societies, and place special emphasis on the important role of women as "agents" of economic and social development.

However, much work remains to be done on smoothing the interface between humanitarian operations and development programmes. There is a need for further innovative humanitarian responses inside countries of origin. By the same token, since the usefulness of humanitarian assistance is by its nature limited in time and scope, development strategies need to be more closely geared to the immediate, as well as the long-term, needs of communities struggling to absorb returning refugees.

The rebuilding of Cambodia and Mozambique has begun, but is far from finished.Preparations for the rebuilding of Angola and Liberia were stopped in their tracks when both countries slid back into conflict.

The rebuilding of Rwanda will present an even more formidable challenge. Between 1959 and 1964, Rwanda produced at least 150,000 refugees. Further *outbreaks* of conflict and persecution in 1973 and 1990 led to hundreds of thousands more refugees and displaced people, followed by over 2 million new refugees in 1994. A huge effort will be needed both by the Rwandese themselves and by the international community to break the cycle of massacre and displacement once and for all. A willingness to invest in social development will be an essential part of that effort.

Source: Office of the United Nations High Commissioner for Refugees

INTERNATIONAL MIGRATION: FOCUS ON WOMEN

Instraw

Situation

In 1985, there were approximately 105 million people who had left their home and family to find sustenance or safety in other countries. Who are these international migrants! Where do they come from! Where do they go! Below are just a few exalmples:

- In 1987, 26,000 Filipino nurses, presumed to be female,

were granted temporary permits to work abroad. Of these, almost 18,000 went to Saudi Arabia.

- Australia, Canada, New Zealand and the United States admit the most migrants, as either citizens or permanent residents. The United States admits the largest number (e.g., 1.5 million in 1992), about half of them women.
- Among the foreign-born population in Europe and the Americas, women outnumber men; the reverse tends to be true in Asia and Africa.

The economic and social impact of migration is significant. On the positive side, in 1989, for example, the estimated $65· billion sent home by migrant workers worldwide provided a major source of foreign exchange for many developing countries.

However, there are also negative effects, not the least of which is the loss of large numbers of productive workers and or highly educated professionals (the so-called "brain tlrain") from the country of origin. And in the new host countries, competition for space, jobs and social services can result in alienation, discrimination, sometimes deteriorating into violent confrontations.

As a result of these pressures on both originating and receiving countries, international migration is now in the forefront of the national and international agenda. The World Summit for Social Development will atldress this problem, especially untler the core issue of "social integration"

Women:

The Unseen Dimension

Despite the large number of women migrants, about 50 million, the debate to date has either centered around male migrants or, at best, been gender neutral. In some cases, the results of this oversight have aggravated old problems in modern guise.

The so-called "white slave trade," the international transportation of women and girls for purposes of prostitution, illegal under a series of international conventions adopted since 1904, was thought to have moderated. Recently, however, cases have been reported in which migrant women, mostly recruited in developing countries as entertainers or restaurant workers, have been forced into prostitution either immediately upon arrival in the host country, or after their visas had expired. Most such cases are thought to go unreported.

While this is an extreme example, the precarious situation of independent women niigrants, particularly temporary workers, is the focus of increasing concern throughout the world.

However, even as economic and demographic statistics reveal the magnitude of population movements, specific data on women are either scarce or non-existent. Although their numbers appear to be increasing steadily, and women areamong the most vulnerable of the migrant populations, only rarely do official figures reflect their true status. In many receiving countries, for example, women migrants are frequently classified as "dependent" even if this is not the case.

Issues

Without detailed facts and figures about the causes and effects of migration, it is impossible for officials to take either preventive or corrective action, or even to set realistic goals for such actions. Although some raw statistics on migration exist in population surveys, exit visas, immigration papers, work permits, etc., most of these figures are not gender-specific, and, where they are, they tend to reflect traditional assumptions on migration.

The economic and social realities underlying the migration of women are often over-looked or undercounted, especially with regard to women who leave home of their own volition. In addition to the economic and social challenges racing all migrants, women are particularly susceptible to physical and mental abuse, as well as to legal discrimination, and are often forced to cope in the shadows of a society without appropriate' protections or services.

Categories of Migrants

There are four categories of international migrants:

- temporary or labour migrants, the newest group of migrants

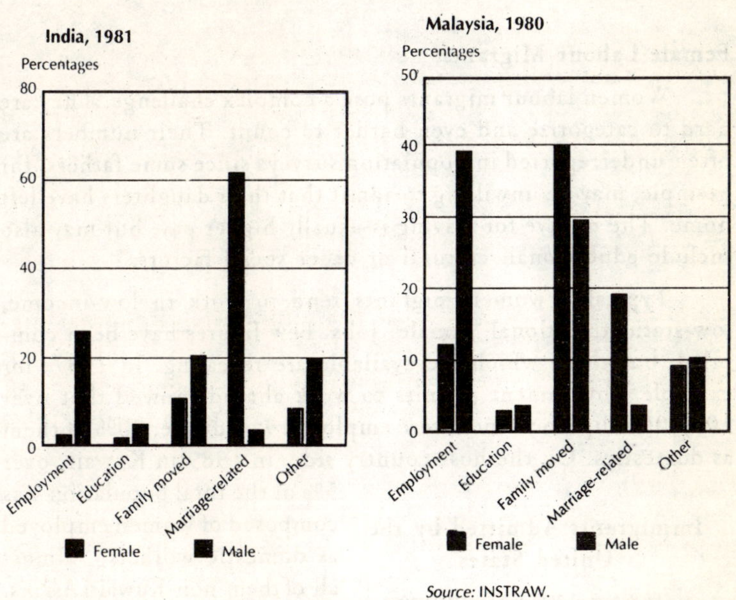

Source: INSTRAW.

who are admitted to a country to fill a specific job;

- refugees, defined by UNHCR as some one who can prove "a well-rounded fear of persecution for reasons of race, religion, nationality, member of a particular social group or political opinion" in his or her country of origin.
- permanent migrants, or immigrants, who are granted permission to stay in a country indefinitely; and
- undocumented migrants, who enter a country illegally or who overstay their visas.

To some degree, all share a common goal, the desire to escape to a better economic, social, or political environment. They also share common needs for physical and legal protection, as well as for social services such as healthcare. And many experience common problems, such as discrimination as strangers in an alien society. Some, in particular women and unaccompanied young girls, are forced to endure the trauma of sexual harassment, rape, or even forced prostitution. Such human rights abuses usually go unreported for rear of retribution.

Female Labour Migrants:

Women labour migrants pose a complex challenge. They are hard to categorize and even harder to count. Their numbers are often underreported in population surveys since some fathers, for example, may be unwilling to admit that their daughters have left home. The motive for leaving is usually higher pay, but may also include educational, cultural or other social factors.

Typically, women migrants tend to work in low-income, low-status traditional "female" jobs. Few figures have been compiled, but those which are available are revealing. In 1987, for example, government permits to work abroad showed that over 100,000 Filipino women were employed worldwide, 80% of them as domestics. On the host-country side, in 1989 in Kuwait, over 5% of the total population was composed of women employed as domestic workers, almost all of them non-Kuwaiti Asians.

Immigrants Admitted by the United States

By Region of Birth and Sex, 1982-1992

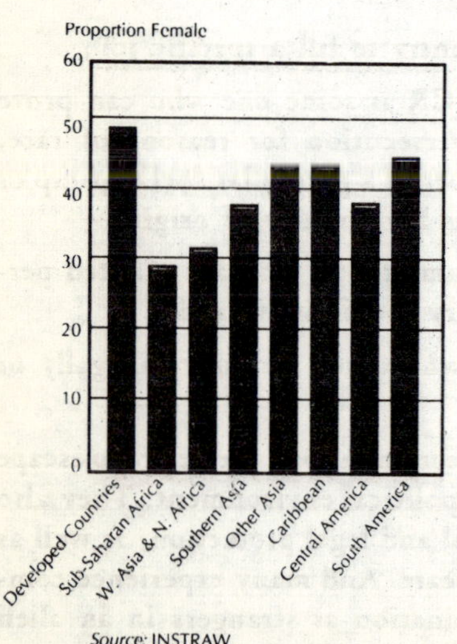

Source: INSTRAW.

Wages for migrant workers, whether legal or illegal, are usually lower than host-country norms. Working conditions may be harsh, with long hours and little or no opportunity to leave the house, meet friends or even talk on the telephone. Nevertheless, their pay scales are still much higher than they would have been at home. Therefore, fear of loss of even the most menial jobs, in addition to the often substantial investment made for travel or other expenses, causes the female labour migrant to endure economic exploitation and physical abuse. Stress and isolation are common and may be frequently compounded by ethnic, cultural, or religious discrimination and negative sex stereotyping.

Women admitted as dependents of spouses or close family members are also considered labour migrants, but of secondary status. In addi- tion to being severely restricted in their access to job opportunities, their residency status as individuals is also uncertain. Living conditions are difficult, with housing often overcrowded and only limited access to social services.

Refugee women:

The plight of refugee women and their vulnerability to exploitation and violence is better known. The generally accepted statistics are stark: over 80% of the more than 20 million refugees around the world today are said to be women and children. That figure is only an estimate, however. The numbers change with each new crisis, as violent political upheavals result in massive, often unpredictable migrations of populations. Accurate population surveys are luxuries in the early stages of a refugee crisis; the estimate that 80% of all refugees are women and children Appears to be based primarily on anecdotal observations of refugees from developing countries with high fertility rates, where the proportion of women and children is normally 74%, to 78%.

Still less is known about the status of newly arrived refugee women as individuals. As refugees they are migraints, although not all migrants are refugees. The distinction has become somewhat blurred. Legally, refugees are defined as those with "a well-founded fear" of political persecution at home; a migrant can be anyone escaping poverty or an environmental disaster, or simply seeking better social or economic opportunities abroad.

Thus, the two categories tend to overlap. Many refugees, like labour migrants, usually only intend to stay in the host country temporarily. Increasingly, however, they are staying longer, sometimes permanently.

Because of their relative lack of skills, education and financial resources, few refugee women are successful in reaching and obtaining asylum in developed countries. Even in developing countries where traditional demographic data do not adequately reftect their social and economic status, women refugees are generally assumed to be dependents whose husbands or fathers are either dead or fighting in civil wars. In reality, even prior to their migration, many women were already heads of households, working as farmers or urban micro-entrepreneurs. Their flight was an emergency decision- made independently.

Permanent migrant women: Permanent migration is generally subject to strict govern- mental regulation and is usually limited to those with relatives in the host country or those with specific skills. These requirements tend to favor men, sometimes accompanied by women who are their dependents.

Independent women migrants are therefore usually restricted to those relatively few women who are better educated. Even so, few independent women leave countries where their role has traditionally been circumscribed, the exception being the continuing phenomenon of the "mail-order bride."

Undocumented migrant women: The undocumentedd migrant is, by deiinition, almost impossible to reach except under sporadic regularization or amnesty programmes. The need to make migration a less attractive option by addressing the root causes of departure is obvious. This is par- ticulariy true for women, whose numbers are thought to be larger than generally estimated.

Suggested Solutions

Understanding both the motivations and consequenctes of international migration are essential to mitigate its effects (e.g., economic, social and psychological dislocations and stress). Besides the obvious gaps in measuring migration by women, incorrectly Gathered or inadequately defined data can also distord and even conceal the actual reality.

For example, in four communities in Mexico, a survey of emigrants focused only on heads of household, "older sons", and women leaving for work in the United States. Women leaving the country for other reasons, such as schooling, were omitted, as was a larger than expected number of undocumented female migrants who were identified only later when they applied for amnesty under a US immigration reform law.

Knowing why women leave home is as important as knowing how many of them leave. Raising salary levels or eliminating wage discrimination at home would probably keep many women from emigrating, as would improving their social and political status—but there are no reliable statistics to prove this hypothesis.

Improved research and training and new statistical methods are the primary tools available to government policy-makers. The key is to supplement raw demographics with improved socio-economie information on migrants, collected separately for men and women. Better basic data in such areas as employment and education levels can yield a more accurate economic profile of a country, its strengths and its weaknesses, and provide the basis for setting realistic goals for future corrective action.

In seeking reliable information on female migrants, the challenge for statisticians is to compensate for the gender bias inherent in current methods of data collection, such as the tendency to survey only male heads of households whose responses can be either untrue (e.g., in a community where women working outside the home is frowned upon) or unreliable (e.g., if the employer does not list his domestic as a resident).

Among the changes and additions recommded for future studies of women migrants are the following.

* **"Gender blind" surveys:** Assure that the same questions are asked of both men and women, particularly questions about their economic activities. Gender-blind surveys should improve the reliability of responses, as well as help overcome the myth of female dependency.

• **Socio-economic comparisons:** Conduct Socio-economic survey undertaken in both countries of origin and destination to ensure that accurate comparisons are made between them. It is particularly important to learn why some women migrated and others did not. The same basic questions should be asked of both groups to elicit parallel information on age, education, marital status, family ties at home and abroad, ability to speak or understand the language of the receiving country, ownership of land, etc.

- **Causes of migration:** Collect information recalled by both groups about their respective situations at the time of migration, and any changes, such as economic or marital status, Since then. The more recent the migration, ideally no more than 5-10 years earlier, than more accurate the date will be.

  Policy analysis: Analyze of the role of government policies in donor and recipient countries, and of the effect of economic and social programmes on migration (e.g., fostering emigration or serving to ease or improve the situation of women at home).

  Research: Study the effects of migration on women who left, as well as those who remained. Among the factors to be inducted ;are: whether the women migrated independently; how they benefited from migration compared to men; whether they were restricted to low income, low-status occupations; and whether or not better economic opportunities arose over time. Comparisons in these same areas should also be made between first generation female migrants and their daughters, as well as the younger generation females in the countries of origin.

Demographers believe that greater awareness and understanding of these issues, and better dissemination and use of already existing data, could provide governments with the foundation for more effective economic and social planning. This would, in effect, complete the circle: better planning would affect women's status in their societies and ultimately influence their decision on whether to leave or to stay home.

Source: United Nations Internatinal Research and Training Institute for the Advancement of Women (INSTRAW)

A NEW AGE FOR OLD AGE

Ageing

The "age of ageing", the "gray revolution", "humanity's coming of age": these and similar phrases are now part of common dicourse and have a clear statistical basis.

In the 75 years from 1950 to 2025, the world's population of elderly people (those 60 years old and over) will have increased from 200 million to 1.2 billion, and from 8 to 14 per cent of the total global population. In the same 75 years, the very old (those aged 80 and above) will have grown from 13 million to 137 million. In short, between 1950 and 2025, the total world population will have grown by approximately a factor of three, the elderly by a factor of six and the very old by a factor of ten.

Rising to the Challenge

The developed countries — whose population are ageing fastest — are adjusting and refining policies and programmes, addressing the needs of older people, including not only how they can be cared for, but how they can continue to participate in society. These countries are attempting to adjust national spending to reflect current and projected demographic ageing and its ripple effects on such sectors as health, housing, education, welfare, employment, and income security.

The developing countries, whose populations are expected to age even more quickly in the coming decades than those of the developed countries have in the past, have begun gradually introducing ageing polices and programmes.

Population ageing in developing countries is a critical problem because of two factors: a weak institutional infrastructure for meeting the needs of increasing numbers and proportions of the elderly and the uncertainty that families can continue to provide care and solidarity for the elderly as a result of many societal changes, such as migration and the increasing participation of women in public life.

A Key Summit Topic

The question of ageing will be an important topic of discussion at the World Summit for Social Development, which is to be held in Copenhagen, Denmark, in March 1995. The General Assembly has designated three core issues for the Summit — social integration, reduction of poverty and productive employment each of which has important implications relating to ageing.

The Summit will consider how to maintain and improve the participation of older people in social and economic activities, how to protect older people from poverty, and how to adapt employment policies to the needs of the elderly.

The policies and programmes recommended by the Summit will be integrated into the continuing activities of the United Nations programme on ageing.

The challenge of ageing to governments of both developed and developing countries falls along two interrelated paths: first, the overall impact of population ageing on aLl sectors and generations; and second, the situation of older people as their traditional status and roles in society change whether it is the "young old" or the very old.

In addressing the situation of older people in rapidly changing societies, the rights and responsibilities of older women, older migrants and refugees need particular attention to ensure that they share equitably in social and economic entitlements.

Despite the complexities of the issue, one clear policy option has emerged in recent years for both developed and developing countries: "help for self-help". a term for government policies that support and facilitate choice for older people to remain active in society as agents and beneficiaries of development. Help for self-help is a policy option that recognize the dignity and capabilities of older people while addressing their need for employment, income security, and social integration.

The Role of the United Nations

The United Nations programme on ageing involves the Secretariat and a number of the Organization's specialized agencies, including the International Labour Organisation, the World Health Organization, UNESCO and others. The effort involves cooperation with Member States, experts and organi-

Changing Age Structure of World Population, 1990-2150

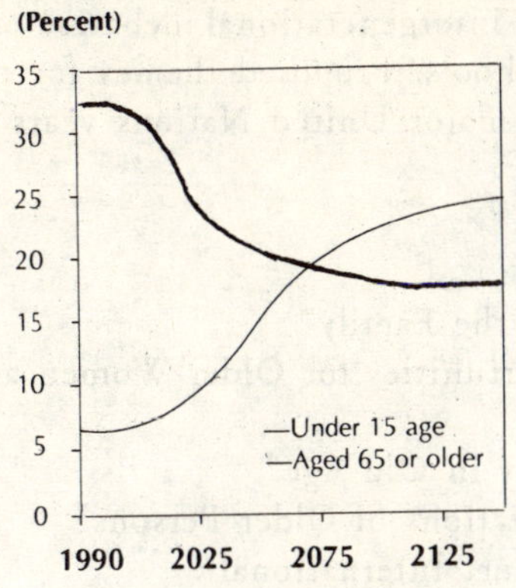

Note: Based on medium fertility projection

Source: United Nations Population Division, Long-Range World Population Projections; Two Centuries of Population Growth, 1950-2150, (United Nations, New York).

zations of the elderly in setting standards and in devising policies and programmes.

The question of ageing was first discussed at the United Nations General Assembly in 1948. It was not evident then *that* the world's population would age so dramatically in the coming decades. Twenty years later, in 1969, the General Assembly re-examined the issue, calling, eventually, for a World Assembly on Ageing to be convened in 1982 in Vienna, Austria.

The World Assembly adopted the Inter- national Plan of Action on Ageing and, later the same year, the United Nations General Assembly endorsed it. This Plan, the first global instrument on ageing, guides the United Nations programme. Every four years, the United Nations Secretariat conducts a global appraisal of progress in implementing the Plan.

The Global Programme

In 1992, ten years after adopting the International Plan of Action on Ageing, the General Assembly endorsed a set of global and suggested national targets on ageing to be reached by the year 2001. Also, the Assembly designated October every year as the International Day for the Elderly. It designated the year 1999 as the International Year of Older Persons.

Future activities of the United Nations programme on ageing will revolve around these events. The period 1992-2001 has been established for reaching a set of global and suggested national targets on ageing. Each event offers an occasion to examine the impact of ageing on society and the situation of older people in that society.

Activities proposed for 1 October, the International Day for the Elderly, include announcements by heads of State, municipalities and organizations; conferences; media discussions; skills exchange among older people; intergenerational debates; and essay and art celebrations in schools. Proposed themes for the years ahead, which tie in with major United Nations years or conferences, are as follows.

1 October

1994 "Older Persons and the Family"
1995 "Employment Opportunities for Older Women and Men"
1996 "Eliminating Poverty in Old Age"
1997 "Celebrating Organizations of Older Persons"
1998 "Older Persons Support International Year of Tolerance"
1999 "Towards a New Age for Old Age: A Society for all Ages"

The International Year of Older Persons (1999) will offer an occasion to assess that needs ahead, particularly in developing countries. A framework for the Year's observance will be elaborated by the United Nations Commission for Social Development in 1995. Two themes are being considered: "a new age for old age", which would address the situation of older people in changing socio-economic contexts; and "a society for all ages", addressing the complexities of society-wide adjustments to population ageing. Country programmes, International campaigns, expert debates and local celebrations are envisaged.

A practical strategy on ageing was endorsed for the period 1992 to 2001. The targets guide current actions on ageing and will give direction to the fourth and fifth appraisals of the implementation of the International Plan of Action on Ageing at the United Nations Commission for Social Development in 1997 and 2001, respectively.

The year 2001 will be a capstone for the century in which developed countries aged and, at the same time, the launching pad for the decades in which developing countries are projected to age with unprecedented rapidity.

Source: Ageing